PLANNING EDUCATIONAL FACILITIES FOR THE NEXT CENTURY

Glen I. Earthman has spent 40 years in the field of education serving as a teacher, principal, executive director for school facility planning in the Philadelphia Public Schools and finally as professor of Educational Administration at Virginia Polytechnic Institute and State University in Blacksburg, Virginia. During his career, Dr. Earthman has served as a consultant to more than 70 school systems across the country and overseas helping them with school facility problems of various kinds. He currently has Emeritus Faculty status at Virginia Tech where he continues to teach graduate courses on school planning. He has also served as the director of the U.S. Department of Education sponsored National Clearinghouse for Educational Facilities. He has written extensively in the area of school facility planning authoring four textbooks and more than 60 articles in periodical publications. His continuing research interests extend to all phases of school facilities, but he has concentrated on exploring the relationship between school building condition and student achievement.

Planning Educational Facilities for the Next Century

® 2000 by Glen I. Earthman

Published in the United States of America
by Rowman & Littlefield Education
A Division of Rowman & Littlefield Publishers, Inc.
A wholly owned subsidary of The Rowman & Littlefield Publishing Group, Inc.
4501 Forbes Boulevard, Suite 200, Lanham, Maryland 20706
www.rowmaneducation.com

Estover Road
Plymouth PL6 7PY
United Kingdom

ISBN 13: 978-0-910170-59-8
ISBN 10: 0-910170-59-2

Cover Photos

Gulf Coast High School, Collier County Public Schools, Naples, Florida.
Photo by Ron Blakeley, world class location photography, courtesy of
SCHENKELSHULTZ Architecture, 8250 College Parkway, Ft. Myers, Florida, 33919.
Phone: 941/481-0200 Website: www.schenkelshultz.com

tableofcontents

figures

preface

SEVEN YEARS AGO WHEN I WROTE THE PREFACE TO THE FIRST EDITION OF THIS BOOK I tried to make two major points. The first was that many books on school planning currently on the market do not address forthrightly the planning process that educators must master to be an effective administrator. Instead, many of the books discuss the building features that should be in a new building as if in some manner this display would show the administrator how to plan for a building. What little discussion of the planning process contained in many books centered on the development of a set of educational specifications. In fact, some books give the impression that once the educator has developed a set of educational specifications, the main task of planning a school facility was completed with little thought of what actions must come before and after. Some of these books are used in courses designed to teach educational administrators how to plan school facilities. With a limited point of view on the planning process, some false impressions can creep into the knowledge base of administrators. The paucity of discussion of the multitude of planning problems educators must face in providing adequate student housing can create a misconceptions of the responsibilities that must be discharged. Naturally, a limited knowledge base does not serve educators very well when they must make decisions.

Educational administrators have a unique responsibility in the planning process for a capital improvement project. They have a distinct leadership position that can help to insure a successful project. Conversely, lack of proactive leadership on the part of educational administrators can greatly hinder the successful completion of the building project. The ability to help a school staff to complete such a project depends upon a solid knowledge base.

There is some value to those books that spend a great deal of time discussing the design of school buildings. They inform the educator of new space possibilities in facilities. They are also a source of interesting trends in school design. Beyond this, the use of these books to inform about the planning process is not the most effective and efficient method of learning about this very important responsibility of educators.

The responsibility of administering the planning process demands some leadership on the part of the educator as well as the school board. In the absence of leadership, someone will step in to fill the vacuum. Sometimes architects and other professionals outside of the school system will fill a leadership vacuum in the school system by making decisions that should be made by administrators and school boards. For this reason, it is very important for the educator to know the various processes involved in planning a new school or major capital project and whose responsibility it is for administering the process. Such a discussion can be done only by a thorough analysis of each process involved in planning schools and the responsibility attached. The content of the present book relies heavily upon a description of the planning process and the role an educator has in it. The book presents, in readily understandable terms, the processes for which educators have responsibility and which they should understand and be able to administer prudently.

The second major point in the previous book concerned the treatment of the educational facility planning process as an integral part of the overall planning process of the school system. Many authors present the planning process for a new school and for any capital improvement project as a separate event in the history of the school system, sometimes not even related to what else the school system does. Some descriptions go so far as to present the project as something done by people outside of the school system for people inside the school system. In other words, the planning for a new school in no way relates to the usual educational program planning processes that go on in the school system. A case in point was presented to illustrate this dichotomy in planning processes. The illustration cited a 1931 school where all of the systems were renovated, but nothing was done to upgrade the spaces where the educative process takes place. This is a classic example of the separation, at least in some people's thinking, of the building structure needs and the needs of the educational program that the building is to house. Although such an example may seem extreme and isolated to some readers, such occurrences do happen quite frequently, even in well-managed school systems. Anytime such planning happens, it is too frequent. Such erroneous thinking occurs too often in school systems, when in reality the planning of any capital improvement project is tied directly into everything else the school system does.

The present text uses the long range planning process of the school system as the vehicle for providing the proper housing for students and programs. The long-range plan thus becomes the key to all planning efforts in the school system, including capital improvement planning. From the long-range plan adopted by the school board, come many other plans that are implemented by various departments and offices in the school system so that all efforts work towards completing the objectives of the overall school system plan. This cyclical effort insures a concentration of available resources to complete objectives and systematic work towards adopted goals of the organization. Under the umbrella of the long-range plan, all employees of the school system work to complete specified objectives which in turn propels the organization in the pursuit of goals. Without this direct link between school facility planning and long range planning, the latter is probably a futile effort and the former a separate event in the history of the school system.

This book takes a very systematic approach to the planning of educational facilities. Each phase of the process of planning capital projects is discussed in detail sufficient for the educational administrator to understand the responsibilities required of those individuals in the schools who make decisions on regarding the kinds of buildings in which students will be housed. The text also speaks to the moral responsibility of educators to make certain students are in safe, functional, and efficient structures.

The inextricable link between the long range planning effort and all physical facility planning work of the school system is emphasized in this work, and can, therefore, be used as a guide to foster effective planning. As a result, this book can be used by the practitioner as both a guide for action and also a staff development vehicle. The text can also be used very effectively for any college or university course in school facility planning because the book gives the potential school administrator an idea of the scope of planning necessary in the school system and how that can be tied into the planning effort for the school buildings.

Glen I. Earthman

Organization and Policy Planning

ALL ORGANIZATIONS NEED SOME TYPE OF STRUCTURE IN ORDER TO FUNCTION effectively and efficiently. This applies regardless of what the organization does and the size of its staff. In fact, the more complicated the task to be done, the more structure is needed. A very small business firm that sells one product needs an organizational structure just as much as a complicated one. All organizations build some type of structure to get the job done.

A school system is no different from any other organization in needing some type of structure to work efficiently and effectively. School systems are organized around the tasks to be done. In this way, those who specialize in a certain subject area or a specific administrative capacity can contribute to the total school effort.

Likewise, specialization allows individuals to become expert in a field of knowledge or a function needed by the organization. Specialization is, of course, one element of a bureaucracy—which is exactly what any school system in the United States is. This is not to deride the fact that school systems are bureaucracies, because a bureaucracy is really the only logical way to accomplish a very complicated task. Sometimes a school system's bureaucracy is blamed for inefficiencies in the organization; but it is not the concept of bureaucracy that is at fault, but untrained or inept employees that cause the breakdown in efficiency.

The more complex the organization, however, the more that specialization is evident in the working force, hence the bigger the organization, the more it reflects the bureaucratic model. Bureaucracy allows staff to specialize. Through this type of organization, employees can become expert in one area and not have to be expert in all. This principle works especially well in the school system where people are employed to do certain highly specialized tasks that require a specified amount of education.

The task of planning for school buildings is a complicated one involving a large number of individuals who possess highly trained skills and knowledge (Kowalski 1989). The head of the planning process for new school buildings, therefore, needs to be knowledgeable about all the facility planning tasks involved so that proper evaluation of the effort can be made. The administrator who heads facilities planning for a school system does not have to be an expert in all of the technical fields involved in planning/designing/constructing a school, but that person should be knowledgeable about those fields and, at the same time, know what the school system expects.

In the area of school facility planning, there are many tasks to complete that require a person to have a high degree of professional and technical skills. In addition, the demand for new school buildings and other capital improvements creates a demand for the size of its staff to do the work. In other words, the larger the demand for new schools and other types of capital projects, the more personnel a school system will employ for this task. Conversely, the less demand for new schools and similar work, the smaller the school facility planning staff. This is reflected in the organizational chart of the school system and in school board policies. All school systems need to have their organization described in the school board policies. Such a description permits the entire school system staff to recognize which office is responsible for which tasks, and to delineate the chain of command.

Large School Systems

In large school systems, the school facilities staff is rather big and includes many individuals with specialized knowledge and skills. This is necessary because of the demand for new schools and other capital improvements.

The facilities department or division in a large school system usually is divided into sections that follow the division of the disciplines in the planning process. Figure 1.1 shows the organizational chart for the school facilities planning department of a large school system of perhaps 100,000 students or more. The top administrator is an assistant superintendent reporting directly to the superintendent of schools. This position should be high enough in the organization to be in the decision-making process of the school system. Generally, someone heading such a department would be in the superintendent's cabinet, council or team. This committee serves as a decision-making group for the entire school system. It's crucial that the head of the school facility planning effort in this decision-

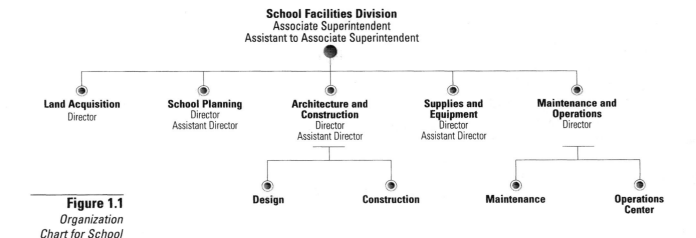

Figure 1.1
*Organization
Chart for School
Facilities
Department*

making body be high enough to be answerable only to the superintendent.

This facility planning department is divided into groups representing the various disciplines associated with school buildings. There is a section responsible for selecting and acquiring the site, another for programming the new school building, and yet another section which monitors the work of the architect. These sections or sub-departments are on the director level. The heads of these sections are supported, as the case may be, by assistant directors and supervisors.

The section responsible for design and construction is subdivided into the architecture and construction groups each headed by an assistant director. The assistant director of architecture monitors the work of the architect, while the person heading the construction group supervises and monitors the firms doing construction work. These groups are staffed with several supervisors who actually provide the monitoring service.

The maintenance and operations section is also included under the facilities department in this school system. This is a common organization variation in a school system of this size. In school systems larger than this example, maintenance and operations may be located in a separate section or department that may or may not report to the same head. The maintenance function is usually located in the facilities planning department because of the overlap in activities such as evaluating buildings, monitoring the design and construction, and writing specifications. All of these functions, plus the planning function, are common to both new construction and many maintenance projects (Castaldi 1994).

The final section in the organizational chart in Figure 1.1 is responsible for procuring equipment for buildings. On the surface, this may seem elementary and not really demanding or needing of a separate section. However, purchasing equipment for school buildings is a very exacting task which requires writing technical specifications, comparing similar pieces of equipment, conducting the bidding, evaluating bids, purchasing, warehousing and delivering equipment to the correct site. These tasks require a great deal of knowledge about the types and kinds of equipment needed for a modern educational program to function well. In addition, the equipment requirements of a new school building represent a large sum of money that must be spent wisely. Job descriptions for the various offices in the facilities department follow. The various tasks to be done are given as a delineation of the areas of responsibility between the offices.

Organization and Objectives of the School Facilities Department

Under the direction of the superintendent of schools, the school facilities department will direct, administer, coordinate and expedite all operations and related activities involved in real estate acquisition, school planning, designing, constructing, equipping, maintaining and operating all school facilities in order to adequately house the pupils, personnel, and pertinent operations of the school system according to the educational goals and instructional requirements adopted by the School Board.

Land Acquisition Section

Objective—To perform the functions essential to the acquisition and/or the disposal of real property in accordance with legal requirements of the state and School Board policies and procedures.

Functions

1. Survey and recommend the selection of new sites or the extension of existing school sites, collecting such data as size, shape, topography, accessibility, proximity to transportation, sewer and drain facilities, utilities, proposed public improvements such as expressways, etc., that might affect the site at some future time.
2. Appraise real property, using approved methods and techniques, and supervise the appraisals prepared by contract.
3. Maintain careful and accurate records of all negotiations, including data that are to be available at all times for public examination.

4. Negotiate for the acquisition of real property on the basis of proper appraisal preparation; perform escrow and title work to consummate the transaction and secure title insurance policies.
5. Cooperate with and assist legal counsel in instituting eminent domain proceedings and preparation of factual data for trial when negotiations are not successful.
6. Lease real property, both as lessor and lessee, and obtain permits for use of real property.
7. Sell real property, including buildings, structures, and other improvements.
8. Process street and alley vacations, assessment matters, tract maps, street openings and widening, and rights of way and easements as both grantor and grantee.
9. Check and study all requests for change or variance of zone properties within the school system to ascertain if and how school properties may be affected. If school properties are affected, represent the School Board before the zoning authorities.
10. Represent the School Board before the Planning Commission and Redevelopment Authority in all matters pertaining to real property.
11. Study all subdivision tract maps filed with the school system as to the effect upon existing school sites and contemplated sites, and make recommendations to city agencies pertaining thereto.
12. Produce monthly reports pertaining to the status of each land purchase program in order to advise the School Facilities Division as to the availability of newly acquired land for use.

School Planning Section

Objective—To accomplish the planning necessary to provide a sufficient number of safe and functional school facilities for the education of pupils at all levels and the housing for personnel responsible for the accomplishment of the approved educational program.

Functions

1. Conduct continuous studies of the actual and anticipated increase or decrease in school enrollment due to growth, demographic, and sociological characteristics including births, immigration, transiency, ethnic characteristics, dwelling unit construction trends, and economic factors, to form a basis for the purchase of new school sites, construction of new schools, and additional facilities at existing schools.

2. Cooperatively plan space requirements for all educational activities prescribed by the curriculum with the Divisions of Instruction and Curriculum and develop school building standards to these requirements.
3. Prepare building program authorizations, schedules, and educational specifications for approval of the Superintendent and School Board.
4. Interpret and translate to architects designing school buildings the space requirements of the instructional program.
5. Develop the justification documents for determining the need for new school sites, additional land, new schools, additional buildings, and alterations and improvements. Develop research material for long range forecasting of future financial needs for school construction.
6. Maintain a database of classroom inventories and school capacities.
7. Serve as a liaison between the Superintendent, Associate Superintendents and District Superintendents, and other school system personnel in all matters pertaining to new sites, new buildings and improvements to existing schools.
8. Direct the development of project lists and expedite a program for alterations and improvements based on a requisition system of requests from schools.
9. Prepare and maintain all official school maps, and school attendance boundaries, and conduct necessary pupil residence studies in order to determine school boundary adjustments.
10. Prepare capital budget building and land programs for the Superintendent's recommendation to the School Board.

Architecture and Construction Section
Objective—To administer the coordination of all activities and operations relative to the design of new school facilities, alterations, and improvements by commissioned architects, engineers, and the school system's design unit, and direct the inspection and supervision of contract construction phases of all building projects.
Functions
1. Administer the preparation of plans and specifications for new buildings, alterations, and improvement projects, and ground improvement.
2. Administer the inspection of new construction, alterations and improvements of buildings and grounds.
3. Administer the operations of the school system design unit in the preparation of plans and specifications for authorized projects.

4. Direct the review of work performed by architects and engineers.
5. Establish time schedules for the preparation of drawings and specifications, advertisements for bids, and construction for all authorized construction projects.
6. Represent the school system in interpreting the technical aspects of a building program to the architect.
7. Maintain up-to-date guide specifications and buildings standard criteria for use by commissioned architects and engineers.
8. Develop budget estimates for proposed capital budget projects.

Supplies and Equipment Section
Objective—To plan, select, standardize, evaluate, and direct the disbursement of supplies and equipment in order to provide the schools the proper type, quantity, and quality of materials to meet the educational needs of the school system.
Functions
1. Administer a standardization program, to include the establishment and maintenance of standard lists of supplies and equipment.
2. Prepare supply and equipment catalogs and printed requisitions for simplified school ordering.
3. Develop and maintain specifications for all school supplies and equipment by continuously researching and evaluating needs, methods, and materials.
4. Direct school system-wide programs to provide new additional equipment and replace existing equipment in order to ensure minimum equipment standards in all schools.
5. Plan, schedule, and direct equipment rehabilitation programs for a number of elementary and secondary schools each year.
6. Plan and develop budget and expenditure controls for supplies, equipment, and replacement of equipment.
7. Coordinate other departments' programs involving equipment and supplies.
8. Establish and adjust the supply apportionment for all schools and coordinate the ordering and delivery of supplies.

Maintenance and Operations
Objective—To repair school system property, including grounds, buildings, and equipment, and to restore school system owned equipment to approximately its original condition of completeness and efficiency. To plan and supervise those

activities necessary to keep the school plant or office in suitable condition for use, such as cleaning, disinfecting, heating, lighting, caring for lawns, trees, shrubs, and flowers and all similar work. To perform work, either by force account or contract, of minor items of alteration and improvement of buildings and grounds, construction of special items of equipment and work of a similar nature in connection with the capital improvement program.

Functions

1. Administer the maintenance and operation of school buildings, grounds, and equipment to insure uninterrupted educational programs.
2. Administer the maintenance and operation portion of the alterations and improvement program.
3. Establish adequate maintenance policies involving emergency repairs and planned long-term preventive maintenance programs, which include contract as well as force account work.
4. Prepare budgets for operation and maintenance of school plants.
5. Maintain fiscal controls, allocate personnel according to needs and established standards of performance, and plan and schedule work.
6. Establish and maintain safety programs throughout the school system.
7. Administer and manage the office policies, personnel and clerical duties.

The above description of a school facilities department in a large school system gives an idea of the scope and extent of work of that part of the organization. In smaller districts, the work is compressed into smaller units: A fewer number of offices assume more responsibilities. Those school planning responsibilities not done by school system staff are contracted out to various consultants.

Smaller School Systems

Small school systems usually do not have the building demands a large school system does and, as a result, do not employ many people on a regular basis to plan new schools. A medium school system is defined as one with at least 10,000 but no more than 25,000 students.

School systems with fewer than 10,000 students are considered small school systems and usually do not employ even one person to guide the planning process for new buildings. When a school system this small builds a new school facility, the school board employs people from outside the system to do the various jobs required in the planning process.

Figure 1.2
*Organization
Chart for Small
School Systems*

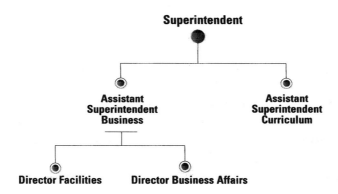

Even a medium-sized school system may employ educational consultants to augment school staff during facility planning. Typically, these systems do not have staff expertise in writing educational specifications, projecting student population growth, evaluating existing buildings, and selecting architects. Since this type of expertise is needed by school systems during facility planning, the system must employ outside consultants.

Figure 1.2 shows the organizational chart for a medium-sized school system and identifies the office and person responsible for facility planning and maintenance. As can be seen, the office is located on the director level, not on the second level down from the superintendent. The position location does indicate, however, the relative importance of new school buildings. The following job description indicates the responsibilities assumed by the head of this office.

Job Description
Director of Facility Maintenance and Transportation
Qualifications
1. Graduation from an accredited college or university with a degree in engineering, planning, or similar discipline and three years of administrative work in a public organization.
2. Experience and knowledge of building and grounds maintenance, construction, operation of large buildings, specification writing, and contract administration.

Reports to—Superintendent or designee.
Supervises—Building maintenance; custodians; construction; contract administration; pupil transportation; and vehicle maintenance.

Performance Responsibilities:

1. Carries out supervisory controls necessary to direct work of personnel assigned to the maintenance division in an overall system-wide maintenance program.
2. Plans, schedules, and inspects work assignments for all maintenance and repairs on buildings and grounds.
3. Makes periodic reports to the Superintendent or designee regarding status of work completed, materials used, labor expended.
4. Responsible for recommendations on projects including cost estimates and materials.
5. Advises on the employment of contractors to perform maintenance services.
6. Assists in the recruitment and recommends assignment, training, transfer, promotion, evaluation, demotion, or dismissal of all maintenance staff.
7. Examines school buildings and develops a program for needed repairs and maintenance.
8. Serves as clerk-of-the-works for all contract work unless otherwise provided.
9. Works cooperatively with the supervisor of purchasing and deputy superintendent in requisitioning materials and equipment, and maintaining records of inventory.
10. Supervises work crews for maintenance and repair of buildings and grounds.
11. Monitors expenditures of allocated funds and adjusts departmental operations within budget limitations and prepares a department budget for recommendation to the Superintendent.
12. Acts as the school system's energy manager. Assembles information, costs, etc., and develops new programs for energy conservation.
13. Ensures that a safe pupil transportation system is developed, administered and maintained to support the total pupil transportation needs of the school system.

School Board Policies

All organizations are governed by policies that specify areas of responsibility and authority. These policies enable people within and outside the organization to know and understand who is responsible for each task assigned in the organization. Thus, policies delineate and circumscribe the responsibilities of various people and offices throughout the organization and, at the same time, award responsibility.

Policies also grant authority to a person or office to do certain tasks and jobs. This authority goes along with the responsibility for completing a task. Both authority and responsibility flow from organizational policies.

School systems are governed by policies popularly termed "school board policies." These policies are resolutions, rules, guidelines, procedures, and regulations adopted by the school board to assist and direct the governance of the system and to eliminate questions of propriety and legitimizing of actions.

Good policies prevent people from duplicating efforts and eliminate staff confusion. For example, school board policies would allocate responsibility and authority to a certain office to select and acquire a site for a new school. For the curriculum development office to select and acquire a site would be duplicative and confusing not only to the entire staff but also to people outside the organization.

In addition to organizational procedures, school policies should also address other phases of school work. Policies should identify areas of concern for the school system and the manner in which things are to take place. For instance, the manner in which purchases are to be made is usually covered in school board policy because this is a very important task. Even tasks that may seem very insignificant might be covered by school policy.

It has often been said that school board policy evolves from problem situations. This means that when a problem arises, the school board solves the problem and creates policy to prevent it from reoccurring. There may be some grain of truth to that maxim; some policies can be traced to such situations, but, for the most part, policies are adopted following deliberation by the school board (Castaldi 1994).

There are many rules, regulations, and procedures imbedded in the school board policies that deal directly with the process of school facility planning. As mentioned above, the general policy on purchasing and bidding governs the work of individuals in the school facility planning department. Other areas of concern for which policies may be needed are:

- Site selection and acquisition
- School name selection
- Site size
- School size and capacity
- Design submissions and approvals
- Student feeder patterns

- Monitoring the design process
- Involvement of the community in the planning process
- School boundaries
- Awarding contracts
- Costing of the capital project
- Bidding process
- Evaluation of existing buildings
- Development of educational specifications
- Capital improvement program planning
- Surety and performance bond requirements
- Change orders
- Construction process and supervision
- Utilization of school facilities
- Protection and guarantees for the school division
- Cooperation with governmental agencies
- Occupancy and orientation of new facilities
- Energy conservation measures
- Architectural and engineering services
- School closing procedures
- Construction records and reports
- Operation of air conditioning systems

Written policies are needed in all of these areas to provide school personnel guidance on how these activities should be executed and who is responsible for doing so. Undoubtedly there are other areas that need policies in certain school systems. Each school system must decide what additional policies are needed. Whatever policies a school system has, they should be periodically reviewed and evaluated for relevance. This is especially true in light of certain recent court decisions and local conditions. Although each school system needs to organize itself to fit local custom, legal requirements and size of its staff, certain elements are common among all school systems. Organizing the school staff for planning a new school building follows certain divisions of labor to fit the disciplines represented. Additionally, there are specified tasks that have to be completed by someone who is competent in the field. That person should be employed by the school system. In this manner, there is a great deal of similarity in the staff who are responsible for planning new school buildings.

The larger the school system, the larger the demand for school buildings, and the more staff is needed to help plan the buildings. As a result, large school systems have school planning staffs that can carry out many school facility planning efforts at one time. Conversely, small school systems do not have a large demand for new schools and thus have little or no staff to handle that task. When a new school facility is needed in these school systems, outside assistance and consultation is employed. ▪

Planning Considerations

PLANNING ACTIVITIES PROBABLY CONSUME MORE OF OUR DAILY TIME THAN ANY OTHER function outside of those designed to maintain our body. Humans spend their lives planning things to do. The level of planning extends from the very basic and simple to rather sophisticated and complex activities. Planning how to go home after work may consume no more than a few seconds of mental activity. On the other hand, planning an expedition to the moon may consume the better part of many lives, People are quite adaptable regarding the level of difficulty of the planning activity in which they engage. While working on a complicated planning task, the same individuals may be planning more simple personal activities without any loss of efficiency on the main task.

Organizations function in much the same way as far as planning activities are concerned, Organizations usually have long-term goals toward which the members work. At the same time, there are many short-term planning activities. Not all of these small-planning activities contribute in the same fashion towards the organizational goals. Because an organization is composed of individuals with personal needs to be met, some short-term plans are designed solely to satisfy the individual and do not contribute to the goals of the organization. In spite of this behavior, the organization moves towards its goals.

Planning is a purposeful activity that helps achieve something. This definition applies equally to individuals and organizations. Without planning, nothing is accomplished, unless by accident. Organizations could not successfully pursue a goal without some sort of planning. Aimless activities would result without planning, and these types of activities are pernicious to the life of an organization.

Plans are devised in order to accomplish certain things. Without plans, an organization could not long continue to offer the services for which it is responsible. There are several reasons for planning, most of which center around the idea of cooperative efforts on the part of individuals in the organization. Random activities on the other hand do not accomplish important things and do not move an organization toward some goals.

Therefore, the purposes of organizational planning are the following:

- To develop and approve acceptable goals,
- To allocate and use available resources efficiently,
- To marshal and conserve staff cooperation and input into goal efforts.

Planning Models

There are two general categories of planning: rational and interactive (Adams, 1991). Rational planning is a linear process with each segment of planning following from the preceding one. This type of planning emphasizes set actions toward predetermined goals or outcomes. Rational planning has definite sequential steps through which the organization should go in developing a plan. This category of planning is thought of as using top-down methodology and decision-making, such as in the hierarchical structure of the public schools. It relies heavily upon hard data and quantification methodology. Many of the problems associated with school facilities such as space allocation, physical plant construction, student projections, transportation assessment, and cost analysis are amenable to the use of a rational planning methodology.

Interactive planning seems to be the opposite of rational planning in that it lends itself best to problems that do not need a high degree of objectivity or quantifiable data. Instead it relies on data derived through ethnographic investigation. Interactive planning is done through decentralized, small, face-to-face groups and it is a team effort as contrasted to centralized planning groups used in rational planning.

Goals in interactive planning models are not permanent, but suggest directions to be discussed. The methodology used in interactive planning is suited to comprehensive and educational policy planning, most institutional planning, curriculum planning, and even resource planning because of the fluid nature of the school organization.

These two categories of planning models seem to be poles apart in their definition. In spite of the apparent contradiction between the two, a third model can be used that incorporates the parts of both. In the composite model, the rational planning model is not developed and implemented just from the top down.

Granted there are many places where all planning is in that direction, but this occurs because someone believes that is the most appropriate way to plan. Many school systems believe in a team approach to planning but use a rational methodological approach. Probably, very few educators could feel confident using soft data, to the exclusion of any other, as would be done in interactive planning. School systems simply do not work that way. On the other hand, school administrators would feel very comfortable using a combination of hard and soft data for appropriate applications.

There are many models of planning available to the school administrator with probably no pure models in existence. The difference between various models may be more in application than in fundamentals. The particular methodology chosen will reflect the ability of the school administrator to define the planning process more than anything else will.

While there is a great deal of leeway in formulating the planning process, there are probably limited processes that can be developed in the local school system. A major difference between models may be the manner in which people within and outside the school system are involved or not involved in the planning process. Another difference may be in the degree of freedom planners have from predetermined goals and processes. If everything from goals to evaluation is set by the top administrators and the data available is limited to certain data sets, there is significantly little the staff can do to affect the process.

The superintendent of schools is the person responsible for the planning process of the school system. If the superintendent wants an open planning system, that will be reflected in the manner in which the planning group does its work. If the school administrator wishes to significantly involve members of the school staff and community, the planning process would reflect that. There are meaningful ways to involve people, and that should be one hallmark of the school system planning process. Secondly, the school administrator should provide leadership to assist the group in defining the parameters of the planning process for all involved.

Planning Types

Lewis (1983) lists three types of planning processes that differ only in the time frame: problem solving, operational and strategic. All of these processes use the same methodology, but they differ in the time spent in the process. There is, however, some difference in the scope of what is to be planned. Problem-solving planning covers activities that can be completed quickly or, at most, within three months. The intensity of planning activities and the focus of work is no less than in other planning processes, but the time frame is shorter.

Operational planning covers activities that last up to a year. Most operational planning is tied directly into the operational budget of the school system (which is also effective for one year).

Strategic planning is used for those goals and objectives that need considerable time to meet. This type of planning lasts from three to seven years. The long-range plan of a school system is directly related to strategic planning methodology.

Some authorities feel that strategic planning should be used to develop a long-range plan for a school system (Norris and Poulton 1991). Strategic planning incorporates the environmental scanning the school system does to analyze the world in which it finds itself. This environmental scanning is the assessment of forces, constraints, social movements, and similar events outside of the school system that might influence what happens inside the school system and how the school system may respond to these pressures and demands.

Much of what is done in the school system lends itself to long-range or strategic planning, especially activities related to housing students in school buildings. Although some of the work of the school facilities department involves short-term and operational planning efforts, the major share is long-range projects. This department actively works to implement the long-range plan of the school system through the capital improvement program.

Not many states require local school systems to produce a long-range plan. Nonetheless, school systems plan for the long term because organizations can not change, improve, or respond to community needs in a short period of time. All school systems have limited resources, and to apply these limited resources wisely to the needs of the community, planning for the long term is necessary.

Planning Steps

The actual steps in planning consist of the activities of an individual or group to accomplish some objective. It is the ordering of events and resources that produces results. Most experts agree that no matter how difficult or simple the planning task, the steps in planning are the same. The nature of planning governs the steps needed to implement a plan. The following are steps in planning, regardless of the activity:

1. Identification and agreement on the problem or goal,
2. Identification of the data needed,
3. Formulation of alternative solutions,
4. Identification of preferred solutions,
5. Implementation of solution or plan, and
6. Evaluation of results.

It is assumed that a constant feedback loop allows the group to go back to a previous step or even to begin again.

Some authorities include an additional step: planning to plan. Some have also suggested another step: identify those who should be included in the planning process. While these two initial steps might be germane in some instances, the first step above includes all of the activities that go into the identification and agreement on the problem or goal. This would include consideration of the people to be involved as well as the method of organizing the effort. Thus, those individuals who are concerned with the goal-setting activity would be involved already. The six steps above speak well for the process and cover all activities needed to plan adequately.

The types of planning activities that occur daily within the school system varies; there are many short-term planning activities, as well as many long-term ones. Indeed, much of the planning activity of the school system could be classified as long term.

Long-term planning affords the school system sufficient time to raise the needed funds for a particular project. In the area of school facility planning, it is impossible to plan, design, and construct a building in less than three to five years. Because of this, long-term planning must take place to have a new school building ready when needed. For a new school project, staff members are engaged in planning activities for several years. Therefore, if the school system needs a new building at a certain place at a certain time, long-term planning must proceed and, to complete the long-term project, many short term planning efforts must transpire first. These short-term planning efforts go together to form the long-term plans.

Strategic Planning

The discussion on the use of strategic planning versus the use of long-range planning is still an important topic for many writers in the field. In spite of the fact that there are a variety of planning paradigms and methods, the major distinction between strategic and long-range planning is still evident in much of the literature on the subject (Donsky 1996). Some of these discussions give the impression that educators have a choice between two types of planning. This is a misconception of the nature and purpose of planning. A common characteristic of all organizational planning modes is that their timeframes and processes are defined by the needs of the organization, not necessarily by changing environmental conditions.

The standard argument regarding the difference between the two planning modes is that long range planning is limited in value to the planning process for educational organizations because the process is so linear and rigid and is entirely data driven. Opponents of long-range planning techniques stress the fact that long-range planning does not take into consideration the environment in which the schools operate. Further, this type of planning does not give direction to the organization.

Strategic planning on the other hand is characterized as being dynamic and active. By scanning the environment and the realities of life, the process produces useful strategies and tactics that will permit the organization to go in new directions. Such simplified descriptions of a very complex process do not give it proper perspective. The most distinguishing feature of the process, however, is the interaction of the organization with the environment with resultant changes in how the organization operates. This feature incorporates extensive data gathering about the environment and a determination of how the organization can respond to service opportunities and possible threats to effectiveness. In this manner the operation and emphasis of the organization might be modified or changed (Kaufman and Herman 1991).

One of the most classic examples of successful strategic planning that resulted in a change of direction for the organization might be in the private sector where through extensive environmental scanning and analysis, a company can and does change directions. Tobacco companies that produce cigarettes and other such products would be a good example. Years ago when the research studies indicating the dangers of smoking became public, the tobacco producing companies could very well see the handwriting on the wall. Then when the numbers of cigarette smokers dramatically dropped as a result of the research findings, they realized something had to be done to maintain profits. The organization had to change dramatically in order to remain a viable organization. One form of change could be to diversify by producing other products a large number of consumers would want so as to counteract the loss of tobacco consuming customers. Such a strategy would change the direction of the parent company making it a more diversified or comprehensive firm. One tobacco company diversified through buying up several food producing and distributing companies. In this manner the tobacco company became a conglomerate rather than a single product firm. The direction of the company was changed as a result of external forces. Although, there is no publicly documented evidence of such strategic planning and implementation, it serves as a good example of the use of strategic planning that changes the direction of an organization.

When the public schools employ rigorous strategic planning such dramatic change in the direction or purpose of the organization is not possible (Donsky 1996). This is mainly because the public schools are a part of the government that has a mandate that can not be changed much beyond what the state legislature or local community desires. This kind of external oversight limits the flexibility of the public schools to dramatically change directions or expand services. Change in direction or purposes of the public schools comes much more gradually and usually through outside pressure and intervention more so than through internal planning regardless of the type of planning.

This is not to say that that the public schools should not use strategic planning to the fullest. Quite the contrary, schools should use strategic planning or some derivative of it when and where appropriate. The key is deciding the appropriateness of any strategic planning. As mentioned above, strategic planning is very complicated and complex. The process requires a great deal of data in order to identify viable strategies and alternatives to consider.

Strategic planning is best suited for a discrete organization. By that is meant that a segment or department within the organization might find it difficult to complete major planning independent of the planning of the parent organization. For instance, a teacher would not attempt strategic planning for the instructional program in the classroom. The planning the teacher does may involve others and employ some recognition of what is happening in the neighborhood of the school which are elements of strategic planning, but the formal process of strategic planning is absent. On the other hand, the principal and faculty can do some strategic planning for the annual school plan and employ much of the elements of strategic planning and management. Even this level of strategic planning is on a limited scale because of time and budget constraints. Nevertheless, elements of strategic planning can be employed on a school building level.

Strategic planning best serves an organization when the time frame is for several years, not one or two years. In addition, the school system is the organizational entity of the community regardless of the size of the public schools. Strategies and decisions emanating from a strategic planning process can be allocated sufficient resources by the school board to be successful. This is not always true on the school building or classroom level. Finally, the local school system, through the school board, interfaces with the state authority that created it and mandates certain courses of study and services to the general public.

Figure 2.1 illustrates a modification of the strategic planning model that would fit a school system planning effort as well as a school building unit. Many of the components of formal strategic planning are included here, and the planning effort results in a long-range planning document that can be used to effect the plan.

Planning for the long term is very characteristic of the public schools. As stated above, a variety of different planning modes are utilized for specific purposes. Much of the day-by-day activities of the personnel within the school system are governed by short term planning. There are, however, very specific long term planning activities in which the school system must engage. Almost all of the capital improvement projects completed by the school system fall under activities

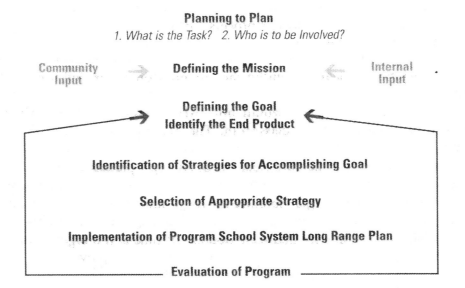

Planning to Plan
1. What is the Task?   2. Who is to be Involved?

Community Input → **Defining the Mission** ← Internal Input

Defining the Goal
Identify the End Product

Identification of Strategies for Accomplishing Goal

Selection of Appropriate Strategy

Implementation of Program School System Long Range Plan

Evaluation of Program

Figure 2.1
Process of Planning

that are considered long term. By that is meant, the activities span several years and involve many sub-plans within an over arching plan for each project. The question then is how do these long term planning activities fit into the overall planning of the school system. If strategic planning is done by the school system, how do the other planning activities fit into the scheme developed through strategic planning.

Public school systems probably do not engage in what might be called pure-type strategic planning, mostly because of the mandated nature of the schools. Public schools do not have the freedom of changing focus or direction as much as other organizations, especially private corporations. As a result, the public schools practice a more moderated form of strategic planning. Nevertheless, the strategic planning efforts of the school system are just as important to the general direction of the schools as to private firms. There must, however, be a direct tie into the other planning activities of the schools from the strategic plan. The key for educators is how to link the strategic planning activities to the more traditional planning efforts, such as the operational plan and budget, the long-range plan of the school system, and instructional planning that spans several years.

Each school system must devise a strategic planning effort that fits that locality. These plans are indigenous to each school system and must account for the degree of latitude of freedom to incorporate new ideas, expertise of the school staff, and the state legislative mandates in operation. From the strategic planning effort, a document should evolve that states quite precisely what the school system will do in the coming years. The exact terminology for this document will vary from state to state depending upon requirements of the department of education or local usage. Some of the terms used to identify these documents include: Comprehensive Educational Plan, School District Master Plan, The Six-Year Plan, Long-range Plan, Long-range Development Plan, Long-range Educational Plan, Educational Development Plan, or School District Educational Plan. Regardless of the name of the document, the contents of the document are greatly similar. ▪

chapter three

Planning in the Public Schools

PLANNING FOR NEW SCHOOL BUILDINGS OR FOR MAJOR RENOVATIONS TO EXISTING facilities requires considerable effort on the part of many highly skilled professional and technical personnel both inside and outside of the school system. In some instances, the working efforts of these individuals comprise separate and distinguishable steps. These steps, however, can be thought of as separate processes that must be completed in order to accomplish the project. In spite of the fact that most individuals speak about the process of planning a school as if it were a single entity, the fact of the matter is that planning for any major capital project consists of a series of processes.

If one could take an overall view of the planning process for any major capital project, it would be possible to view it as a series of separate steps or processes that comprise a whole process. If it were possible to image that on a certain date in time, the superintendent of schools and school board came to the conclusion a new school or a major renovation was needed to accommodate an increasing student population or a planned major change in educational program. The question immediately comes to mind, what are the steps that they must go through before the project becomes a reality? There are many identifiable separate steps or processes the school staff and school board must go through to complete the task and end up with a new or renovated facility.

Planning, designing, and constructing a capital project can be thought of as a rather complex process composed of many steps or processes. These processes have certain requirements that must be met. For instance, hiring an architect is one major step, but there is also a process the school board must go through before the architectural contract is signed. Moreover, the work of the architect is a different step than employment and again, the school board and staff have some responsibilities to make certain the design meets the needs of the school staff.

Each of the steps can be perceived as a separate process that certain actors must complete in order for the capital project to be constructed. In the usual progression of events, the school staff and school board must complete the following steps or processes:

- Organize the school staff
- Determine the size of the student population
- Select and acquire a site for a new school building
- Select and employ an architect
- Develop a funding package
- Develop a set of Educational Specifications
- Monitor the design
- Advertise and bid the project
- Monitor the construction phase to completion
- Orient the staff to the building
- Evaluate the building and planning process

These are the usual steps a school system must go through to complete a new building. These steps or processes may not strictly follow the order listed above, although that is the normal progression of events. Sometimes political decisions might delay one or more of these processes that throws the entire process out of order. Nevertheless, some of these processes can proceed independent of other processes. For instance, the school staff may develop a set of educational specifications long before either a school site is selected or an architect employed without serious consequence. There are, however, some processes that must proceed or follow others, such as securing sufficient funds before a site is acquired. Likewise, a school system would not want an architect to begin designing the facility before the necessary educational planning is completed. There is, however, a certain amount of fluidity in the order of these processes.

The school system staff and school board must properly supervise and administer all of these processes. Outside personnel are normally contracted to complete some of the processes above, but the overall supervision and direction rests with school personnel. In small school systems, most of the processes above are completed with the assistance of outside expertise because the school does not have the staff to complete the work. Even in these systems there must be sufficient school personnel to properly interface with outside consultants and design professionals.

Planning Responsibility

In every school system, someone must be responsible for all planning efforts on an organizational level. In a small school system, the responsibility might be lodged in one person who is an administrative assistant. That person organizes the school staff to produce the long-range plan. In large school systems, there may be an office of research and planning that assumes the planning responsibility. In a very large system, the department of planning may service the entire school system.

Regardless of who or what office is directing the planning effort, there will always be a certain amount of discord resulting from the planning efforts. The planning office or person will always be perceived as planning for others rather than planning with them. This cleavage is normal but disquieting because planning which involves staff should truly be a cooperative affair. Unfortunately, this is not always the case, especially when staff members feel they do not have a say in how planning takes place. To forestall such feelings, the planning office or officer should actively seek ways to involve staff early in the process. The planning process should produce a plan that is acceptable to everyone and that staff members will work toward, and, at the same time, should be one that represents the needs of the school system.

The planning efforts directed toward a long-range plan never come to an end. The planning process for a long-range plan is cyclical in nature in that there is no beginning and no end. Changes in the current long-range plan will take place periodically through the normal process of review. The minute one long-range plan is adopted, work begins on modifications and changes so the document is continually updated. In this manner, a school system always has a current long-range plan from which it is working.

Developing a long-range plan is not an easy task, especially considering the number of people involved. Considerable lead-time must be allowed to complete the document early enough for review and adoption. The office in charge of planning must adopt a schedule and publish it widely to gain support and cooperation in getting the tasks completed.

Long Range Planning Document

Planning is a purposeful activity designed to reach an objective. Planning activities within the school system assist in accomplishing certain things within the overall long-range plan. The long-range plan serves as a means for all of the departments in the school system to work toward common goals. It serves as the authority for the activities of all segments of the organization for a number of years. The long-range plan, therefore, should address the goals of the school system, the recipients of the services, and the resources available.

The requirements for the content of the long-range plan vary from state to state and from school system to school system. There are, however, some essential elements that must be included in any long-range plan. As stated above, the purpose of the document is to identify goals and apply resources to those goals; therefore, the long-range plan should contain considerable information about the school system. At a minimum, the document should address the following major headings:

- The Community — Location, resources, constraints
- The Educational Program — Number and kinds of programs
- The Number of Students — How many and kinds of students
- The Facilities — Number and kinds of teaching spaces
- The Financial Plan — Sources and amounts of funds

These headings are convenient divisions of the school system's total plan. Each heading contains considerable information about what is to be done and the resources available to the school system.

The Community

The long-range plan should describe the community in which the school system is located. This description should include a listing of resources available to assist the schools in doing their job. The community description should also detail the socio-economic problems people face and their effect upon the schools. Where the schools have tried to mount programs to assist the general population with their community problems, these programs should be identified.

The results of the environmental scanning could be presented here because this description is in effect analyzing external influences upon the schools. The description of this scanning should be of considerable value to those working within the school system. This section should present sufficient information so that readers not associated with the school system could gain an accurate view of the community and its effect upon the schools.

The Educational Program

This section deals with the type of educational program offered by the schools. The description must be precise so that the entire scope of the educational activities is listed. The main thrust may be of the kindergarten through twelfth grade program, but all of the programs for which the school system assumes responsibility should be described and each program must in some way relate directly to the goals identified for the school system.

The section dealing with educational programs should contain a very specific description of programs starting with the goals of the school system and translating them into enabling goals, and finally into objectives and behavioral objectives. Subject matter included in the various programs should be included in the description. Readers should have a very detailed view of the educational program offered by the school system.

New educational programs and activities that are projected to be started during the life of the long-range plan should also be identified. A description should include the population to be included, the numbers of individuals or groups, and the number and kind of staff needed. In addition, the year of planning and implementation should be identified. New initiatives will require funding at some point. Identifying these programs and their impact on staffing will allow the personnel department to mount a human resource plan to procure the needed staff.

Further, information contained in this section will affect the financial plan developed to fund the long-range plan. Therefore, this section should be in great detail so that all pieces—needed staff, materials, space and funds — will come together and be available at the appropriate time.

Student Projections

The number of students the school system will serve in the future is an important piece of information. The school system must plan for the appropriate number of students and adults the system will expect to have in the next few years. This is necessary in order to have the right kinds of educational spaces and in the right locations at the propitious time. Planning and constructing a new school building consumes many years, and a school system needs lead time to complete the task. This section of the document should show how enrollment projections in the school system will grow or decline, in what locations, and the kinds of students that will be in attendance.

School Facilities

This section should describe the educational spaces available in the school system. To prepare this document, all of the school facilities owned and operated by the system should be evaluated. The results should indicate the number of classroom spaces that can be used and how many students they can hold. The difference between the number of instructional spaces available and the number projected to be needed would indicate the need for new space. If the school system is experiencing a decline in student population, surplus instructional spaces should also be identified. In this situation, decisions must be made for the disposition of the surplus either in identifying different uses for the spaces or by disposing of the surplus through sale. In any event, there should be a comparison between available space and number of spaces needed, and a plan devised to deal with the difference no matter which direction. The financial impact of either should be addressed.

The Financial Plan

The final section should deal with the financial package developed to fund the long-range plan. This funding plan should deal with both operational funding and capital funding.

When adopted, the operational funding plan becomes the operational budget of the school system. Even though this budget is for only one year, projections of operational budgets for the future should be made so that the school board can see the future financial impact of the proposed program. This is important, because it allows the school board to anticipate financial need (assuming the educational program is implemented).

The other part of the financial plan should deal with the need for capital funds. In as much as capital funds are obtained differently than operational funds, a plan detailing how these funds are obtained must be presented. If a new school is needed, the plan should provide a way to obtain capital funds through whatever means available to the school system. Most school systems rely upon general obligation bonds to pay for new facilities. This means a bond issue will need to be floated. If state programs exist to aid local school systems in constructing a new building, the plan should include anticipated funding from this source.

Capital funds are usually under a separate budget from the operational budget, but the pay back for bonds is included in the debt reduction section of the operational budget. The impact of the bond issue re-payment on the operational budget should be examined. The financial analysis should also look at the existing bonded indebtedness of the school system and the effect on the district's capability to go further in debt. All of these considerations should be discussed thoroughly in the financial plan section of the long-range plan.

Action Plans

The long-range plan itself is never intended to be implemented directly. This rather large compendium of data gives direction to the entire school system, but the actual implementation of what the long-range plan stipulates is left to more refined and precise documents. After acceptance of the long-range plan by the school board, the departments, offices, and individuals within the school system must breakdown the long-range plan into manageable parts to actually complete what the overall plan contains.

The document that will actually serve as the implementation tool is called an Action Plan or Work Plan. Sections of the long-range plan are divided into discrete portions and assigned to personnel who have expertise in that certain field. These sections are then converted into work instruments with precise objectives that can be accomplished.

Each segment of the long-range plan contains work that must be done in order for the plan to be completed. These segments have a cluster of responsibilities that will need special expertise, such as the finance plan will need individuals expert in many different areas of financial planning. Figure 3.1 illustrates the actual department or individual that has responsibility to develop and implement an Action Plan. As can be seen, these responsibilities cover the entire spectrum of the functions of the school system. In smaller school systems, several of these functions may be incorporated under one person or office. Nevertheless, the Action Plan must be developed and discharged for each of these responsibilities. Regardless of the size of the school system, all of these jobs need to be completed by someone.

The long-range plan of the school system permeates all segments of the organization. These segments in turn develop action plans to be implemented. The most obvious manifestation of these Action Plans is in the individual school building where the principal and staff formulate and complete an annual school plan. These individual school site plans complement the school system long-range plan, yet display the necessary individualization of planning to meet the needs of the children in each school building.

The exact format of the work plans may vary according to each locality. The plans, however, should contain several segments that enable the department, office, or individual to: (1) identify the job to be completed, (2) the objectives of the job, (3) measures of effectiveness, (4) costs associated with attainment of the objectives, and (5) deadlines for completion. These plans might also contain statements relating to the further division of work and task responsibilities into

LONG-RANGE PLAN SECTION	TYPE OF ACTION PLAN	RESPONSIBILITY
1. Community Characteristics		
2. Educational Plan Description	Curriculum Development Instructional Development Human Resource Plan	Director of Curriculum Director of Instruction Director of Personnel
3. Student Projections	Demographic Study for SDE Funding	Director of Research
4. Facility Needs	Capital Improvement Plan	Director of Facilities

5. Financial Plan	Budgetary Plans
	   Operating Budget
	   Capital Budget
		Director of Finance

	Annual School Site Plan	Principal & Staff

Figure 3.1
Action Plans

smaller units, the quality of the product that is needed, and sources of assistance available. There may also be statements relating to certain limitations, handicaps, and constraints the department will have to overcome to be successful.

One important aspect of the Action Plans is the need for assigned resources to complete the objectives. These resources are in the form of personnel, time, and funds. Without these resources, the work under the Action Plans can not be accomplished. This resource allocation is in the form of department, office, school site, or individual budgets that are derived from the general operational budget of the school system.

The Action Plans usually have a life of one year, but new Action Plans are developed each year. Those tasks or objectives not completed in year one are then re-cast into the plan for the following year until they are either completed or changed. An objective can be declared redundant because of changing circumstances and dropped from the plan. This would result from evaluations of the Action Plan and would reflect back on the changes in the long-range plan which seeps into that document each year. These changes can result from a number of influences both inside and outside the school system. Naturally changes emanating from the state department of education, for example, could influence the long-range plan immensely. Such changes are not a negative aspect of the long-range plan, but a simple recognition of the fact that the long-range plan is a living document that can change as circumstances inside and outside the school system may change.

Each department, office, school, and individual is evaluated according to the amount of work completed. This evaluation can take the form of formal reports to the superintendent and school board to informal conversational evaluations on a personal basis. Each school system must develop a system of accountability and evaluation to determine the success of those involved in this work. Successful work towards the completion of the Action Plan for each department or office is expected. Rewards of some sort should then be supplied to effective managers who complete the Action Plan. Conversely, remediation in some form is applied to those individuals who can not or did not accomplish the work assigned under the Action Plan.

The work of the school system proceeds through the implementation of each Action Plan. In this manner, the long-range plan of the school system is implemented. Completion of all objectives and tasks under an Action Plan indicates the school system is moving successfully towards the general goals. This movement is more of a gradual accomplishment than sudden rushes and spurts of activity. ■

chapterfour

Long-Range Planning:
Program Development

THE FIRST PART OF THE LONG-RANGE PLANNING EFFORT EXAMINES THE COMMUNITY in which the school system is located and the type of educational program delivered to the youth of this geo-political area. This examination can take many forms and can use various types of instruments for gathering data. Data may be solicited from sources within and outside of the school system.

The community in which the school system is located contains many elements that impinge upon as well as support the individual school organizations (Graves 1993). For the long-range plan, however, the description of the community should report both assets and liabilities. The educational program developed by the school system should reflect the particular needs of the community. For example, in areas with social problems, many times school systems develop educational programs to lessen the impact of those problems on the citizens and students of the community. Essentially, the community problems influence the school system to respond to a particular problem. In this manner, the educational program of the school system is influenced by community problems. Therefore, identifying community problems is a very important part of the long-range plan.

Likewise, the community has assets that various school organizations can use to augment the educational program. Examples of this include museums, zoos, transportation systems, and parks and recreation programs that the community operates. In addition, there are private sector assets that schools can and do use. Examples of this are private museums, musical and sporting organizations, social groups, and medical associations. These, too, should be described in the long-range plan.

In each community there are various social and governmental programs and services designed to assist citizens who need them. The extent of these programs and services depends upon the community itself. In some communities, there are very few services, but in others, the range is extensive. In many cases, the school system depends upon these services and programs to assist in the development and growth of students. Many of these programs and services aid the lower income population of the school system or those who have trouble helping themselves, but some programs serve the entire range of school age population in the school system.

Nevertheless, all of these activities assist the school staff in educating children who live in the school system. Because of this, precise documentation of these programs and services is important for it will enable school system employees to become familiar with these assets and how they might assist in their work.

Because each community is unique, the community asset description is place specific. Much of the educational program then is effected by the availability (or the lack) of these programs and services in the community. This is the reason an enumeration and documentation of community assets and problems should be printed in the long-range plan of the school system.

The second item to be addressed in the long-range plan is the educational program. On first thought, describing the educational program of the school system must seem like an impossible task if done properly. A simple listing of subjects on each level might be more appropriate and less time consuming. But the curriculum is more than the subject matter taught in the schools, and for that reason, more detail and precision is needed in the description than a simple listing of courses and subject matter. This section of the plan should not only describe in detail the present educational program, but also the program that will be implemented in the next five to seven years or through the end of the long range plan. The latter is very important because of the implication for change in the school system in the future.

Much of the educational program of the school system is now mandated on the state level. In the last 20 years, each state has exercised its control over its school systems by mandating more and more courses of study and services. The number of courses or subject matter prescribed by states during this period has increased greatly. Therefore, the differences between school systems have decreased over the past two decades. This is not to say, that all school systems are alike; such is not the case. But there are many similarities and considerable uniformity throughout the states. This means that each school system needs to describe its educational program in detail to delineate the differences.

Each school system changes and adds to the program offered students. This is a never-ending process of improving the educational program. Each school system improves its offerings by adding services as well. While one school system may have a certain course of study or service, another may not have it, but will be working to acquire that course, or some other. Each of these program changes or improvements must be described in the long-range plan so resources are allocated to achieve that improvement.

As stated in the previous chapter, the long-range plan serves as a stem from which other plans of action branch. These action plans may be in staff development for a new program, in human resources to secure new teachers for the changed program, in the curriculum department to develop curricular materials, or in the school facilities department to develop a capital improvement plan. Therefore, it is necessary to spell out the changes to the school system's educational program envisioned in the immediate future.

The first task in describing the educational program is to identify the goals and purposes of the school system (Mackinzie 1989). These statements relate why the organization exists and what it does. The goals and purposes guide the organization in its task of educating the youth of the community.

Each organization has generalized statements about what it does that are printed in a document. These statements give direction to the workers and to identify what the organization does to those who are outside of it. Such statements also limit the scope of operation and focus the efforts of workers. This dual purpose is served equally by these goal statements.

In extremely small organizations, a definition of purpose can be understood by all concerned without a purpose or goal statement. This is because everyone knows what the goal is and how to work effectively to the goal. The more complex the organization becomes, the less likely it becomes that all employees will know what the goal is or how they are to work towards it unless there are written statements they can refer to occasionally. In a very complex, large organization, such as a school system, the purposes and goals need to be identified and written for the edification of everyone.

There are many ways of writing the purpose and goals of an organization. These statements may be expressed as a vision statement, a mission statement, philosophy of education statement, goals, and behavioral objectives. While these terms have specific meanings, many school systems use the terms interchangeably with little distinction between them. Such indiscriminate use of these terms does not facilitate clarity.

There are precise distinctions between the terms cited above. Each describes a specific part of the organization's goals and purpose in decreasingly global aspects and scope. To lessen confusion about their use, the following section will examine these terms.

Vision Statement

Recently an even more global term has been coined to describe what the organization does. Designed to point the organization to a more distant future, this term has been called a vision statement.

A vision statement guides the organization to a better world. This statement is of a rather grand order and describes what the organization would like to work towards and how it can contribute. Although a vision statement may be constructed to be something like a blue-sky wish, it must conform to the area of responsibility of the organization. The vision statement can not deal with all of the problems of the worked, but must confine itself to education, as in the case of the school system. A vision statement is something everyone concerned with the organization would like to see in the future. The following is an example of a vision statement developed by a state board of education:

Vision Statement—Every child can learn. Each child has unique talents that our schools must identify and develop. The Commonwealth's most important investment in the present and in the future is to provide for all its children an education based upon excellence and equity.

This statement identifies two general areas in which that particular organization would like to see the state move, i.e., excellence and equity. Both of these qualities are worthwhile and need to be included in the vision people have of a good school system. This vision statement is also global in that it addresses the future state of education.

Mission Statement

The mission statement is much different from the vision statement, as well as from the philosophy, goal, or purpose statements that are frequently used. Where a vision statement points the organization to the future, the mission statement explains what the organization is all about. Likewise, the mission statement does not address goals of the organization specifically, nor the belief system in operation in the schools, nor the goals towards which the school system is working.

The mission statement may be akin to the purpose statement in that the mission of a school system also is its purpose. The purpose and the mission statements may, in fact, be the same thing, however, the term "mission statement" seems to be in favor with educators today.

The mission statement of a school system must answer the twin questions of why this organization was formed and what it is supposed to do. In essence, the mission statement cites the legal basis of the organization of the school system.

In all states, the legislature has created local schools for a specific purpose—to provide an appropriate educational for all the youth of the community. That is, indeed, the purpose and mission of the local school system rather than to maintain law and order such as the sheriff's department does or to provide recreational services which is the responsibility of the recreation department. But the local school system, as represented by the school board, may also wish to express the type of educational program to be offered in the community based upon the needs of the people to be served. In that case, the mission statement must also reflect this local need.

A mission statement of a state board of public education is shown below. This statement alludes to the state constitution as the source of authority and power for the board, but the statement also addresses the specific work of the board as that body sees it. This specific mission statement should be read in conjunction with the vision statement cited above in this chapter:

Mission Statement—The mission of the Board of Education is to ensure for all children in the Commonwealth an education that enables them to become informed and productive citizens in a democratic society. In keeping with Article viii of the Constitution of the State, the Board establishes standards of quality, subject to revision only by the General Assembly, and exercises general supervision of the public school system. The Board has primary responsibility and authority for establishing educational policy. To that end, the Board provides leadership and actively involves citizens and school systems in formulating the policies necessary to meet its educational commitment.

This mission statement is for a state board of education and addresses the responsibility statewide. In a local school system, the responsibility is to the citizens of the geo-political area served by the schools. With slight changes in wording, this mission statement could serve a local school system. The mission of a school system is to provide an appropriate education for all youth in accordance with the constitutional provisions of the state school system. Every school system should have a clear and concise mission statement, whether or not there is a vision statement. Such an expression provides everyone concerned with a clear idea of what the organization does.

Philosophy

Of course, defining what is an appropriate education has to follow from the philosophical statement and the goals identified for the school system. The mission statement simply tells what the organization is and defines its purpose. Defining what is meant by education must stem from other statements. This is where both the philosophical statement and goals carry on the mission of the organization.

Philosophy deals with belief systems and tries to explain certain phenomenon, such as:

- How do individuals learn?
- What is knowledge?
- Where does knowledge come from?
- What are values?
- Where do values come from?

These are very important questions for school system employees, because much of what is done is governed by the beliefs these individuals hold about these questions. What is taught in the schools is determined to a large extent by what we believe is knowledge. Likewise, how an individual believes children learn will greatly determine the methods used to teach. The values teachers try to instill in their students depend to a large measure upon what values the teachers believe important. In spite of the fact that each teacher must have answers to these questions, the school system also has an interest in these questions and should have some answers to guide the teachers and administrators when they work with students.

This does not mean that the school system should force teachers and administrators to hold common beliefs, but there should be a common statement that answers the questions above to which all can ascribe. There should be room for individual belief systems within the overall philosophical statement of a school system.

The philosophical statement of a school system should confine itself to answering the questions of belief listed above. This statement should not address the purpose of the school system, nor the goals towards which the organization is working, but rather how individuals learn, the type of setting or environment that is conducive to learning, and the larger picture of values and where knowledge originates. These are the only areas that a philosophical statement should cover. To include other items in a philosophical statement is to miss the real meaning of the belief statement that a school system should have.

Goals

The next level of expression of what a school system should be doing addresses goals. These statements express how an organization should direct its efforts and what the program can do for individuals. In other words, the school system will direct resources to assist individuals to become more productive or gain certain knowledge, skills, and attitudes. The goals of an organization can never be achieved but are something toward which an organization works. For example, if educating the youth of the community is a goal of the school system, then that goal can not be achieved until the last youngster in the community graduates and there are no more left to be educated, a situation which is most likely never to occur.

The goal statements should reflect all previously developed statements. If a school system has developed vision, mission, and philosophical statements, then the goal statements are usually thought of as program goals. A set of goals might be: *The Goals of the Washington Public Schools are the following:*

1. To develop in each student, by relevant, interesting and diversified instruction, a command of the basic skills and the ability to think clearly, communicate effectively and learn easily.
2. To help each student to be creative and make cultural and recreational activities a part of his/her life.
3. To give each student a clear and honest understanding of the United States, including contemporary urban problems, historical interpretation and international relations.

These program goals reflect what the school system works towards and where it will commit its resources. The goals identify activities legally within the purview of the school system and focus on the individual student. As goals can never be fully met they are stated in generalized terms rather than by using measurable or quantifiable terms.

Enabling goals sometimes augments the goals of a school system. These are statements, which direct the organization to do certain things so that the general goals of the school system can be addressed. For example, certain services must be available before any instructional program can be activated, so an enabling goal would focus on the services. Enabling goals are assumed by certain segments of the school system to assist the instructional segment of the organization; the enabling goals move the organization toward the general goals.

Examples of enabling goals are:

- To develop an efficient, responsive and flexible organization with the motivation, ability and resources to meet the needs of each student, teacher, and administrator.
- To engage in every effort to attract, train, and retrain the most competent personnel.
- To provide functional physical plants, in which teachers can utilize modern teaching methods, students can effectively learn, and to which community residents will come.

As with program goals, enabling goals are never fully met but are something towards which the organization works until such time the goals change. For example, the third goal is something towards which the school facilities department continuously works. The goal will never be fully achieved because there will always be a continuing need to provide modern, functional buildings to house students. This particular goal drives the maintenance program to provide such housing for students. So long as there are buildings, the enabling goal will be relevant and there will be a need to have a maintenance program.

The other two enabling goals address the organization of the school system and its staffing. Both these areas are of vital concern in working towards the program goals. Without an efficient organization and staff, work efforts would be handicapped. Other enabling goals may be needed to augment the program goals. These should be developed in conjunction with the major program goals.

Behavioral Objectives

Assuming goals cannot be achieved as such, there must be some way to measure the effectiveness and efficiency of the organization in working towards its goals. To do so, the goals of the organization must be translated into statements that are measurable. These statements are termed behavioral objectives.

Behavioral objectives are written in terms of observable student behavior that can be measured by some type of instrument. This means the student will be measured or examined to determine how much of a predetermined amount of knowledge has been gained after appropriate instruction. Behavioral objectives

Figure 4.1
Behavioral
Objectives

Organizational Goal 1.0

Develop in each student, by relevant, interesting and diversified instruction, a command of the basic skills and the ability to think clearly, communicate effectively, and learn easily.

Program Objective 1.0

During the XXXX-XX school year, each student will master the basic learning skills of reading at a level commensurate with his/her ability as measured by norm-referenced tests.

Behavioral Objectives

1.1—As of June XXXX, approximately eighty-six percent (86%) of students in grades K-3, will have demonstrated mastery of certain basic learning skills of reading at a level commensurate with his/her ability, as measured by the State Basic Learning Skills Testing Program.

1.2—Students in Grades K-3 who have not demonstrated mastery of certain basic learning skills of reading at a level commensurate with his/her ability will receive remedial instruction through the Title 1 Remedial Reading Program, State Primary Remedial Program, and regular classroom instruction.

1.3—As of June XXXX, approximately seventy percent (70%) of students in grades 4-7, will have demonstrated mastery of the basic learning skills of reading at a level commensurate with his/her ability, as measured by the State Basic Learning Skills Testing Program.

1.4—Students in Grades 4-7 who have not demonstrated mastery of certain basic learning skills of reading commensurate with his/her ability will receive remediation through regular classroom instruction and the Title 1 Remedial Program.

1.5—As of June XXXX, approximately eighty-nine percent (89%) of students in Grade 9 will have achieved a mastery score of seventy percent (70%) or more on the State Reading Minimum Competency Testing Program.

1.6—Students unable to obtain a mastery score on the State Reading Minimum Competency Tests will receive remdial instruction through the Metra-structured Reading Tutorial Program, individual and small group tutoring assistance and special service personnel when applicable.

1.7—All students deficient in the basic learning skills of reading will be identified, diagnosed, and remedial instruction will be prescribed and provided. Student performance will be assessed on a systematic and routine basis.

1.8—Enrichment activities in reading will be provided to students identified as academically gifted in this area.

are derived from the program goal, which in turn was developed from an organization goal.

Figure 4.1 is an example of the breakdown from an organization goal to a program goal and finally into a series of observable behavioral objectives.

The behavioral objectives shown in Figure 4.1 measure how well students are performing and, in turn, indicate how effectively the school system is performing and working towards its identified goals. These objectives are for only one program. Each program of the school system should have such behavioral objectives to measure student achievement. Only through this form of measurement can the school system accumulate data regarding achievement.

From the educational goals, program objectives, and behavioral objectives, the educational program can be systematically attached to them. The actual description of the educational program for the long-range document, however, is by subject area. Special programs and activities of the school system should also be included in the description of the educational program for the long-range plan.

Program Development

Local school systems are required to offer all state-mandated programs and services (unless especially exempted). As state program mandates have increased rapidly in the past decade, much of the educational program offered in any school system is a result of state action. While there is no reason to believe this trend will abate; school boards do have some freedom to incorporate programs and services demanded by the local constituency. Examples of both state-mandated and local-requested programs abound in the curriculum of the public schools. Family life education and driver education might be examples of the former, while English as a Second Language might be included because of local demand or need.

Most program options adopted by the local school board are the result of pressure from some group. Pressure may come from local, national or states groups, or from the school staff itself. An excellent example of a national pressure group exerting influence on school boards is the President's Program of Physical Fitness. This program is not mandated by the state but is included due to outside pressure.

The curriculum of the local school system is constantly changing because of these types of pressures. Through a well-developed long-range plan, the curriculum changes can be orderly and anticipated well enough in advance to provide the resources necessary for full implementation.

Needs Assessment

The school board desires at times to know how the community feels about the effectiveness of the school system. In such circumstances, school boards may conduct a community attitude assessment. This assessment can take many forms, but the purpose is to determine how people perceive the school (Graves, 1993). The results of these assessments can prompt the school board to extend or reduce an existing program, or to establish a completely new program. The results may also serve to confirm existing goals or provide data to revise certain goals.

This is a way of finding out if the community believes there is a difference between what the school is doing and what they believe could be done. Such assessments provide the school board with valuable community input into not only the program offered, but into the goals of the school system (Romney 1996). Many school systems conduct assessments on a regular basis and thereby accumulate data for a longitudinal study of trends.

Not only members of the community, but the staff of the school system should have an opportunity to have strong input into the goals formulated by the school board. One of the most influential resources is the superintendent, who should have a great deal of input into the process as well as into the final product. Sometimes a school will select a particular candidate for the district's superintendent because that person is believed to possess enough vision and insight to help the school system clarify new goals.

All of the sources of change and goal formulation are important to the school system, and all must be incorporated into the process of educational program development. The long-range plan should reflect the needs of these sources by funding the program detailed in the document. The long-range plan is not a static document, but one that changes as needs change. The long-range plan is usually developed for a five-to seven-year period. In spite of this length of time, the document changes to meet certain needs. Each year of the long-range plan resources may be re-allocated to meet specific identified needs. ▪

Long Range Planning:
Student Enrollment Projections

EVERY SCHOOL SYSTEM NEEDS TO KNOW HOW MANY STUDENTS WILL BE ENROLLED in the future to do any worthwhile planning. During the planning process, the school system identifies and develops the educational program to be offered in the areas served by the organization. The next step is to determine the number of students that need to be educated—both now and in the future. In this manner, school buildings can be located to accommodate population increases or, in the case of a declining enrollment, how to reconfigure the student population in fewer buildings.

Purposes of Projections

The number of students to expect in the future is needed in order to address the four F's of administration: funding, faculty, facilities, and function. Each of these aspects of school administration centers around how many students a local school system will educate. State funding for the educational program is based on the number of students enrolled. The number of students also determines the number of faculty members. Of course, the number of classrooms and buildings a school system uses is a function of the number of individuals enrolled. Even the function of the school system, meaning the type of program, is determined by the type and kind of the student make-up within the school system. Not only student enrollment, but also the types of individuals that comprise the student body are important in the planning process. The extent and types of special services employed in the school system are directly related to the numbers and types of students in the serving area. Every aspect of administering schools is tied into the number of students enrolled.

For the most part, school systems cannot respond quickly to needs for programs and/or housing for students. Planning a new educational program may take the better part of a year (plus advanced notice for funding), before it can be successfully implemented. In as much as it takes from two to five years to plan, design and construct a new school building, school systems need to project far in advance the number of students who will enroll in the school system. For these reasons, school systems need to look to future enrollments to plan the work of the organization.

Basis of Projections

Projections of student enrollments are not glimpses into the future or precise revelations of things to come. Unless one believes in crystal ball gazing, tarot cards, dream interpretation or some other device for looking into the future, student enrollment projections can only be, at best, an educated guess. This is precisely what student enrollment projections are—a guess, but one based upon the most accurate available data.

In developing projections, administrators must keep in mind that they are dealing with two of the most unpredictable areas of human behavior: procreation and the ability to move from one geographical location to another. In some locales, the latter behavior is not as unpredictable as the former; nevertheless, either behavior is something demographers can only guess based upon previous behavior.

Social phenomena affect both human behaviors in a very direct way. For instance, several decades ago an electrical black-out in New York City resulted in an increase in the birth rate approximately nine months later, and then to an increase in kindergarten enrollment five years later. As humorous as that episode may seem, similar occurrences can be documented throughout the country. Some social phenomena have an immediate impact, such as the case above, while other social phenomena may take a longer period to appear.

Economic factors may cause a gradual movement of individuals and families from one area to another with a subsequent loss or gain of students spread over a period of time. The opening or closing of a factory in a town may be the direct cause of a student loss or gain, but often the social or economic factors operating in a community are so intertwined that it is difficult to identify one cause as the main source of change in enrollment.

Demographers try to look at the entire community when developing projections. Many times, the environmental scanning of the community, done during development of the long-range plan, will help identify factors in the community that may affect enrollment at a later date.

The main thing to keep in mind when developing enrollment projections or in using the results of projections is that they must be developed based upon previous behavior of individuals. Demographers assume that based upon previous behavior, individuals will continue to act in the same manner. Without this premise, projections of future student enrollments can be misinterpreted and misapplied.

Projection Assumptions

Student projections, like any population projections, are based upon certain beliefs about how the area will grow or decline. These beliefs are drawn from data gathered about the area studied. Based upon this data, certain assumptions or beliefs are developed. These assumptions serve to guide demographers in deciding which methodology to use in developing projections and the direction of change in current enrollment.

For instance, if a community shows definite signs of growth in certain segments, it might be safe to assume the community will continue to grow in the same manner for a period of time. All projections must be based upon some assumptions of growth or decline; otherwise, projections of any worth can not be developed. In discussing the projections, demographers must identify these assumptions as the rationale for the manner in which projections are cast.

As long as the developed assumptions reflect the pattern of growth in a community, a greater reliability can be placed upon the projections themselves. The set of assumptions developed are not static; assumptions can become obsolete quickly if changes in the community do not continue to support them. Demographers must continually monitor the community for signs of growth or decline.

Indices such as housing starts and completions, telephone and sewer connections, and postal receipts give the demographer an insight into the development of a community. As these indices are the same ones used originally to develop the assumptions, changes in the indices will cause the demographer to re-consider the original assumptions and change or modify them if necessary. Areas in which assumptions may be developed include:

- Immigration/emigration rates
- Employment rate and certain economic factors
- Social conditions in the community
- Fertility rates

- Number of students attending private schools
- Drop-out rate of the schools
- Ratio of births to deaths in community
- Number of military or federal installations in community.

All of these factors have a direct impact upon families and, in turn, student enrollments and their projection. Therefore, demographers must decide whether or not there will be any change in these factors and in which direction changes will occur. Without addressing these areas, reliable projections cannot be developed.

Projection Data

Hard data is needed to forecast the approximate number of students a school system will have in the future. This data may be of the number of people in a geographical area or a selected group of persons, such as children between certain ages in a selected area. Whether all the individuals in an area or just a portion, a count must be taken upon which the projection will be based. The basic data of a set of projections is an accurate count of the people included in the projection. This accurate count comes from a census enumeration, which is simply the actual counting of people at a certain time and place.

A basic fact of projection methodology is that future trends in community development may be derived from past development. In other words, the community will develop the same way in the future that it developed in the immediate past; past trends indicate development trends of the future (McKnight 1990). This is the very heart of all types of projections, regardless of the population.

Other types of data are also used in projection methodology to provide indicators of possible growth or decline. Housing starts and completions, postal receipts, sewer and telephone connections all provide information about the development in a community. The more housing starts and completions, the more new families, the greater the increase in student enrollment. A definite rate of growth can be developed from the data of several years of housing starts and completions. This rate of growth can be used in several methodologies to determine the population growth rate. This growth rate can also be compared to growth rates developed using a different methodology.

All of the indices of community development can be used to compare with student population to determine congruence of patterns of growth, stabilization, or decline. The most influential community factors affecting immigration and emigration in the community are the availability of adequate, affordable housing and employment opportunities that draw families and individuals into a community. The absence or decline in these factors cause movement away from the community. These factors should be monitored continually by school administrators and others who develop student enrollment projections.

Census Enumeration

Every school system is required to conduct a census enumeration of the students within its geographic area. The census may cover students from certain ages such as 2 to 18 or from birth to 21. State law may actually stipulate school-age children only, but recent court decisions regarding the availability of educational services to special populations may mean the school system is required to count every person from birth to age 21 to have an accurate picture of those needing educational services

If the school census enumeration data is to be the basis of projected enrollment, then an accurate count of those individuals from birth to adulthood should be taken. Without this data, projections can be only a partial view of the clientele to be served. With birth data and an accurate count of all pre-school children in the community, the school district gets a count of all future clients of the organization and this can form the basis of future needed services.

Many states stipulate when the census should take place. If this is the case, local leeway is eliminated. There may be some benefit to allowing local school systems to set the date of the census enumeration because of certain local factors. For instance, in some communities seasonal workers immigrate to the community for a time and then leave, greatly effecting student population. If the workers and their families are in the community during the school year, educational services must be provided to these migrant students. This cohort then becomes a significant population to account for in making projections. If there are no local circumstances that would demand a census enumeration at a certain time, a fall enumeration coinciding with the first report to the state on student enrollment would be a propitious time.

Usually the highest enrollment of the school year is in the fall, with enrollment peaking during the third month of the school term. Most school systems must report enrollment to the state by the end of the first month of the school term. Census enumeration at this time probably produce the best results for the district, as the system has nearly the largest enrollment of the school year. Once started, it is crucial to take the enumeration at the same time each year to ensure comparable data.

A census enumeration card can be used to gather data for the school system. This card lists all individuals living at the address, the ages of each person, and any disabilities school-aged children may have. This last point is important because the school system must identify disabled students early and serve these children in some cases even before they are enrolled in school. Figure 5.1 shows a census enumeration form a school system could use for data gathering.

The school census is organized and conducted by an office or person in the school system. Usually this responsibility is lodged in the office of research and planning, the pupil services office, or, in some rare instances, in the school facilities department. In small school systems, this function may be housed in the office of the administrative assistant to the superintendent or pupil personnel. No matter which department conducts the census enumeration, the resources to do so must be in the operational budget of the school system for the year in which the census count will take place.

To perform the census, the school system must actually canvas individuals. This may be done by organizing lay people to actually go from door to door to gather data. A systematic visit by a representative of the school system to every residence in the geographic area served by the district is needed for an accurate count.

For a door-to-door, house-to-house count, usually the school district is divided into smaller areas using the elementary school areas. Alternative geographic designations, such as census blocks or political wards, may be followed. The elementary school attendance areas are usually sub-divided into smaller units for ease in making visits. A leader is assigned to each area and a series of workers are assigned to each sub-unit. Data gathered in the sub-units are combined to form a total elementary attendance area count of individuals. Counts from these units form the basis of the projections for each elementary school attendance area and subsequently for secondary school attendance area projections. In large attendance areas, a sub-leader may be used to provide sufficient supervision for the complete house-to-house visit. The accuracy of the count for each area can be assured only through closely monitoring the canvasser.

Census data is eventually combined to form the total school system census count. This data is the basis of total school system projections. Most of the time, the projections are started on the elementary, middle school and high school levels, eventually combining to form the total school system projections.

Figure 5.1
*School Census
Enumeration Form*

Virginia Triennial School Census

January, 2000

Washington County Schools

Message to Washington County Residents:

The Triennial School Census is an enumeration of all individuals ages 1 to 20 and all handicapped persons ages 1 to 22. The Census is the basis on which the counties, cities and towns of the Commonwealth of Virginia receive their fair share of the one-percent state sales tax and other tax monies. All individuals ages five through nineteen and handicapped persons ages two, three, four, twenty and twenty-one are counted for revenue purposes. Counts of individuals ages one to four are used for educational planning by the state and locality.

The enumeration of (a) all persons between ages 1 and 21 and (b) all handicapped persons between the ages of 2 and 22 will be reported to the State Department of Education in a summary form. Names, addresses and telephone numbers of individuals are required to be held by the Washington County School Board in a confidential file, available only to the state auditor of the Census, until destruction of the file three years later. The Washington County School Board is required to conduct this Triennial School Census in accord with Sections 22.1-281 through 22.1-286 of the Code of Virginia. Prompt return of the Census Form received at your address will help Washington County Public Schools to meet state legal requirements and to plan effectively for educational facilities and programs.

School Census Form—2000

Figure 5.1
*School Census
Enumeration Form
(continued)*

Name of parent/guardian/resident:

_____

Street Address:

_____ Apt _____

_____ Zip _____

Telephone:

Day _____ Evenings _____

Residence is located near which elementary school:

☐ Main Street Elementary School

☐ Elmwood Elementary School

☐ Washington Elementary School

☐ Monroe Elementary School

☐ Carver Elementary School

☐ Moore Elementary School

Complete one line for each person in this family whose primary residence is at this address and whose date of birth falls on 1/1/78 or 1/ 1/99 or any date in between, including persons away from home in a school, college, reformatory, hospital, prison, or armed services.

Name of person	Date of birth	Sex	Disability	Type of school

Projection Time

Population projections can be developed for different times depending on the purposes intended. General projection time periods are set for convenient and practical reasons. Governments many times require population projections for a longer time period than other organizations. It is not unusual for a government to need to project population change 20 or, even, 50 years in the future.

School systems generally plan for much shorter periods of time. There are some very practical reasons for a shortened planning time. Generally, the shorter the projection time, the more accurate the projection. In most cases, there is a turnover in school board members every five to ten years. In addition, the chief school administrator's tenure is sometimes shorter than the planning period of the school system. However, trends in growth for a sustained period of time enable administrators to plan for the eventuality of the population.

School population changes on a short cycle. Every six years, the population of the elementary school changes completely as does the entire population of the secondary schools. The needs of the community the school system serves changes quickly necessitating changes in the educational program. Such forces require a shorter period of planning and implementing programs.

A five-year student enrollment projection might have served the needs of a school system many years ago. Today, school systems need to project further into the future. Some states even require the local school system to project the student enrollment for 10 years or even up to 20 years. Extending projection times will undoubtedly increase with increased demands for a longer planning period. These longer projection periods will not increase the accuracy of projections. A 20-year student enrollment projection can only provide a guide to growth trends and will not indicate the actual number of students that will be enrolled two decades hence.

The accuracy of student enrollment projections is directly related to the accuracy and currency of the data. Assuming that the data is accurate, the more current the data, the better the projections. In addition, projections must be updated each year with fresh data derived from the school system. Only in this manner can the projections approach actual count of students.

This also means that the accuracy of the projections can be guaranteed only one year at a time. There can be a reasonable degree of accuracy in the first five years of projections, but beyond that, accuracy falls quickly.

Projection Methods

Many methods are used to project populations. The methodology is usually determined by the purpose of the projections. Projections for short periods usually do not require complicated methodologies, but the longer the period of projecting, the more complicated and involved the methodology is. Some governmental agencies and commercial organizations project populations for an extended period of time. In such cases, rather sophisticated methodologies are used, but such methodologies are not necessary for shorter periods of projections.

Both the purpose of the projection and the population involved determine the methodology. The basic questions to be asked in generating student enrollment projections are:

- Will the enrollments increase or decrease?
- Will the increase or decrease be like similar increases and decreases as have occurred in the past?
- If the increase or decrease will not be similar, in what ways will it be different?

There are a limited number of basic methodologies used for projections but there are a larger number of variations on these basic methods. Thomas Hoy (1947) listed the following methods of projecting school populations:

- Forecasting school enrollment from total population
- Forecasting by analysis
- Forecasting by mathematical techniques
- Forecasting by the Bell Telephone Company method in which the rate of increase in the total population is assumed to apply to increases in school enrollments
- Forecasting by the multiple factor method, which assumes that fundamental relationship exists between certain economic factors and school enrollment
- Forecasting by analogy

MacConnell (1957) expanded these methods and identified more than nine methods that could be used to project student populations. Some of these methodologies can be classified as variations rather than separate methods:

- Forecasting by analysis
- Forecasting school enrollment from total population
- Prediction based wholly on past census data
- Method of analogy

- Multiple factor method
- Bell Telephone Company method of index analysis
- The "Law of Growth" Principle—Pearl-Reed Logistic Curve
- Projecting natural increase
- Combined method

Other authorities have separated the methodologies into a fewer number of methods. Shellenberg and Stephens (1987) state there may be two general approaches to be used in projecting populations. One general approach uses historical enrollment data as the basis of projections. This data is then projected by using previous trends that are believed to apply to the future. This is basically the survival methodology. The other approach combines historical data with selected variables believed to impinge upon student enrollments. This is some form of multiple regression analysis.

In addition to these two approaches, there are other projection methods that are not based on student historical enrollment data. These methods rely on data derived from sources other than the school base, such as the number and kinds of individuals who live in a house. This kind of data is developed by an enumeration of the housing units of a school system, then by determining the composition of the persons living in each house. This factor becomes the basis of projecting population by applying it to each house in a certain geographical area.

There are three basic ways of projecting student populations. Some are more appropriate than others in trying to project student populations:
- Forecasting by retention or survival of the population
- Forecasting by use of multiple regression analysis
- Forecasting by use of geo-referenced data

Of the three approaches, the first is the most widely used and applicable for school purposes. Some school systems in countries other than the United States sometimes use the multiple regression method to project student populations; however, few if any school systems in the United States use that method. Almost every state uses the survival method of projecting students.

Even though the multiple regression analysis is perhaps more accurate than the survival method, school systems and state departments of education have not used this methodology to any extent. However, some projection methodology experts contend that the survival method is as accurate as the regression models and it is simpler to use. Every state uses a form of the survival method for projecting student enrollment in succeeding years. In as much as the survival method is so universally used, both on the state and local level, it is important for the school administrator to be able to produce and interpret results using this methodology.

For school population projection purposes, the survival and georeferenced methods are probably the most useful and widely used. There are three variations of the survival method that should be considered for use in school systems in certain circumstances. These variations all use some sort of rate of survival of a designated group or groups to produce projections or data for further analysis. Examples of this last group include methods of forecasting from analogy and from the total population. These two, combined with the grade or age survival ratio and the geo-referenced methods, seem to be the best methods of projecting student enrollments available to school systems.

Forecasting By Analogy

This method of projecting student populations assumes that growth characteristics between two different, but similarly situated, school systems will correspond. This method is best used in suburban settings where there are discernible rings of growth from the center of the population density. Projectionists assume, based upon an analysis of community characteristics that their school system will grow in the same manner as a neighboring school system has already grown. Thus, the rate and direction of growth of the neighboring school system can be determined and applied to the school population of the subject school system. From this application of rate and direction of growth, a set of projections can be derived. The rate of growth will be a mean of the percent of growth for each year. This mean is then applied to the present student population for each year to be projected to determine the future student population.

The direction of growth is not directly applicable to the projection of numbers of students in the future but can enable planners to do some extrapolation of where growth may take place. This would be a very rudimentary exercise. Direction of growth usually follows arterial highways or other forms of transportation, such as forms of public transportation, into and from the population center of density.

The forecasting from analogy is an easy-to-use method of projecting student population because the data is easily available from the neighboring school system. With a minimum of mathematical manipulation, the mean rate of growth per annum can be determined and applied to a known student population. This method is perhaps the easiest to perform. The accuracy of the results may be less than desired. There has to be a very strong assumption that the subject school system in fact will grow in the same fashion as the neighboring school system. This assumption should be based on a thorough analysis of the two school systems and the unequivocal conclusion of comparable growth.

The advantages of this method is the ease of obtaining data and the simple manipulation of the data. The disadvantage is the doubtful accuracy of the projections. So long as the assumption that the two systems will grow alike remains viable, the results may prove valuable. When the slightest change in growth patterns occurs, the accuracy of the projections is suspect. This method of projection should probably be used as a check or back up for another type of student enrollment projection methodology.

Forecasting Student Populations From Total Population Projections

This method of projection is based upon the assumption that an observable ratio between total population and school enrollments has existed in the past and will continue in future populations. From previous census data, the exact percentage of each age group of the total population can be determined. This percentage is then applied to previously prepared projections of total school system populations. Various government units, such as city or county planning commissions prepare total population projections for geo-political areas. But usually these projections do not contain any breakdown according to age groupings. Projections of the total population are usually made through a survival ratio applied to previous total population counts derived from the Federal Census. The school system uses the figure for the total population to determine what percent each age group will be in the future, assuming the percentages will remain the same. The approximate number of students in each age group can thus be determined.

Here again this methodology is very simple and easy-to-apply. Data is readily available from a governmental agency with no conversion necessary. The mathematical manipulation of the data is not complicated, and the results arc straightforward. There are, however, several disadvantages to this method.

The first disadvantage is that the age groupings of the Federal census are not consistent with the enrollment policies of the school systems. The census is broken down according to full age groupings. For example, individuals will be included in the age four grouping whether the child is 4 years old, or 4 years and 11 months. School systems usually enroll all individuals in the kindergarten up to 4½ years. In addition, there are 17½-year-old students who are still in the high school, and in some limited instances students who are 18 years old. The federal census breakdown does not accommodate these divisions within an age grouping. Because of this, the results must be extrapolated to arrive at a sensible enrollment figure. This extrapolation exacerbates the possibility of inaccuracy of results.

The school organizational levels such as elementary, middle, and high school are not consistent with the age groupings of the Federal census either. This causes a problem in the distribution of students. Here again, one must extrapolate the results to fit into the organizational levels.

Another difficulty is that a total population projection can not be fit into individual school attendance areas. Demographers must develop a percentage approach for dividing the projected student population for each school building. This is done by determining the percent that each school building enrollment is of the total school population and then applying this factor to the projected student population. There is always a margin of error.

In some areas the school system's boundaries do not coincide with the county or city boundaries, so there may be more than one school system within a local governmental area. Here again, a percentage of the total population each school system contributes to the whole must be developed and then applied to the school population projections. The margin of error in this mathematical process may present a problem in accuracy of results.

The dates when the total population projections are done by the planning commission or other governmental agency usually do not coincide with the needs of the school system. Usually the planning commission projects on a decade and not on a shorter term. Most school systems rely more upon short-term projections than long term, even though the school system may be required to develop ten-year projections. In addition, often the local planning commission projections are tied directly into the beginning of each decade to use the census data obtained through the Federal enumeration. This exact projection date may not be helpful to a school system that is developing student projections beginning three to seven years into the decade. Obviously, this would cause some problems in the length of time of the projections.

Table 5.1 presents a set of student enrollment projections developed by using total population projections obtained from a county planning commission. These were developed to confirm the direction of growth in a set of projections developed using a different methodology.

Table 5.2

*School Enrollment
Projections From
Total Population*

		2002	2003	2004	2005	2006	2007	2008	2009	2010	2011
5-9 Year	*Total*	1416	1446	1460	1429	1417	1427	1442	1465	1504	1610
Population	*School*	1395	1321	1301	1264	1292	1301	1315	1336	1372	1468
10-14 Year	*Total*	1468	1439	1413	1437	1450	1465	1480	1488	1487	1484
Population	*School*	1499	1446	1434	1488	1473	1488	1503	1511	1510	1508
15-19 Year	*Total*	1574	1599	1617	1576	1537	1494	1452	1416	1423	1458
Population	*School*	721	679	672	731	676	657	639	623	626	642
Special Education		87	95	107*	73	83	83	83	83	84	87
Total		3682	3541	3514	3556	3524	3529	3540	3553	3592	3705

* Includes Alternative Education classes

Forecasting by Cohort Survival Ratios

This projection methodology is also known as age, class, or grade retention rates, or grade progression ratios. Other terms used for this methodology are: percentage of survival, percentage of retention, grade persistence, forecasting by analysis, survival-ratio method, and retention ratio projection. Regardless of the terminology, the method uses the survival of the members of a designated cohort or group as the basis of predicting the size of the cohort or group in the future (McKnight 1990). A cohort is simply a designation of a certain group of individuals such as the entire first grade class or some other group. There is always a ratio between the size of a group one-year and the size of that same group the following year. This ratio is the basis of the projections in this method. As a kindergarten class moves through the school system and eventually emerges as graduates of the twelfth grade, the composition and number of students in the class change. These changes result from students moving into the school system and joining the group or moving out of the school to decrease the group.

These annual changes represent growth or decline of population in the school system. Under the assumption that the group's size in the future will reflect the changes of similar groups in the past, predictions of the size of any class or group can be made. This is the basic assumption of this methodology. This is no different from the assumptions used for all other methods of projecting when existing census data are used.

The first step in building a database for cohort survival ratios is to determine the kindergarten enrollment in the future. There is always a relationship or ratio between the number of live births occurring in one year and the enrollment of kindergarten students five years later. The percentage of live births that enroll in the public school is effected by the number of individuals who enter private schools or move out of the school system boundaries. In either case, the percentage of live births that will end up enrolling in the public schools must be determined. The live birth count can be obtained from the state or county department of vital statistics. The birth count for the prior most recent five years is obtained, and the percent of that group who will enroll in the public schools is applied to that figure. This becomes the expected number of kindergarten students in the first five years of the projections.

These figures are the base data for the remaining projections. In some cases, accurate live birth count is not possible to obtain, or the projections are to be done on a school building by building basis, in which case the live birth count for the whole school system cannot accurately be dispersed to each school building. In these circumstances, an alternative method of deriving the kindergarten count must be used. A linear survival ratio can be developed in such cases. The linear survival ratio is simply the difference in percentage of the number of individuals in a grade one-year and the number of individuals in the same grade the following year. This is not the growth or decline of a single group of individuals but rather the change in size of groups occupying a grade from one year to the next. There is a sizeable but subtle difference in the two approaches. The survival ratio of a group is more accurate than the difference in the size of a group from one year to another. Nevertheless, this approach can be used if live birth count is not available or accurate.

The survival ratios for the remainder of the grades are developed by dividing the number of students in one grade into the number of students in the next grade a year hence. Students in the first grade one year are in the second grade the next year, or at least a percentage of the original number are then in the second grade. Students who were retained in the original grade, students moving into the school system and those moving out are accounted for through this mathematical process. The growth and decline of the group is thus accounted for as it progresses through the school system.

The ratio between a cohort in a grade and that same cohort in succeeding grades is developed for all grades kindergarten through twelfth grade for the number of years data are available. For example, if there were one hundred students in the kindergarten class one-year and only ninety-nine students in the first grade a year later, there would be a loss of students, and we would say that only 99 percent of the students survived. If this kind of ratio were developed for each kinder-

garten class for a period of five to ten years, there would be an appropriate number of ratio factors. Each of these ratio factors would be used to obtain a mean ratio between the kindergarten and first grade cohorts for the period of time.

This arithmetical average would be used to project kindergarten cohorts into the first grade for succeeding years. Similar mean ratios would be developed for each grade, using the number of students in one cohort divided into the number of students in that same cohort a year later. The number of years of student enrollment history available will determine the base years for the mean ratios. The more years included in the database, the better the results of the projections.

A mean survival ratio should be developed for each grade kindergarten through eleven by using the same mathematical process of dividing the number of students in one grade cohort into the number of students in the next grade cohort for the succeeding year. The mean survival ratio should then be applied to the current enrollment in each grade of the school system. The mean survival ratio is applied for each year the projections are to be developed, five or ten years. The result will be a set of student enrollment projections kindergarten through grade twelve for a specified period of time that can be used for a variety of planning purposes throughout the school system.

Linear ratios can be developed between the size of a grade cohort one-year and the size in succeeding years. These ratios can be used to develop a complete set of student projections. This is done by dividing the number of students in the particular grade in one year into the number of students enrolled in the grade the next year and following. This ratio simply tells the differences between the size of groups in various years. This methodology does not track a single group through the years to determine the change in size. This variation in methodology is probably best used to determine kindergarten enrollments as described earlier. Such a set of projections could be used best for comparison purposes with other methods of projection.

The cohort survival method of projecting student enrollments is the most widely used method in the United States (McKnight 1990) Almost every state uses the cohort survival method to determine future enrollments because this method is quite simple and easy to calculate. Data needed for the mathematical process is very handy and available. There is also a great deal of accuracy in this method. Although some demographers believe the regression analysis is more accurate than the survival ratio, an equal number believes the survival ratio method is just as accurate as the regression analysis. The survival ratio methodology accounts for the individual factors influencing enrollments such as movement into and away from the school system, retention, death, annexation, housing changes and employment changes. These, coupled with the ease of handling data and the universality of the method, surely speak for continued use of the methodology throughout the school systems in the country.

There are some disadvantages to the methodology, however. Sudden growth or decline in the community may be moderated to the point of not having sufficient influence upon growth patterns in the future. If a community is growing rapidly in the most recent years, a ten-year database may not identify or allow the real impact of recent growth or decline to influence future enrollment figures. In such cases, demographers must augment the cohort survival ratios with supporting community growth indices to corroborate the original findings or to modify the projections to account for previously unidentified community developments. In addition, unless the survival ratio is continually updated with current enrollment histories, any small margin of error is magnified in succeeding years. This is true of any set of projections regardless of the methodology.

Table 5.2 contains a set of projections derived through the cohort grade survival ratio methodology. Table 5.3 illustrates the results of a linear survival ratio methodology and Table 5.4 shows a comparison between grade survival, linear survival, and projections from total population.

	2002	2003	2004	2005	2006	2007	2008	2009	2010	2011
Kindergarten	216	242	200	213	241	240	240	239	238	238
Grade One	335	269	275	248	249	291	290	290	289	288
Grade Two	272	297	265	270	237	239	280	279	279	279
Grade Three	279	285	300	276	259	237	239	280	279	279
Grade Four	334	282	281	294	278	261	238	240	282	280
Grade Five	234	320	280	295	282	273	257	234	236	277
Grade Six	288	259	332	301	316	263	254	239	218	220
Grade Seven	309	265	251	311	288	307	256	247	232	212
Grade Eight	364	318	262	256	327	289	308	257	248	233
Grade Nine	311	337	321	271	275	324	287	306	255	246
Grade Ten	266	238	257	239	238	222	262	232	247	206
Grade Eleven	280	229	208	229	247	214	200	236	209	223
Grade Twelve	221	254	214	204	246	237	206	192	227	200
Special Education	80	87	95	92	73	81	82	78	78	76
Total	**3789**	**3682**	**3541**	**3514**	**3556**	**3478**	**3399**	**3348**	**3317**	**3257**

Table 5.3
School Enrollment Projections 2002-2011 Grade Level Cohort Survival

	2002	2003	2004	2005	2006	2007	2008	2009	2010	2011
Kindergarten	216	242	200	213	241	240	239	238	238	238
Grade One	335	269	275	248	249	246	243	239	233	230
Grade Two	272	297	265	270	237	232	227	222	217	212
Grade Three	279	285	300	276	259	250	241	233	225	217
Grade Four	334	282	281	294	278	272	269	264	259	254
Grade Five	234	320	280	295	282	280	278	276	274	272
Grade Six	288	259	332	301	316	313	310	307	304	301
Grade Seven	309	265	251	311	288	285	282	278	275	272
Grade Eight	364	318	262	256	327	329	332	335	338	341
Grade Nine	311	337	321	271	275	273	271	269	267	265
Grade Ten	266	238	257	239	238	237	237	236	236	235
Grade Eleven	280	229	208	229	247	254	261	268	275	282
Grade Twelve	221	254	214	204	246	255	264	274	284	295
Special Education	80	87	95	92	73	83	82	83	82	82
Total	**3789**	**3682**	**3541**	**3514**	**3556**	**3549**	**3536**	**3523**	**3507**	**3596**

	2007	2008	2009	2010	2011
Grade Level Cohort Survival	3478	3399	3348	3317	3257
Linear Cohort Survival	3549	3536	3523	3507	3596
Percent of Total Population	3529	3540	3553	3593	3705

Computer Driven Projection Programs

Computer software programs are currently on the market that can be used to project student enrollments using the cohort survival methodology. Such programs are available from a number of commercial concerns and even universities. In addition, educational consultants can develop such software for a school system. Some school systems have developed indigenous survival ratio programs to fit local concerns.

The programs developed by most commercial firms are what might be termed generic software in that they are developed with the mathematical processes to serve as many applications as possible with no modifications for local demographic factors or conditions. By using the mathematical process of the method alone, questionable projections may result. The mathematical projection of a set of enrollment figures may produce results quite out of proportion to what is perceived by knowledgeable local school personnel.

When a school system is in the market for a commercial software package, school personnel should determine the exact method of projection that will be used and whether or not the program can be modified to fit local conditions. Based upon answers to this question, school systems should be able to make an intelligent decision regarding applicability of the program. School systems may also wish to obtain the services of a knowledgeable educational consultant to assist in the evaluation. The school system may employ an educational consultant to develop a program that will fit the needs of the school system just as economically as purchasing commercial software.

Forecasting By Use of Geo-Referenced Data

This method of projecting student enrollments is sometimes called the land saturation analysis method because the line of projections proceeds to the time when all land in the school system is used for the intended zoning purpose, and a count of students can be made. This method is usually considered the most comprehensive of all methods of projecting student enrollments in a limited geographical area.

The premise upon which this methodology is based is that eventually all land in a given geographical area will be used for some purpose, and that projections can be made from that utilization. Each parcel of land in a school system has some designation for use given by the zoning board of the local government. This zoning designation allows the owner to use the land for the purposes requested and to build appropriate structures upon it to accommodate the purpose. Thus, if a parcel of land has a zoning of R-1, the owner can build a single dwelling upon the site. The owner may not build a car wash or apartment on the site because of the zoning regulation. Zoning regulations cover all types of land use from farming to commercial and heavy industry to a variety of residential zoning designations. These regulations allow an owner to use property for designated purposes and at the same time prohibit that person or company from using the land for purposes other than the designated one.

Land in the school system that contains some type of housing is of most concern to the school planners because these are the types of property from which students are generated. Exact counts of individuals living in existing housing can be made through a census canvass. Base data for the geo-referenced system comes from the census that a school system conducts. Almost every school system in the country is required to conduct some type of enumeration of youngsters in the service area. These canvasses may be on an annual, bi-annual, or tri-annual basis. Data obtained from this canvass provides the school system with base information about the makeup of the various sections of the school system. Most school systems conduct a very thorough enumeration of the residents and, as a result, have an excellent database. Unless diligence is exercised in gathering census data in these canvasses, the school system may be handicapped in trying to project student enrollment in the future. In some instances, particularly in large urban school systems, the United States Census data are used as the database.

The reason for this is the enormity of the task of counting every individual in a large metropolitan area. The expense of the effort and the amount of time needed to organize and execute such an undertaking makes it mandatory to use United States Census data. There are problems, however, that must be overcome in using these data. In most situations, the boundary of the census tracts do not match either the individual school building attendance area or the school system boundaries. Extrapolation and adjustments have to be made in the data to conform to the boundaries of the school system. Regardless of the source of data, an accurate count of individuals will provide invaluable data about the composition of the school system.

From this data an index or factor can be developed describing the family that lives in each dwelling. Various family indices can be developed to reflect differences in type of housing. For instance, the family index may be different for families living in multiple family units than in single family units. A single family dwelling unit on a one-acre tract might produce a different family composition index from a dwelling situated on one-tenth of an acre or on a five acre tract. Each living unit type can produce a different family index. After analysis of the census data and the development of family indices, this factor can be used to project the number of students generated by new housing developments of any sort. Each dwelling unit is multiplied by the specific family composition index to determine the total number of individuals the new development will produce.

The family composition index should also indicate the breakdown within the housing unit. The index should describe the number of adults who are in the family and the number of dependents by age grouping. For instance, the school age grouping should show what percent of the family would be pre-school aged, primary school aged, and elementary and secondary school aged. If the family composition index was 2.97, the breakdown should include what percent of that number would be in each age group —1.65 adults; .10 pre-school child; .67 elementary school child; .45 middle school child; .10 high school child. These percentages can then be applied to new housing units to project the number of students that will be generated by that type of housing. In this manner, total student projections of sections of housing and of the entire school system can be developed.

Growth in the school system will result from changes in land use or development of vacant land. When land that is zoned residential is developed, such plans must come before the local governing body. Likewise, changes in the zoning from one to another must also be approved. Thus, sufficient notification of proposed changes in use or zoning of any tract of land can be detected by the school system by perusal of the official minutes of the local governing body. Changes in zoning designations can be made upon application to the proper governmental body and office. Application is usually made to the zoning board and if approved, the local governing board ratifies the approval so that the comprehensive planning map of the area can be officially changed. Such changes occur when economic conditions warrant a different use for the land. For instance, suburban farm owners may change the zoning designation of the farm to that of a residential area so that new housing can be constructed to accommodate a growing population. Such abrupt changes in zoning designation require more that a simple letter of request by the owner, When such changes occur, the development of the land by means of a plat plan is required by the zoning board. This document assures fidelity of the land development to requested changes in zoning ordinances. Each plot on the plan is examined to assure proper land coverage, utilities, traffic, land impaction, social and civic services and other requirements. All such changes must first be passed by the zoning board and subsequently by the governing board so that such action may become public knowledge.

The success of a land saturation analysis system of projecting student enrollments is predicated upon close cooperation between the local government offices and the school system. Proper and timely notification of changes in land use and zoning is essential if the school system is to obtain the type data needed to organize and keep the system up-to-date. Information on proposed changes is passed on to the school system through the official minutes of the zoning board and local governing board, copies of tentative tract maps, staff memoranda, and even informal communications. The land saturation analysis system was originally developed to predict the rate and nature of residential growth in undeveloped school systems (Gilmore, 1979).

Other types of development such as urban renewal can also result in growth. Although the data regarding this type of development is area specific, it nevertheless needs to be monitored to provide a comprehensive view of the school system. The basic resource of community growth is residential development on zoned land, regardless of where it is situated in the school system. Specific data needed for land saturation analysis may vary from one school system to another, but the basic information will include:

- Current zoning by parcel or study area
- Gross acres of undeveloped land by zoning type
- Net acres of undeveloped land by zoning type
- Projected number of dwelling units by parcel or study area predicted on zoning density allowances
- Estimated year of development for each tract
- Number and type of new dwelling units projected per year for planning time frame—5, 10, 15 years
- Number of bedrooms per dwelling unit
- Address and location description
- Developer's name and address
- Price range
- Rental range
- Critical development factors such as sewer line extension, new roads, industry, flood plain work, annexation
- Yearly development estimate by study area
- Survey of proposed sub-divisions under consideration
- Undeveloped acreage by school attendance area
- Breakdown of projected yearly dwelling units by attendance area
- Proposed general zoning plans which could change density allowance
- Urban redevelopment master plan
- Survey of requested and issued building permits
- Survey of issued occupancy permits

A number of advantages are associated with the land saturation analysis methodology. A good deal of confidence can be placed in the results of the projections. The nature of the increase in student enrollments and the direction of growth can be predicted with a degree of accuracy. The timing of the growth can also be anticipated to a high degree based upon estimates of completion of housing developments and upon actual completions as verified by occupancy permits. Just as this may be an advantage, there is also a disadvantage in the timing because there is no way to precisely predict when a housing development will be completed and occupied. Many factors outside of the control of the developer govern the sale of property, particularly housing.

There are, likewise, some disadvantages to this methodology that limit its use. In the first place, such a system works only where zoning ordinances exist. As strange as it may seem, many rural areas in the country do not have official zoning ordinances to govern land development. Obviously, where such does not exist, a geo-referenced system can not be used. The land saturation analysis would probably be inappropriate in a large rural area where there is little or limited housing development. Probably the most beneficial application of such a system would be in a growing suburban area, although an urban area could most certainly put such a system to good use (Gilmore 1979).

Another disadvantage of the geo-referenced system is the cost to implement and maintain the data base used for making projections. Unless the system is constantly updated with current data, the system becomes obsolete in a matter of days or weeks. A school system must commit sufficient resources to have a first rate system; otherwise the funds are not well spent. Obviously, a good computer hardware and software system is needed, and this increases the cost, but the personnel costs needed to implement and maintain the system are perhaps the most expensive. The availability of good data for decision making by school personnel, however, should more than compensate for such costs. In addition, the extension of the geo-referenced system into other areas of administrative decision making of the school system could well justify the cost of the system. There are many possibilities of extending the land saturation analysis system into a more sophisticated system of management information that could assist in areas other than student enrollment projections. The land saturation analysis system data are attached to each parcel of land in the school system and also to the people who inhabit the structure on that parcel. The kinds of data attached to the dwelling and subsequently to the individuals can be as extensive as needed. The school system maintains considerable data on each student that could be attached to the dwelling in which the student lives. Examples of such data might include:

- Schools in which the youngsters are enrolled
- Distance from elementary and secondary schools
- Number of the bus and the routes used by students
- Types of programs in which students are enrolled
- Number and kinds of disabled persons
- Racial and sexual designation
- Grade level

Other data about either pre-school children, school-aged youngsters or even adults could be generated and attached to the particular family group, but all data would be attached to the dwelling in which the family is located. Data about the structure in which the family lives could also be useful for planning purposes. The following data about the housing could include:

- Size of the building lots in acres and square feet
- Size and shape of all structures
- Assessed valuation/true market value of the structure
- Additions to the original and date of construction
- Utilities available and used
- Type of zoning

Other types of data about the particular dwelling might be identified and used, depending upon the planning needs of the school system.

An information system such as this ties selected student and census data to demographic and geographic data forming a comprehensive information system which is sometimes referred to as a geo-coded or geo-referenced system. From such a system, many administrative and management decisions could be addressed. For instance, proposed changes in the bus routes caused by student increase could be analyzed through data manipulation. Proposed decisions could be developed and the implications of such decisions analyzed before being implemented. Location of new school buildings could be identified easier through such a data system. In addition, the closing of a school building, with all of the ramifications, could be analyzed before the fact so that all exigencies could be anticipated. Savings of time and effort could result with the availability of such data, and decisions could be enhanced greatly because of the amount of data.

The heart of any land saturation or geo-referenced information system is the data related to each parcel of land and its location. Much of these data can be obtained through the United States Census Bureau's DIME (Dual Independent Map Encoding) file (Gilmore 1979). This is a geographic base file defining a street network in terms of segments, nodes, enclosed area, and non-street features such as railroad tracks, municipal boundaries, and rivers. By matching the addresses of students and other demographic data with DIME street segments, the coordinates of a student's house can be interpolated into the system. This enables the system to identify and isolate each dwelling by location for further analysis. Each of the codes can be tied into the existing school attendance areas for compilation into school building groups on elementary, middle and high school levels.

Much of the data needed in the system for each student is currently available within the information system of the school system. These data can be hooked into the geo-coded database. The technology and databases needed to implement a geo-referenced information system are currently available. All that is needed is to tie the two systems together which can best be done by using the United States Census DIME file to marry with the information the school system currently has to form an integrated information system.

Summary

The importance of student enrollment projections to the planning process of a school system can not be underestimated. Such data are necessary for all types of decisions, including where and when new school buildings are needed. In addition, decisions in other areas of the school enterprise use future student numbers as a basis. The prudent administrator, however, recognizes the limitations of any set of student enrollment projections. All such projections are based upon certain assumptions about the development of an identified geo-political area. For the most part, demographers assume that future development will reflect past development. To the extent that assumption is correct, a great deal of reliability can be placed in the projections. This reliability can be enhanced by having current data, but there are always limitations that should be placed upon use of exact numbers contained in projections. Although projections give an idea of the numbers of students involved and the direction and rate of growth, school planners should observe caution in using the results of any set of projections for decision making.

In this chapter, four methods of projecting student enrollments were discussed. Each method has advantages and disadvantages that should be recognized. While there is no one best system, neither is one method necessarily the most accurate, although some methods have more promise than others. Each method is used by school planners and has a place in the planning process. ■

Long-Range Planning:
Evaluation of Existing Facilities

THE LONG-RANGE PLAN CONTAINS A DESCRIPTION OF THE EDUCATIONAL PROGRAM to be offered in the school system in the present and over the next few years. In addition, that plan projects present and future student populations that will need to be housed. Once the program and the anticipated number of students are set, the next task is to determine how they will be housed. One aspect of this task is determining what buildings are currently available and what will be needed for future changes in educational program and number of students coming to school.

Long-range planning can only be done by evaluating all the buildings used for educational purposes. This evaluation should establish the capability of each building to sustain the program needs and student population of the school system. For example, if a school system decides to convert to a middle school program, there are strong implications for building change. All of the intermediate or junior high school buildings in the school system will have to be evaluated for possible structural changes and conversions needed to accommodate the educational program change.

If the program change is to be accomplished within the period of the long range plan, building changes must be made in a timely fashion. This way the program can be implemented before the end of the current long-range plan. In addition, the grade configuration change from a junior high or intermediate organization to a middle school organization may impact the capacity of the buildings scheduled for change. This inextricable tie between educational program, number of students and building must always be recognized.

To properly understand how the present inventory of school buildings can fit the expected program each structure must be evaluated. The purposes of evaluating the existing buildings are:

- To determine which existing facilities will be able to accommodate the desired program with the given number of students.
- To ascertain what improvements are necessary to enable the facility to work better.
- To develop a list of building improvements and maintenance items to be included in the capital improvement program.
- To provide data on which to base subsequent designs of new buildings or additions.
- To determine to what extent each facility aids in desegregation and reacts to population shifts and declines.
- To verify existing available teaching spaces in the school system or to gather data to implement such an inventory (Earthman, 1990).

Evaluation Teams

The building evaluations should be carried out by a team headed by a representative of the school facilities department. Team members should include the principal and selected teachers from the particular building. Team members should be knowledgeable about instructional methodology, curriculum, educational technology, and structural and mechanical engineering.

The team should have a representative from the central administration curriculum and instruction office as well. It is important that the central administration be represented because of possible educational program changes that will be implemented system-wide during the long-range plan. In addition, representatives from the architecture and construction section of the facilities department should be included (if such personnel are available). Small school systems, which do not have such personnel, may wish to employ an outside educational consultant to assist with the evaluation. This practice is common in both large and small school systems.

If the task warrants such, this evaluation team can be augmented by curriculum specialists drawn from various sources. The task of the team is to evaluate the building to gather data for use to improve the building. In some extreme cases, data can be gathered to assist the school board in deciding whether or not to keep the building in service or to convert it to other purposes.

Frequency of Evaluation

The frequency of evaluation depends on the purpose of the evaluation. Several levels of evaluation should be performed during the life of the school building. Repeated evaluation throughout the building's life ensures the building is maintained in good repair, and that it adequately houses the students and educational programs over the years.

The initial building evaluation is conducted when the building is first constructed, then periodically, the building must be completely re-evaluated in terms of number of students and type of program housed. At the beginning of each long-range program, each building in the school system should be assessed by an evaluation team as described above. The basis of the evaluation is the program description in the long-range plan, but the general condition of the building should also be inspected. All of the building's systems should be inspected and evaluated to determine their current condition and any need for improvement.

Systems such as the heating, ventilation and air conditioning, lighting, plumbing and communication should be reviewed for efficiency or need for improvement. Even basic structural components like the roof, floor, walls, and fenestration should be reviewed. Such an evaluation will require the services of an architect and engineer. If the school system does not have such services on the staff a consultant will have to be retained.

Some systems also think it wise to obtain the services of an educational consultant, especially if their staff is relatively small. Outside educational consultants can bring a sense of objectivity that district employees cannot, and according to research findings, outside consultants can better identify facility changes needed to accommodate the given educational program than can the building principal (Akers, 1982).

Maintenance Evaluation

Another level of appraisal is the annual evaluation for maintenance needs. The building principal, custodian, and a representative of the teaching faculty should do this evaluation. There may be times when the principal desires the services of a subject matter specialist or other expertise from the central administration to assist in the evaluation. This might be appropriate when there are educational program changes in the offing.

This annual review should be used to identify maintenance items that have developed during the year but which are not of an emergency nature. Emergency repairs such as broken windows, clogged plumbing, broken doors, and the like, of course, require immediate attention and are handled through a different system. Items that might be addressed in the annual evaluation include conversion of a room, construction of shelves, change of lighting, or additional water service.

Items identified through this evaluation are sent to the office in charge of the capital improvement plan for inclusion on the list of changes and improvements scheduled for that building. After this, the items are again prioritized cooperatively by the central administration and building principal and become part of the capital improvement program.

Special Evaluation

At times a special evaluation needs to be made of a facility outside of the regular appraisals conducted in conjunction with development of the long-range plan. Rapid changes in student population, major changes in educational programs or the failure of a structural member of the building are all reasons for a special appraisal. Depending upon the circumstances, the school system may need new data on several buildings, all buildings or just one building. Sometimes special evaluative instruments are used to gather the data. These occasions may require the services of an educational consultant to construct an appraisal survey and conduct the evaluation. This is frequently the case when a school system has failed to conduct frequent and periodic evaluations of its buildings and the effort becomes a bootstrap operation to bring the school system up to current expectations.

Appraisal Instruments

An appropriate appraisal instrument is needed to effectively evaluate a building. Building evaluation instruments assist the team in reporting the condition of the facility by summarizing and organizing what the evaluators should observe. Items covered include the configuration of the building, furniture and equipment available, lighting, temperature, general conditions, specific features needed for specialized programs, accessibility by handicapped persons, numbers and kinds of spaces available, and support services just to mention a few.

Building evaluation instruments have been developed by states, individual school systems, professional organizations, and by individuals. Examples can be found in any textbook on school facility planning. In addition, the Council of Educational Facility Planners International publishes an appraisal guide.

Examples of appraisal instruments are:

- Appraisal Instrument for School Facilities by Steve Akers (1982)
- Appraisal Guide for School Facilities by Harold Hawkins and Edward Lilly (1990)
- MEEB: Model for the Evaluation of Educational Buildings by Carroll McGuffey (1974)
- Model to Assess School Buildings and Facilities for the Physically Handicapped by Roger Thurston (1979)

These guides can serve as a starting point for a building evaluation. Each must be modified to meet the particular needs and desires of the local school system as well as the regulations mandated by the state in which the school system is located.

Many school systems develop an instrument for local use so it can take into consideration local conditions, such as facility demands of local pedagogical practices. Many states require large tracts of land for school sites; however, urban school systems must accommodate buildings on small, heavily impacted sites. Locally developed guides can take this disparity into account. A locally developed evaluative instrument can be used over a period of years providing consistent data on each school building in the system. Development of such an instrument can be done by the school districts facilities department. Appendix D contains a building evaluation form developed by a school system.

Most standard evaluative instruments use a pre-determined number of items that are given a numerical score to indicate how well the item meets certain requirements. The most commonly used scale ranges from 1 to 5. Such a scale ensures uniformity of evaluation because each space in the building as well as the site has a specified number of items to evaluate, and each item requires a score. Such a scale allows a person to check the appropriate evaluation and arrive at a total.

This uniformity is further enhanced by listing each space with predetermined items to evaluate. In this way, such instruments enable successive evaluators to consider the same items using the same scale. This permits the school system to have a certain degree of uniformity in the evaluations for each building over time.

Evaluative Data

Each evaluation produces data about each building in the school system. The data consist of a list of projects or tasks to be completed to keep the school building in a state of good repair, and to provide the kinds of spaces and accoutrements that enables the educational program to function properly. These projects need to be incorporated into the capital improvement program.

Most school systems separate regular maintenance projects on existing buildings from other capital improvement projects such as additions to existing buildings and new buildings. Often, the maintenance program is separate from the regular capital program and even funded differently, from the operational budget of the school system. In unusual circumstances, maintenance projects may be funded through bond funds; however, this may not be the best use of these funds because of the long term pay-back and the interest costs over a period of years and the short term nature of the project. Major maintenance projects such as new roofs and heating systems may well be funded under capital funds because of the long life of these items. The periodic and annual evaluations of school facilities will produce items that can be classified as typical maintenance projects and at the same time identify needed capital improvements to the building. All of these must be prioritized if included in the maintenance list.

Central administration and building personnel should work together to prioritize items; deciding which to fund first and which to fund later. Some items identified by the central administration staff may have priority over other items because of prior knowledge of the condition of the building or because of a district-wide preventative maintenance program. In other cases, items related to program or particular circumstances in the local school organization may determine the priority. In any event, both the building principal and staff and the central administration personnel must be satisfied with the final priority list.

Following this, the items are placed on the maintenance list or schedule of the school system and funded in order of the priorities set. The funding pattern may well extend the entire five to seven years of the long-range plan. Both the annual and periodic evaluation of the school building should include an appraisal of the following areas:

- Ability to support the educational program
- Adaptability of the building
- Aesthetic quality of the building
- Structural soundness
- Site conditions
- Operational and maintenance efficiency
- Condition of mechanical systems
- Compliance with safety rules

Only through a system of periodic and annual evaluations will the school system identify projects needed to maintain its facilities in good repair. Through prioritization, the items on the maintenance schedule will be accomplished in a timely fashion. In this manner the facility needs of the school system can be met within the resources available. The school facilities are a valuable community resource that need to be kept in the best possible condition at all times. Proper evaluation of the facilities will provide the necessary data to assist school personnel in completing this task. ▪

chapterSEVEN

Long-Range Planning:
Financial Planning

THE FINANCIAL CONSIDERATIONS FOR A LONG-RANGE PLAN SHOULD BE COORDINATED with other planning efforts. The success of any plan is defined by having the necessary financial support exactly when it is needed to pay for implementation. Without this coordination, the planning effort is severely blunted and becomes an expensive exercise for the school system.

Individuals and offices responsible for the financial support of the long-range plan should provide their input to the planning process from the onset. Beyond initial planning, advice on the financial resources and constraints of the school system is always needed by school planners at crucial points along the planning schedule. Coordination of efforts is best done through a planning council of the school district. The planning council usually reports directly to the superintendent of schools. In small and medium-sized school systems, the planning council might be a very small group representing the major areas of responsibility in the district. Periodic meetings of the council will keep members current with the process of the planning effort and, at the same time, address problems. The coordinating mechanism of the planning council will assist the school system in producing a tightly written long-range plan that reflects the needs and resources of the school system and its clientele.

The financial portion of the long-range plan must identify resources for both operational and capital projects. This means that both the annual and longer term funding of capital projects is addressed. Even though the long-range plan covers several years, only one year of the plan is funded at a time. Consequently, the financial portion of the long-range plan deals with resources for two major aspects of operation: the day-by-day running of the school system and the longer-term capital projects.

The idea behind the funding package of the long-range plan is to know the sources of revenues and how to apply them, then to put this together into a cohesive plan of action. Funding for the operational portion of the long range plan comes from both state contributions through some type of formula, local contributions from taxation, plus whatever federal funding that is available.

Capital projects funding are developed in much the same fashion. The local financial planner must be knowledgeable about the types and sources of funding for capital projects in the particular state and how to obtain them. The success of not only the long-range plan, but also the capital improvement budget depends on the availability of sufficient funding at the proper time to complete each project.

The funding for capital projects can come from a variety of sources: a new school building may be financed from a single bond issue while, an addition to an existing building might be funded from the annual operations budget of the school system. Both projects, however, are considered capital projects. Operational funds can also fund major renovations and the purchase of school sites, busses, and major equipment. All of these projects are capital expenditures. A school system could, if resources were available, construct a new school building from the annual operating budget. Such expenditures, however, are extremely rare because the large cost of a new school means that such a financial impact could not be sustained. The example does show the flexibility in the use of operational funds. Capital funds do not have that flexibility of use.

The designation of capital and operational funds is derived from the manner in which the funds are obtained. Both funds come from state and local tax revenues. Operational funds are obtained through the annual tax collections on both levels, while capital funds are derived from the local school system going into debt for a specific purpose. When this is done, the funds obtained can be spent for only the stated purpose: constructing a building or completing a similar project.

Funds left over from the project, if any, must be returned to the taxpayer unless the school board can legally re-allocate the funds to another capital project that can be completed with the excess funds. In some states, this action must be taken only through a referendum of the voters. In this manner, the control of capital funds is derived from how funds are obtained. Capital funds can not be used for operational purposes such as the daily conduct of the school system.

The entire maintenance program of the school system is funded through the annual operational budget. Maintenance projects identified through the school building evaluation completed for the long-range plan are included in a maintenance and alterations schedule that is tied into the funding package of the long range plan. Some of these projects are quite substantial in scope and cost, but if the projects are to keep the building in a state of good repair, they should be funded under the operational budget.

There is an inextricable tie between the long-range plan and the capital improvement plan developed to house the educational program. The long-range plan follows a very logical pattern of development to describe the type of educational program offered in a geographic area. The long range plan further describes how many students will be involved in the educational program which gives a clue to the number of facilities that will be needed to properly house the number of students. After an evaluation of the existing buildings to determine how many students can be accommodated, the deficit (if any) in classroom space must be recognized and eliminated by constructing new space.

This correlation between program offered, number of students, and available spaces produce the number of new school buildings or classrooms that will need to be constructed. This need for new construction must be addressed through the financial portion of the long-range plan. School systems receive funding for programs from many sources, including all three levels of government. In addition, sources other than the government contribute to the operation of the public school systems of the country. Such is not the case for capital project funding. The sources of funding for such projects are very limited.

Federal Government Funding

The Federal Government provides limited funding of public schools. Federal funding is usually restricted to program initiatives and personnel development programs. The programs assisted are usually those that impinge upon the welfare of the country. This rather unique position results from the provisions within the U.S. Constitution. The Tenth Amendment, known as the Reserve Clause, reserves to the states any power not designated by the Constitution to the Federal Government (Alexander and Alexander 1992). Education, or the responsibility for providing an education, is not mentioned in the Constitution and is therefore a responsibility of the states and not the Federal Government.

It is important to keep this in mind when considering the financial effort of that level of government in assisting local school systems in housing educational programs. Because of this clause, the Federal Government has not been noted for providing construction funds to local school systems on a general basis. Only in very specific cases has that branch of the government provided funds of any consequence for such an effort.

Undoubtedly, the first effort of the Federal Government to assist the local school system in building schoolhouses could be considered the Northwest Ordinance of 1797 where the 16th and 32nd townships of government lands were donated for local purposes (Alexander and Alexander 1992). This could be considered the offering of a site for a school building. Such offers were made to each territory when it became a state, and many local school systems were organized around that geographic location.

Perhaps the most recent effort to assist local school systems with school building problems was during and immediately after World War II. Under the Impacted Aid Program of the Landrum Act of 1941, the Federal Government provided funds to local school systems to purchase sites, construct buildings, pay for fees, and equip the schools. Only school systems that were affected by the impaction of federal workers in the area were eligible for such funds; the vast majority of school systems were not eligible. School systems near military bases, armament factories, or other war efforts were the only ones to receive assistance. The greatest funding for this program was during the war years with the effort dwindling down as the need lessened. In 1983, $80 million was appropriated for this program, but in 1984 only $20 million was allocated. During the last five years, very little money has been allocated for construction purposes under this program.

The Federal Government has, from time to time, provided construction funds for vocational schools. In 1963, Congress passed the Regional Vocational High School Act that provided funds for planning and constructing regional vocational schools throughout the country. Originally, planning funds were available with the possibility of matching funds for construction following. The Act was not sufficiently funded to complete the planned projects, and the lack of local funding on a regional basis meant that very few building were constructed.

In the same vein, the government provided construction funding for vocational schools in selected impoverished areas. Under the Appalachian Regional Development Act of 1965, construction funds were allocated for such institutions. Only limited funds were allocated each year. In 1976, for example, just $10 million was available for the entire Appalachian region, insufficient to make an impact upon the diverse population in such a large geographical area. Since then, no construction funds have been available under that legislation.

Another piece of special purpose legislation was the Emergency Relief Act of

1974 and 1983. The latter version of this act provided construction funds to localities to rebuild governmental and public buildings destroyed by flooded conditions in Virginia and West Virginia. In this area, the damage to the local infrastructure was so complete that the Federal Government felt compelled to provide funding under the general welfare clause of the Constitution. School building replacement was included under this program of restoring the local infrastructure. This one-time program is no longer funded.

The removal of asbestos from public buildings is considered a national problem that deserves attention from the Federal Government. The asbestos removal program funded by the Federal Government provided planning funds to allow local school systems to identify sources of asbestos and develop a plan for its removal. Funding for the actual removal of asbestos in the public schools, however, was extremely limited which forced local school systems to provide matching funds. The mandatory provisions of the legislation that require removal, provide a strong incentive to quickly sanitize every building. Most school systems have either completed such an incentive for the school system to implement a program of asbestos removal or are well on their way to completion.

The Federal Government also has an interest in the education of special populations. Most of the funding has been for educational programs of various sorts and for personnel retraining. The government has, however, taken the leadership in making buildings accessible to the handicapped person. Through the Education for All Handicapped Children Act of 1976 and Section 504 of the Rehabilitation Act, the Federal Government has made provision for handicapped students to have access to buildings owned and operated by the local school system. Funds available through these acts, however, are for planning purposes and not for the actual renovation of the building. These pieces of legislation have not been funded at a sufficiently high enough level to provide relief to the local school system in complying with the mandatory provisions of the acts.

One of the most far-reaching pieces of federal legislation concerning school facilities was the Housing and Community Development Act of 1968. Under this act, local school systems were reimbursed for certain costs associated with land banking of school sites identified in the long-range plan and purchased in advance of need. Funds were available for reimbursement of settlement costs, relocation costs, and interest on bonds used to purchase parcels of land. The concept of acquisition of sites in advance of actual need was quite far-reaching and encouraged long range planning by the local school system. School systems apparently did not take advantage of this opportunity because the 1973 Capital

Improvement Budget document of the School District of Philadelphia stated that only one other locality made an application for funds under this act. This legislation was not funded in subsequent years.

The Federal Government has provided funds for new construction on college and university campuses at different times. Such legislation, however, has been for special disciplines. The Higher Education Facilities Act of 1963 provided funds for the construction of science and mathematics buildings. In the implementation stage, $230 million was appropriated for a three-year period for such projects throughout the country for both public and private institutions of higher education. Subsequent revisions to that legislation in 1992 reduced the amount available to colleges and universities.

From time to time, every governmental level has surplus property that must be disposed. The Federal Government began such a program shortly after World War II when it divested a great quantity of war-produced material and equipment. The Federal Surplus Property Program transferred all types of property to different levels of government and to individual private citizens. Real property was disposed by offering the site to other governmental levels first and then disposing of it to the private sector. Several military camps, arsenals, training sites, and similar facilities were transferred to local school systems. This program is still in operation, but there is virtually no real property included as surplus today.

Because the Federal Government's role in providing for education is limited by the Constitution, it has provided only limited funds for educational purposes. What little has been provided was usually designated for special programs. The housing of students has not been seen as a responsibility of the Federal Government and, as a result, very little legislative provision has been made for assisting local school systems in providing safe, modern school buildings for students.

In 1995-1996, the United States General Accounting Office issued a series of reports on the condition of the school buildings in the country (GAO 1995, 1996). These reports presented a picture of great need for almost all school buildings to be upgraded. Dismal pictures of the conditions of buildings were painted in these reports. The reports stated it would take approximately $112 billion to bring all school buildings up to standard, and these were 1995 dollars. The amount of funds needed today is even greater.

Because of these, and other reports, the Federal Government has recognized the vast need of all localities to provide adequate school housing for students. In recent years, several laws have been passed to provide funding for either school buildings or some form of relief from the interest payments caused by going into debt. Some of the more recent initiatives include: Improving America's Schools Act of 1994 (P.L. 103-382), School Repair and Construction Act of 1997 (S. 1472), Education Facilities Improvement Act of 1997 (S.1160), The Partnership to Rebuild America's Schools Act of 1997 (S.456), and The Taxpayers Relief Act of 1997. Only two of these legislative initiatives have been passed and signed into law, the rest of the initiatives have not passed Congress.

Sentiment on local governmental levels seems to be that almost all of the individual school systems in the country do not have the resources in themselves to bring the school facilities up to standard. As a result, the state and federal levels of government will need to provide some assistance. What form this assistance will take is not known at this time, but there are several schemes that can be used today in combination that can reduce significantly the burden of providing safe, functional, and efficient school buildings by local taxpayers.

State Government Funding

Each state has the responsibility for providing some form of education for all citizens. As a result, each state has developed a system of local schools and a scheme for funding them. Naturally, the funding system reflects the importance the citizens place upon education. In addition, each state has made a decision regarding the extent of funding for school buildings. Not all states have opted to provide funds to the local school system for school buildings.

If the financial commitment for school buildings provided by all states were averaged, the conclusion would be that states do not provide a very significant amount to local school systems for school construction. There are several reasons for this. First, there is the belief that the localities should provide housing for students rather than the state. This belief is rooted in the colonial period when each family in a locality had to make provision for housing the schoolmaster. Secondly, the title to the school building is usually held by the locality so it is felt that state funds should not go into property that is owned by the local government.

These reasons may seem trivial in light of present day thinking. Yet these beliefs governed the actions (or inaction) of state legislatures for decades. The matter of equity of program and facilities is a recent phenomenon that is only now struggling for acceptance. Likewise, the philosophy that the state government is responsible for providing equality on the local scene is yet to be implemented throughout the country.

The amount of assistance a state gives local school systems for new school construction ranges from absolutely no state funds in 12 states to full funding of capital projects in Hawaii. (Hawaii, however, has only one local school system and the funding scheme from the state reflects this single entity.)

Thirty-five states provide some type of state assistance that confirms the idea that most states believe in some sort of shared responsibility for providing housing to students. Five states have loan provisions and ten states, Colorado, Iowa, Kansas, Louisiana, Montana, Nebraska, Nevada, North Dakota, Oklahoma, South Dakota, and Texas provide no support to local capital projects and all funding must be borne by the locality.

There are a variety of plans for providing state assistance, but generally falls into two basic categories: grants-in-aid and loans. Grants are funds that are given outright to the local school system. Loans must be paid back to the state agency; the locality simply uses state funds for a period of time, usually under favorable conditions.

Grants-in-Aid

Under this type of assistance, the state funds are given to the local school system and do not have to be paid back. Grants may be outright gifts with no qualifications of the recipient school system. In this instance, each school system qualifies for a certain amount of assistance. Usually grants are on a per pupil basis, such as a certain amount of capital funds received by the school for each student in membership.

Grants can also be made on a classroom basis where the funds are distributed according to the total number of students divided by a set number of students per classroom unit. For instance, 25 students may be the factor used to decide the number of units a school system has with payment based upon the number of classroom units into which the total student body can be divided. Educational program grants can also be awarded in like manner for state support, but this funding is separate from capital funding.

Grants-in-aid can also be awarded according to some qualification of the school system on a matching basis. Under this provision, a local school system may qualify for a set amount of funds, but that would have to be matched with local capital funds. In some states, the original amount of state funds would be determined by the amount of square feet in the building, certain building components, number of students to be housed, or similar criteria.

In addition, a financial aid factor may compensate for wealth or lack of wealth in a local school system. Under these programs, school systems classified as poor would receive additional compensation over and above the normal grant amount. About 25 percent (27) of the states have enacted such grants-in-aid programs to provide state assistance to local school systems. There is an equalized grants program in 16 states, and the rest have either a flat or matching grants provision (Camp, 1983).

Grants can be given for capital outlay or for debt service. In the latter case, school systems must go into debt and construct the building before any funds are available. Under this type of program, the state provides a grant for the debt thus created upon application by the local school system. These grants go to pay off debt. Under the capital outlay grants programs, the school system usually has to expend funds up front before receiving aid from the state. Some sort of grants program for debt service, either equalized, matching, or flat exists in 16 states (Educational Writers Association, 1989).

Some states provide grants to local school systems for capital construction based upon a per pupil count. These grants are awarded regardless of need. Usually the grant amount is very low and, as a result, the school system must advance considerable local funds for any major construction project.

Loan Programs

The second way local school systems receive state assistance for capital projects is through loan programs. Under these programs, a fund is established from which school systems may secure loans. The loans are secured by the title to the property on which the school is sited. The local school system may borrow a set amount of money to be used in constructing a school building. The payback for the loan is usually over a 20-year period.

State loan programs' interest rates are usually below the rates obtainable on the open market, in some cases as much as 3 percentage points below. Both low interest rates and favorable payback conditions make this a favored program. The amount of funds that can be secured under these programs is usually not very high. As a result, school systems must contribute local funds to complete the project.

At the present time, six states have such a loan program: Arkansas, California, Indiana, Minnesota, North Dakota, and Virginia. With the exception of California, none has any grant-in-aid program. In addition, California and Minnesota have a forgiveness clause in their loan program that means the local school system does not have to repay the full amount of the loan.

School Building Authorities

School authorities are vehicles to circumvent certain restrictive legislation. An authority is a quasi-governmental corporation, incorporated under the laws of the state and with state backing (Camp 1983). These are single-purpose organizations with a public governance structure appointed by the governor, legislature, mayor, or city council. A building authority can do two things: raise funds for local school systems, or actually construct buildings for the system and lease them back.

The Virginia Public School Building Authority raises funds for local school systems. The authority can get a better rate of interest on a large bond issue than a small school system could get with a small bond issue. The authority can usually command a better credit rating than small school systems, which also results in better interest rates.

Some building authorities plan, design, and construct buildings for the government. The Chicago Public Building Authority, for example, does all of the work entailed with having a building constructed to the exact specifications of the school system. The authority then enters into a long-term lease with the school system to pay back the cost of the building. At the end of a specified period, the building's title reverts to the local school district, and the authority uses the funds received to construct other buildings. This is in effect a turnkey project for the school system.

Local Government Funding

The local school system has the largest responsibility for funding school construction. In addition, the local school system has a very limited tax base upon which to secure needed funding for capital construction. The local real estate tax is the sole source of revenue for school systems for both operational funds and capital funds.

This places a heavy burden upon the citizens of the locality. Most schemes for raising funds for school buildings rely upon debt to be paid over a period of years. This seems to be the most equitable method because the payment for the building is assumed by not just one generation. Not all methods of raising funds for school buildings are legal in all states, and the school administrator should make certain, through legal advice, which ways are acceptable for raising funds.

Pay-As-You-Go

This method of raising funds for school buildings stipulates that when funds are available, building takes place. Funds must be provided through the operational budget under this method. Paying for construction when funds are available saves the money that is normally spent on interest payments, which can represent from 40 to 200 percent of the cost of construction. Saving this much money is indeed a sizeable gain.

At the turn of the century, this was a popular method of financing public schools. Of course, school buildings at that time did not approach the cost of such facilities today. There are not many school systems these days that can allocate sufficient funds from day-to-day operations to pay for a new school building. So few, if any, school systems use this method of raising construction funds.

Sinking Funds

This method is also called the capital reserve fund. A sinking or reserve fund is much like a savings account: funds are placed in an account for future construction and when the amount needed to build a school is reached, planning and construction takes place. A specific amount of money is set aside each year to build up the sinking fund for the amount of funds needed. Since this spreads the cost of the building over a number of years, high interest payments are avoided.

There are two reasons school systems do not use this form of raising revenue. First, it takes many years to accumulate sufficient money to pay for a new building. If the student population increases rapidly before there are sufficient funds to construct a building, the school system faces a housing problem that may consume more funds than are in the sinking fund.

Additionally, the money in the sinking fund can only be invested in suitable governmental investment instruments. The interest paid on this type of saving usually does not keep up with inflation. As a result, the sinking fund can never grow large enough to cover the cost of construction. At one time this was a common method of raising revenue for school buildings, but today it is not seen as a viable method. In fact, in some states, the sinking fund is not legal.

General Obligation Bonds

General obligation bonds or municipal bonds are the traditional method school systems use to finance capital construction. The proceeds from the sale of general obligation bonds can be used for any purpose involved with planning, designing, and constructing a building: contracting planning expertise, design work, construction, equipment, site purchase, the employment of in-house educational planners and so on.

The municipal bond is a debt instrument backed by the full faith and credit of the local government unit or school system. It is not a lien against the property of the school system, rather it is an obligated debt of the government. The authority for issuing these debt instruments is obtained by a public referendum of the voters. Voter approval of the sale of bonds indicates it is the wish of the community to go into debt.

When a school system decides to go into debt, certain actions must be taken. A bond referendum must be held so that the voters have an opportunity to express their wishes. The school board and administration must observe the legal procedures involved with the process of going into debt. This includes limitations of indebtedness, vote of approval, type of bonds to be issued, payment of the principal, maximum term of payment, maximum rate of interest, restrictions on the sale of the bonds, tax rate, time limits for election notices, and voting procedures.

The first step is for the school board to pass a resolution that a bond referendum is to be conducted. In some states, the school board must request a local court to conduct the bond election. Upon official notice from the school board, the court makes all preparation to conduct the election. Tellers are appointed, polling places established, ballots printed, ballot boxes readied, election dates and times established and posted, and official notices of the election posted and printed in the newspaper. The court conducts all of these steps.

After the election, the court notifies the school board and publishes the results. However, in many states, the local school board can conduct the election. In these locales, the school board does everything listed above. The results of the election are then certified to the local court and to the office of the city or county treasurer. School systems fiscally dependent upon a local government must have approval from that body before going into debt.

The ballot is a simple statement asking voters if they approve going into debt for the stated amount of money. In most states, a simple majority—50 percent plus one vote—is needed to pass a capital bond referendum. In some states, majorities of up to 60 or 66 percent of the voters are required to pass a bond issue.

There are some very limited exceptions to the normal method of going into debt through a referendum. In some instances school boards or city councils can bond themselves to a certain limitation of the assessed value of the property. In Virginia, if the school board uses either state loan funds or funds from the public school building authority, voter approval is not required. In some communities, the city charter permits local city councils to go into debt without voter approval. But these are the exceptions to the rule of voter approval for debt.

When a school board first seeks a referendum, it secures the services of a bond attorney. Such services can be obtained through a reputable bonding house—a company that buys and sells bonds and other debt instruments. The bond attorney determines the legality of the bond by investigating the procedure used by the school board to go into debt. The bond counsel also assists in preparing the actual bonds, and making certain the correct terminology is used.

Once these preliminary actions are completed, the bonds are printed. Each bond is a valuable negotiable commodity and must be personally signed by a legal representative of the school board.

When the bonds are delivered, they are sold at public bidding. The school board sells the bonds to a commercial firm that, in turn, sells the bonds to the public. A notice to bid on the sale of the bonds is submitted to the legal newspaper of the locality. The time and date for receiving the bids is contained in the notice. When the bids are received and opened, the best offer to purchase the bonds is accepted by the school board.

Usually the best bid is for the lowest percent of interest for the school board to pay on the bonds. The bank, investment house, syndicate, or brokerage firm that submits the lowest bid is awarded the sale of the bonds to the public. That company in turn puts the bonds on the public market for open sale. Many pension funds invest regularly in such municipal bonds. Mutual funds devoted to the purchase of tax-free bonds are also firms that purchase such bonds. People invest in these pension funds or mutual funds and receive the benefit of tax-free income.

Municipal or general obligation bonds are usually offered in $5,000 denominations. At that price, few people can afford to purchase them. That is why mutual funds offering access to these investments are popular. In some unusual circumstances, municipal bonds may be offered in the $1,000 denomination, specifically designed for those individuals who might want to purchase this type of investment.

Types of Bonds

Four types of bonds seem to be viable vehicles for local governmental agencies: term, sinking fund, serial, and amortized bonds each use a different method for repayment. Only one type of bond is printed under an issue as the method of payment should be uniform over the life of the bond.

Term Bonds

This type of bonds is issued for a predetermined period of time at the end of which all bonds are redeemed. The interest on the bonds is paid during the term of the bond. At the end of the term, the school system must raise the entire amount of the bond issue to redeem the bonds. This balloon payment at the end of the term is often a sizeable amount and difficult to raise.

Sometimes this leads to issuing additional bonds to finance the original issue that can lead to permanent debt. Most schools do not issue this type of bond because of the difficulty in raising the entire bond amount at the end of the term. Payment of the principal amount of the bond issue often places the burden of payment on the next generation of taxpayers.

Sinking Fund Bonds

These bonds are actually term bonds in that the principal of the bond issue is paid at the end of the term. A set amount of the principal of the bond issue is set aside each year and placed in a sinking fund to draw interest during the life of the bond. At the redemption date, the full amount of the bond issue is paid. Interest accrued during the life of the bond is used to reduce the amount of principal the school system has to raise for redemption. In some states this type of bond is not legal.

Serial Bonds

These bonds are redeemed at various times during the life of the bond issue: A set number are redeemed during the first five years, another group in the next five years, and so on until the entire issue is retired. Interest is paid on the bond until it is redeemed. With several maturation dates, the school board can raise sufficient funds to retire a portion of the total bond issue without the burden of raising the entire sum at one time.

The serial bond is the most favored type of bonding used by school systems. One reason is that a large balloon payment is avoided and, at the least, the various payments are not excessive. The repayment of the entire bond issue, including principal and interest, is spread over the time of the bond issue. This permits the school system to determine a set annual tax rate to repay. The burden of repayment is shared equally over the life of the bond. Investors like this type of bond because of the varying dates of maturity.

Amortization Bonds

These bonds are similar to serial bonds in that there are no balloon payments. The repayment schedule for these bonds provides for retiring part of the principal of each bond over the life of the bond. A semiannual payment to the investor contains the earned interest plus part of the principal. The payment schedule on this bond is much like a government backed housing mortgage where principal and interest are returned with each payment. An additional advantage with this mortgage is that with each payment, the debt load of the school system is reduced proportionately

Credit Rating

The interest rate on a bond is directly related to the credit rating of the school system. The lower the credit rating, the higher the interest the school system has to pay the investor holding the bond because the bond is considered more at risk. Each school system that has bonds for sale has a credit rating developed by one or more of the major credit reporting agencies.

The more common agencies are Moody's Investors Service, Standard and Poor, and Fitch's Investors Service. These agencies rate school systems and other branches of government according to their ability to repay debts. These ratings and the factors used in establishing them are much like the credit rating of an individual. Many items enter into the rating for the school system, such as amount of current debt, ratio of debt to assets, history of repaying debt, ratio of assessed valuation of property to number of students in school, number of outstanding bills, record of payment of bills, stability of leadership, history of successful bond referendum, and even the percentage of favorable vote on the last bond referendum.

Credit rating scales of the school system are indicated by letters from high (AAA, Aaa, A) to low (CCC, Ccc, C, D). In this manner, the bonds then carry the rating of the school system. Credit ratings are important to the school system, and everything that is possible should be done to keep the rating as high as possible.

Bond Capacity of the School System

Each school system has a debt limit that is called a bond capacity. This means the system can go into debt to a certain limit through offering bonds for sale. Either the constitution or statutes of the state most often define the bond capacity of local school systems. These limits may be a certain percentage of the assessed value of the taxable real estate in the school system. The limits range from a low of 5 percent to a high of 15 percent. In some cases, school systems may exceed the debt limit by appealing to the state legislature or some other state office.

Management of Bond Proceeds

The proceeds of a bond issue are not always used immediately. The planning and design work for a new school must precede the actual construction. Thus, the bulk of a bond issue may not be needed for two years after the bonds are sold and the proceeds realized by the school system.

Prudent administration of these funds indicates that the funds are kept in a safe place, but one where some interest can be gained. It is not unlawful for school systems to invest part or all of the proceeds of a bond issue into interest-bearing instruments. There is a limit, however, as to the type of instrument that can be used. All investments must be into an instrument issued by another governmental agency. For instance, local school systems could invest in state or federal government bonds, notes, or bills. School boards may not invest in any instrument that places the principal amount of the investment at risk. In addition, school boards may not engage in arbitrage of any sort.

Alternative Funding Plans

The vast majority of capital improvement projects are funded through the issuance of general obligation bonds. These are usually called municipal bonds because they are issued by a local governmental agency. Over the decades, this type of funding has been adequate to fund the needs of school systems.

In recent years, with the growing need to upgrade existing school facilities and accommodate a growing student population, many school systems are in a financial situation where they have difficulty properly financing all of the capital needs. In addition, the large increase in the cost of school facilities has created a strain on the financial resources of the school system. The latest report on the condition of the financial need to upgrade all schools in the country placed the amount at $112 billion (GAO 1995). This amount is just what it would take to place all existing school buildings in satisfactory condition. It does not address the need for new school buildings in certain school systems. This large financial burden can not be born entirely by local school systems. To remedy this situation, many local school systems and states have tried a number of alternative funding plans to relieve the financial burden of providing adequate school buildings.

Alternative funding sources have become very popular in selected localities. Some very creative ways of using streams of dedicated revenue to leverage debt or other enhancements have been successfully used. In addition some models of alternative funding from sources other than school system have been modified. For instance some alternative funding schemes used to implement the Clear Water Act have been suggested for use by school systems. Modification of financial schemes in other segments of the government have been implemented in certain localities.

Some caution has to be used in discussing alternative schemes to fund educational capital improvement projects. The first caution is that most alternative funding plans are site or place specific. In other words, the alternative funding plan can be used for a specific school building, but can not be used universally to other school sites in the school system or to school systems in other locations. Moreover, most alternative funding plans can not raise the entire cost of a single capital improvement project. In addition, funds realized under any alternative funding plan are usually limited in the amount raised.

Nevertheless, such alternative funding plans as are applicable to any and all capital improvement projects should be used to the fullest advantage. This will mean that administrators will need to be aware of possible plans that may be available to their particular state and locality because not all plans are universally applicable. What might be permissible to employ in one state, may not be in another state.

State Revolving Funds

State Revolving Funds are an effective mechanism for bringing low-cost financing to meet community needs. These funding mechanisms are also considered loan programs in that the state would loan funds to local school systems to pay for capital improvement projects. The return of principal and interest from the local community would build-up an ever larger fund balance. Under such plans, the state lends the funds at below market levels with favorable repayment rates. A revolving fund is a loan and is technically not a debt that could be counted against the debt limit of the school system.

Several states currently have provisions for a loan program to local school systems. The rate of interest charged by the state is usually low and the term of the loan may be upwards of 20 years. These are indeed favorable repayment terms. Most states have restrictions on the amount a school system can borrow and there is usually a backlog of requests for the limited capitalized loan fund. Even with these limitations, state loan funds are very attractive and useful to the school system.

There are some variations of this scheme in that some authorities are suggesting that the Federal Government provide each state with matching grants to capitalize the State Revolving Fund. A state could create an independent revolving loan fund to facilitate the same end. In either case, the return payments would increase the total capitalization of the fund and provide an increasing supply of money to lend to local school systems (Council of Infrastructure Financing Authorities 1998).

State Credit Enhancement Programs

These types of programs basically use the credit rating of the state rather than the local school system to sell bonds (Standard & Poor 1998). Most local governmental units, such as the schools, have a lower credit rating than the state in which it is located because of a number of factors. Because of this, the local school system would pay higher interest rates on bonds they issued. State credit enhancement plans are essentially the substitution of the credit rating of the state for local governmental agency to sell bonds. Significant benefits in lower interest payments can be realized through this substitution. Credit substitution programs are created through a state constitution provision, legislative statute, or both. This legal basis provides a surety of payment by a state government.

One major factor in these programs is that through the legal provisions of enhancement, the state provides a cure for default on the part of a locality. The state in essence pays for any default on the part of the school system. This cure may be in the form of withholding state aid from the local school system or the debt is paid through a state school building fund. Thus, the bondholder is assured that the debt will be paid in a timely fashion. While credit ratings assess the probability of full and timely payment of the debt based on economic, financial, management, and debt factors, credit enhancement plans can also reflect legal provisions of public law that protects bondholders from possible default.

The extent of credit enhancement depends upon the exact nature of the program of the state. In some instances, the state guarantees payment to avoid default by the local school system. In other states the responsibility of debt repayment rests with a state aid intercept program that diverts standard education payments from the school system to make debt payments. Both of these methods of payment are a very effective way to guarantee payment. At the present time, there are 22 states, listed in Appendix J that have some form of credit enhancement program. States other than those listed are contemplating implementation of a state credit enhancement plan. School boards and administrators need to explore the use of this credit rating when contemplating the issuance of bonds.

Tax Credit Plans

Under a tax credit plan bondholders are rewarded for purchasing municipal bonds by allowing them credits against possible tax liability. In these plans, tax credits can be used against Federal tax liabilities and are substituted for the interest bondholders would normally receive from the school systems. One such plan that has been approved by Congress under the Taxpayer Relief Act of 1997, is called the Qualified Zone Academy Bond. There are variations of this plan being proposed in other legislative measures.

Qualified Zone Academy Bonds

Under the Taxpayer Relief Act of 1997, a new category of no-interest bonds are created. The state and local governments can issue qualified zone academy bonds to fund the improvement of eligible public school buildings. An eligible holder of a qualified zone academy bond receives annual Federal Income Tax credits in lieu of interest payments from the school system. These annual credits compensate the holder for lending money and, therefore, are treated like taxable interest payments for Federal tax purposes. The benefit of these bonds is that the school system would not have to pay interest to the bondholders. This would in effect reduce the overall cost of the building. In many cases, the interest payments for any construction project normally exceed the original cost of construction by at least two times. Thus, over a twenty-year period of time, considerable revenue could be saved.

Under the proposed qualified zone academy bonds, there are a number of requirements that must be met for a bond to be classified for tax credits. The first is that the bond must be issued pursuant to an allocation of bond authority from the state educational agency. Second, at least 95 percent of the bond proceeds must be used for renovation or acquiring equipment at a qualified zone academy.

A qualified zone academy is a school that is designed in cooperation with business and is located in an empowerment zone or enterprise community or attended by students at least 35 percent of whom are from low-income families. The third requirement is that private business organizations must have promised to contribute to the qualified zone academy certain property or services with a value equal to at least 10 percent of the bond proceeds.

Qualified School Modernization Bonds

These bonds are similar to the qualified zone academy bonds in that state and local governmental units can issue qualified school modernization bonds to fund the construction and renovation of school facilities. These bonds were defined in the Partners to Rebuild America's School Act of 1997 (S.456) that was not passed into law by Congress. The holders of these bonds would receive Federal income tax credits in lieu of interest payments from the bonds themselves. In turn school systems would not have to pay interest on these bonds thereby reducing the total cost of a school building construction project. The credit rate of these bonds would be set by the Secretary of the Treasury and the bonds would have a term of only 15 years.

To be classified as a qualified school modernization bond, the issue would have to meet three requirements. The first requirement is that the U.S. Department of Education must approve the school construction plan of the state or eligible school system. This plan must be based upon a comprehensive survey of construction needs throughout the state and there must be a guarantee the proceeds of the bonds will be used for modernization of school buildings. The second requirement is that the local school system must receive an allocation for the bond from the state. The third requirement is that 95 percent of the proceeds must be used for construction or renovation of school facilities. Private business establishments would not be required to contribute goods or services to school systems under this program.

Impact Fees

Almost every local government can enact ordinances relating to the proper development and use of land. These ordinances take the form of imposing an impact fee on a developer to pay for public services such as schools. An impact fee is different from a tax because the fee is based upon the police power of the government to regulate private activity to protect public health, safety, and welfare. Impact fees are a form of development extraction where an extraction is a condition of permission that requires a public facility or improvement to be provided at the expense of the developer. An impact fee is:

1. in the form of a predetermined money payment;
2. assessed as a condition to the issuance of a building permit, an occupancy permit, or plat approval;
3. pursuant to local government powers to regulate new growth and development and provide for adequate public facilities; and
4. levied to fund large-scale facilities to serve new development (Ducker 1994).

Alternatives to Construction

It is natural to think that whenever additional students need to be housed, the school system should construct a building, but such thinking may not result in the best solution. For the most part, it is a good solution to construct a school building, but each situation should be evaluated to determine if other options might be more beneficial to the school system. Several alternatives to new construction are available to school systems and should be considered.

Long Term Leasing

In certain situations, it may be more economical to lease a facility rather than build a new facility. Comparing the initial cost of the facility, the interest payments, and the cost of ownership to a leased facility for 20 years may be to the advantage of the school system. Only by completing such studies will the school board know which decision to make. Such studies employ a life-cycle comparison of an owned versus leased facilities. This is where all costs of the facility are used for the comparison.

There are many available spaces that would lend themselves to a lease arrangement. Church educational classrooms, speculative buildings, and private school facilities may be used to great advantage to both the school system and the owner.

Long term leasing of facilities is legal in all states and should be considered a viable alternative. Leasing permits the school system the use of school facilities without the burdensome debt that can negatively influence their credit rating, because costs for leasing come from the operational budget. Another advantage to leasing is that the building remains on the tax rolls and the school system receives tax revenues paid by the owner.

Conversion of Existing Buildings

Some existing buildings can make very good school facilities. Conversion of an existing building to fit the needs of a school is a good alternative to consider. Buildings that have large open spaces make excellent schools. Warehouses, shopping areas, and supermarkets are all good spaces in which to put a school because, with a minimum of conversion, the facilities could house students. If the structure and systems are in good working order, then with the installation of carpeting, wall treatment and lowered ceiling and lighting system, the facility is ready. The cost of conversion of the existing building is many times less than constructing a new building on a new site.

One drawback to such a solution is that existing buildings often are not located where the bulk of the students live. When this happens, additional transportation is necessary which adds to the total cost of housing students. In urban areas where a site is either not available or the costs are prohibitive, conversion of an existing building could be a good solution.

Inexpensive Buildings

Inexpensive buildings are not cheap buildings. These are buildings constructed with material that makes them inexpensive. One such application is the air structure, which is actually a balloon supported by air pressure. A typical building foundation is laid which might rise to three or four feet above the ground and above this a balloon structure is attached, and the building is maintained by air pressure. Auxiliary pumps are in place in case of failure of the main air pumps.

Such a structure could cover large expanses such as a swimming pool, tennis courts, and even a practice soccer field. Several applications of this type of building have been used for several decades. This solution, however, has limited application.

Systems Buildings

Some school systems have tried to reduce the cost of a school building by using what have been called modular structures. Such buildings are composed of various systems that are constructed in the factory and then assembled at the site. This combination seems to reduce the overall cost of a building. Factory built components can be constructed faster because there are no stoppages of work because of weather, and an assembly line can be created for the construction process.

There are constraints on the use of modular buildings. One is that the spaces within the structure are either a square or a rectangle. Also, most modular buildings are single story; however, there are some companies that can produce a multi-story building.

Community Facilities

It is very common for students to use community facilities in their education. Field trips have been a part of education since the early part of this century. But the idea of locating classes of students in community-owned facilities is quite different. However, every community, has spaces in both commercial and public buildings that are vacant and could be used to house a class of students. Municipal buildings, libraries, museums, and commercial buildings are examples of where space can be found to house students.

The School District of Philadelphia housed 500 students in such facilities within the city. This was known as the Parkway School. A rented office space served as the headquarters and homeroom for the students, but the subject matter classes were taught in such facilities as a newspaper building, courtroom, science museum, and insurance office. All of the facilities were close enough for the students to move from one building to another in much the same fashion as college students. This solution, however, may have limited applications.

Contracting for Service

In some localities, housing developers must provide either a school site or, in its place, a monetary consideration to the school system in order to have the plan adopted. In some cases, a developer can construct a school building less expensively than a school system can. The developer could then lease the building to the school system for their use. The building would be built to the specifications of the school system.

The economy would come from the fact that the developer has the equipment and workforce on the site that would work for economy. Tax write-off advantages would accrue to the developer; the land would still be on the tax rolls, and the school system would have a school ready when the children arrive. Further, the school system would not have incurred a debt, but at some point in the future, the school system could purchase the building, if needed.

A further extension of this concept might be not only to lease the school building from the developer, but also to contract to provide the entire educational program. The school system would enter into an agreement with the developer who would provide not only the building but also the staff, materials, and supplies. The curriculum would be provided by the school system. Such an agreement is legal in all states and in some special situations, might be a viable economic solution. ■

chaptereight

Development of the Capital Improvement Program

THE LONG-RANGE PLAN OF THE SCHOOL SYSTEM IS THE BASIS OF OTHER PLANS OR programs. This document serves as a general guide so the entire organization can work cooperatively towards the identified goals. Because of the size of the long-range plan, other more manageable plans must be developed. The enormous tasks identified in the long-range plan are broken into component plans that can be completed.

The actual work detail needed to complete the long-range plan is contained in subsequent plans developed by various offices and departments after the final adoption of the plan. These offices and departments then assume responsibility for executing the plans for which they have responsibility. Each department or segment of the organization contributes to the long-range plan during the formulation stage for those areas which the department has responsibility and expertise. After the plan is adopted, it assumes responsibility for execution of that portion.

For example, part of the long-range plan describes the instructional and classified staff needed to implement the desired educational program. This description of needed staff is comprehensive in that types and numbers of staff are identified even according to the level of instruction. Based upon the description of the staff needed in the plan, the personnel office must fashion a Human Resource Development Plan to secure the number of individuals needed. This plan will cover the same time span as the long-range plan and be completed at the same time as that document. Over the years the personnel department will systematically implement the Human Resource Development Plan in support of the long-range plan. This will happen in other departments of the school system as well.

The long-range plan also stipulates the educational program to be carried on and the number of students expected over the years. These factors determine the scope and size of the school system program. In addition, the plan describes the number of classrooms this combination of program and students will need to be properly housed in adequate facilities. The previously completed evaluation of existing facilities owned and operated by the school system identified the current inventory of classroom spaces available. The difference, if any, between the number of classroom spaces available and those needed for the given student body represents the number of new classrooms that need to be constructed. Also, the distribution of the student population will indicate where the additional classrooms will need to be located.

In school systems experiencing a decline in student enrollment the problem of surplus space and what to do with that space will be identified in this section of the document. All of this represents data needed to produce a plan to provide suitable housing for students.

Just as the long-range plan is the basis of subsequent plans to employ the needed teaching staff, develop curricular materials, re-train the staff, and other efforts, it is also the basis of the school system's capital improvement plan. Data for the capital improvement program is derived from the evaluation of all facilities conducted earlier and described in previous chapters.

If a comprehensive evaluation of all facilities has been conducted and complete data on facility needs obtained, the necessary ingredients for a capital improvement program are available. This implementation plan, which is called the capital improvement program, is developed as a response to the need for classroom space.

Capital Improvement Plan

The capital improvement plan (CIP) is a set of proposed actions to provide housing for the school system's students (Castaldi 1994). This document is often called the capital improvement program. The plan or program covers the work of several years, and its span coincides with the time span of the long-range plan.

The completed program will consist of a number of different kinds of capital projects including: new school buildings, additions to existing schools, major renovations of older schools, the purchase of sites or buildings, and major improvements to schools.

There are always more capital improvement projects than the school system has funds to complete, so each project must receive a priority for when it will be completed. Many factors enter into setting the timing for each project. When prioritizing, the most important factor is the need to house either a growing or declining population. If a school system is growing rapidly, the construction of new schools may take precedent over all other projects. In different circumstances, other factors may carry more weight.

The exact timing of the project is determined by a cooperative effort between the school facilities department and the superintendent. The fiscal officers of the school system also participate in this process because they can give advice on the availability of funds.

Some office must be responsible for actually compiling the document and having it published. This office may be in the school facilities department if there is sufficient financial expertise. In large school systems, there is generally an office devoted just to the preparation of the capital improvement program. This office provides coordination services to other departments and offices that have a direct input into the prioritizing process. This office also has direct relationship to the department responsible for development of the capital improvement budget which is the instrument used to actually complete capital projects.

The capital improvement budget is a different document from the capital improvement program. The capital improvement program is a set of proposed actions to provide housing for students in the school system and can be classified as a plan for doing certain things. The capital improvement budget on the other hand is a document that authorizes actions through the expenditure of funds. The capital improvement budget is an approved expenditure plan for capital projects.

Any budget is defined as an adopted expenditure plan along with a revenue plan, and the capital improvement budget deals specifically with funding for school buildings. Without the budget, the school system staff would have no authority to spend funds for any project no matter how worthy. Capital improvement budgets that are being offered to the school board for consideration are, in fact, proposed capital improvement budgets. Only after the document is approved by the school board and proper authorities, can the document be called a budget in the true sense.

The capital improvement program lists all capital projects the school system wishes to complete over five to seven years. These projects are described in the long-range plan developed previously through the facility. Each project has a description of the scope of and need for the project. In addition, the cost estimates for each part of the project are obtained either through an estimator on the school staff or in small school systems, through the expertise of a person outside of the school system such as an architectural or construction firm. The description tells how this project fits into the overall scheme for the school system. The various components of the project are listed as well as the suggested time for completing them. Not every project would contain the same components, but a new school building project would have a site to purchase, would need to obtain some educational planning, architectural services to secure, a building to construct, and some furniture and equipment to complete the building. The listing of each capital project would look somewhat like Figure 8.1.

The capital improvement program entry in the figure shows the total anticipated expenditures for the project over the five years and the suggested outlay of funds needed to complete it. A total of $24,780,000 will be spent on the construction of a new high school. The design work is spread over a number of years and shows the heaviest concentration of work in the year immediately preceding construction. The site is purchased two years in advance of the beginning of construction, sufficient time for preparation of the site. The last major purchase is for loose furniture and equipment. In as much as the $1,940,000 is not needed until the beginning of the fifth year of the project, that amount can be invested

Project B0156
Potomac High School

Figure 8.1
*Capital Improvement
Project Description*

Description: A project is required to plan and construct a 60-station high school in the northern Potomac area to be completed by the year 2004.

Justification: Rapid residential housing construction in the area to be served has required construction of five schools in the last four years. Enrollments are projected to increase in the next five years.

Expenditure Schedule (000's)

Cost Element	Total	2000	2001	2002	2003	2004
Plan/Design	1,200	270	700	100	90	40
Land	900	900				
Site Improvement	500		500			
Construction	20,280			20,280		
Furniture/Equipment	1,900					1,900
Total	*24,780*	*1,170*	*1,200*	*20,380*	*90*	*1,940*

in proper instruments to realize some funds with which to offset inflation for the period of time. Even the $20.7 million for construction will not be needed until the beginning of the third year and an investment strategy can be developed to realize some funds for that period of time. A proper investment program for all funds should be established based upon the above schedule.

Capital Improvement Program Approval

There are several levels of approval for the capital improvement plan. The points of approval are both within and outside of the school system. The initial level of approval is with the central administrative staff who has the responsibility for compiling the document. This level of approval is the first hurdle for the CIP.

The basis for prioritizing all of the projects suggested for the CIP is the need to house students properly in modern school buildings. Growth in student enrollments in a school system can mandate the priority system, or a program initiative in a stable school system can be the deciding factor. There is always the pull in prioritizing projects between the need to implement a new program and to provide sufficient classrooms for the student body. Undoubtedly, in a growing school system, that need takes precedence over new program implementation, if it is a matter of only one being served properly, but there is always the need to provide the right kinds facilities so a program can function properly. Nevertheless, initially central staff has to put each project into proper sequence, taking everything into consideration. After the document is put together with the suggestion prioritization, it is reviewed by the administrative council, team, or cabinet of the superintendent for their approval. This body of administrators is very knowledgeable about the needs of the school system as a whole, and about the political environment in particular. From this group may come some suggestions for changes in priority, but for the most part, such changes will impact very little upon the overall thrust of the capital improvement program.

Following this internal review and approval, the superintendent recommends the capital improvement program to the school board for their formal approval. After the document is explained to the school board in sufficient detail, a series of public hearings is set. The school board conducts these hearings for citizen input. There may be one or several meetings throughout the school system. In some states, there are rules and legal regulations regarding the public hearings on all programs that must be observed, but the public hearing for a capital improvement program or plan is different from the public hearing on a proposed capital improvement budget. The budget represents a public expenditure of funds whereas the capital improvement program is simply anticipated actions based upon prioritization.

Following the public hearing meetings, the school board meets in regular session and approves the program by resolution. This approval simply gives the staff the right to proceed with the projects in the order listed but does not give authorization for the expenditure of funds. The approved program, however, becomes the official document to judge progress in completing the work of the school facilities department.

In some states and localities, governmental agencies other than the school system may either have approval responsibilities over the capital improvement program or may have a review capability.

Such agencies as the art commission or the city/county planning commission may have review capability. Even if these agencies do not have any responsibility for reviewing or approving the document, they should be brought into the process to provide a review. The more widespread the review of the capital improvement program is, the better the dissemination of information throughout the school system.

Capital Improvement Budget

The proposed capital improvement budget is developed from the capital improvement program. In a school system that has many capital improvement projects, the various projects in the capital improvement program are spread over several years to allow for the orderly development of each project and completion of every phase in a timely fashion (Montgomery County 1998). In addition, the projects are spaced over the years so that the school staff can handle the projects without over burdening the employees.

The projects listed in the first year of the capital improvement program then become the projects to be funded through the capital improvement budget. In the example of the capital improvement program discussed earlier in this chapter, the first year projects, which included the purchase of a site and employment of an architect, would become the projects funded in the capital improvement budget. All budgets for a school system are for one year at a time and do not carry approval for more than one year. The appropriations in a budget document are only for the year in which the budget was approved.

At the end of the first year, all of the projects in the capital improvement budget should be completed. When that happens, the projects listed for the second year become the projects in the capital improvement budget for the following year. This process of completing projects listed in one year and then proceeding to the following years in systematic order allows the school system to complete the capital improvement program.

The process of approval for the proposed capital improvement budget is the same as for the program. The state usually has legal requirements for public hearings. The hearings normally must be held ten days prior to consideration by the school board. When such hearings are completed, the school board approves the budget by resolution. The approved capital improvement budget becomes the authority by which school staff can commit funds to projects. Until the budget is approved, contracts cannot be signed, materials and supplies not purchased, nor employees hired.

Maintenance Schedule

During the annual evaluation of a school building by the principal and/or central staff, many items of repair are identified. These items may be as simple as a door not working correctly or a broken light switch or as major as a roof replacement or mechanical system improvement. A list of all projects big and small are gathered into one list for each school building. Items needed for preventative maintenance are also included. All items, regardless of source, become part of the maintenance schedule of the school system.

Most school systems have a program for preventative maintenance (PM) and replacement of major systems in a school building (Kowalski 1989). Such programs rely upon regular servicing of equipment to prevent untimely obsolescence and breakdown. In addition, specified replacement of equipment and parts of buildings prevents interruption of the use of the building by school personnel and students.

School systems usually develop a list of the items in a building that will need replacement after a specified period of time. For instance, heating systems usually have a definite lifetime. After that, the system will undoubtedly fail. To forestall that happening, school systems regularly replace boilers as well as roofs, lighting systems and other systems at the end of their useful life regardless of condition. This allows the maintenance staff to replace the system at the convenience of the school staff and not cause an interruption in service.

As with most organizations, the maintenance needs of the school system are more than can be completed in one year. Thus, the school staff has to develop a maintenance schedule for a certain period of time, usually a five-year period although the schedule can be for a shorter period of time.

The maintenance schedule is on going and never completed. As soon as all the items for one year are completed, there is another group of items to be added to the schedule so that it is extended for another year. This process of constantly adding maintenance projects to the schedule continues throughout the life of the school.

Each item is prioritized by the central administrative staff and individual school building staff. After this prioritization and approval internally, the schedule is submitted to the school board for their review. The school board does not have to approve the maintenance schedule specifically, nor do they need to have any public hearings because this is an internal matter. The funding of the maintenance schedule, however, depends upon the operational budget that the school board has to approve.

During the operational budget approval process, all budget categories, including maintenance, are open for public review. However, only the amount of funds proposed for maintenance work is identified, not specific projects. The funding provided for maintenance projects depends on the school board. Sometimes limitations are put on the amount of maintenance funds available because or certain factors which have nothing to do with maintenance work.

In school systems with a high regard for the school buildings and the investment they represent to the community, sufficient maintenance funds are always available for needed work. Sometimes during financial emergencies, the school board seeks to conserve limited funds for the program of the school by reducing the amount of maintenance funds. This action is shortsighted both in the immediate and long-range future. Proper maintenance of school facilities demands a focused program of identification of need and completion of task with appropriate funding. Only in this manner can the buildings of the school system be kept in a state of good repair. ■

Employing the Architect

THE ARCHITECT IS ONE OF THE MOST IMPORTANT CONTRIBUTORS IN THE PLANNING/ designing/ constructing process for a new school building, an addition to an existing building, or a major renovation. This person actually puts into form what the educators need and desire to house the stated educational program. As a result, considerable staff time and effort should be expended to secure the services of an architect that can serve the school system well.

Some large school systems have architects on their staff. These people do design work for the district, however, seldom, if ever, design entire school buildings. This is because, to complete the project, an architect designing an entire building needs considerable support staff, such as consulting engineers and technicians. These support staff, along with sufficient workspace, would have to be provided by the school system in order to design a major building project. This is rather difficult to do because of limitations of staff and the volume of new work completed in these systems.

Usually staff architects are used to design small renovation projects or to design additions to existing buildings. Some staff architects supervise the development of design work by outside architects under contract. This supervision is very crucial to the development of an appropriate, timely design for a new school in a large system. There are five basic services that can be expected from an architect when that person is hired:

- Schematic design
- Design development
- Contract document development
- Bidding advisement
- Bidding Construction monitoring

Architects provide a client other services such as pre-planning, evaluation, feasibility studies, programming activities, and orientation to the building. All of the services outside of the basic services, which are covered by the contract, cost extra (Graves 1993).

Sometimes architectural firms will provide educational consultant services as part of their total services. Although this is an excellent way for a school system to obtain needed educational consultation on a certain project, the cost of such additional services are borne by the architectural firm which in turn bills the school system for these services. It is often far better for the school system to hire its own educational consultant to insure the type of services needed and the objectivity required.

School administrators may think the educational consultation received through the architect is a free service taken out of the total cost of the architect, but this is not true. All of the services outside of the basic five cost the school system extra. Whatever additional services the school system needs should be discussed and decided upon at the time of the contract negotiations so that the responsibility for the cost can be determined early.

Schematic Design Process

During this stage, the architect develops a concept for the building and works to place all of the components within the structure observing proper relationships between the components of the building. The concept is developed and refined through repeated reviews of the initial work. At the end of this stage, the architect has a drawing of the building showing all spaces within the building, relationships between spaces and functions, and the general configuration of the building (Brubaker 1998).

Completion of the schematic design represents the first milestone for architectural design work. This is a very crucial stage because the perimeter of the building is set at this time. Further changes to the exterior of the building could demand a re-design at extra fees. Interior design can change during the design development stage, but basically the outside walls of the school building and the basic shape of the structure is set at the conclusion of this stage. In addition, the building has been located on the site and circulation patterns established. When the schematic design has been approved by the school board, the architect will have completed approximately 10-15 percent of the total work of the project and is paid accordingly.

Design Development Stage

After the schematic design has been approved, the entire scheme needs to be further developed and refined. This is where the fine points of the design are established. Systems other than structural, such as electrical, plumbing, and HVAC, are designed and refined. During this process, some of the spaces within the building may change shape or size, but the building's configuration remains intact. At the end of his stage, final drawings are complete. This phase represents approximately twenty percent of the total work effort of the architectural team.

Construction Documents

This stage of work proceeds along with the design development. The construction documents consist of the final or completed drawings and a set of technical specifications which lists all of the materials used in the construction of the building. This phase of the work, approximately forty percent of the work effort, is usually completed by architects, engineers, and technicians who are familiar with the properties of the materials used in the design and who can describe them in functional terms (Vickery 1998).

Bidding Advisement

As part of the agreement, the architect will provide services during the bidding process. Such services might include helping the school system to secure an adequate number of viable bidders for the project, evaluating the bid in terms of the budget and the capability of the bidder, recommending areas where reductions in the project may be made when a bid is over the budgeted amount, and recommending to the school staff whether or not to accept a bid or to negotiate with the lowest bidder. These services represent five percent of the effort and are well within the scope of responsibility of the architect.

Construction Monitoring

This work takes place after the bidding and while the contractor is building the structure. The task consists of providing periodic review of the status of the building project and on-site supervision of the work of the contractor. Developing shop drawings and providing material review is also included in this phase. Both a Clerk-of-the-Works and the architect provide this service, the former on a periodic basis, such as weekly or bi-weekly basis, and the latter at certain stages of construction. Approximately twenty percent of the total work on the project is expended in this phase.

Selection Method

Several methods are available for selecting the architect or any other professional for service to the school system:

- Non-Competitive method
- Comparison selection
- Design competition

The most frequently used method of selection is the comparison of several candidate firms; the least used is the design competition. All of the methods are used at some time by school systems throughout the country.

Non-Competitive Method

This method of selection is also called direct employment because a school system usually employs an architect who has done satisfactory work for the system before or is the only architect available because of geographic conditions. Some school administrators find it easier to continue to work with the same architect who last did some work for them. There is no review of candidates or their credentials, because the evidence of a good building is already located in the school system.

Some school systems, because of their rural and isolated location, find it necessary to employ the only architectural services available. Additionally, the architect might know the school system and school board, which could greatly facilitate development of the design and approval of it. There are many cases where architects have successfully served a school system over a period of years and this method of selection of an architect continues today.

In spite of the ease of selecting an architect through the direct method, there are some decided drawbacks. The most important disadvantage is the likelihood that the architect who does repeat business in a school system might tend to use the same solution to building problems over and over again. This means the architect tends to design the same building regardless of the location, specific educational requirements, or the type of program offered. The school system then tends to end up with one type of building throughout the system.

When the school system uses one architect to the exclusion of others, they may have to wait on a design if the firm is heavily engaged in other large projects. Such reliance leaves the school system at the behest of the architect when a building is needed. These are sufficient reasons not to use this type of architectural selection, wherever possible, in favor of one that will allow the school system to employ different architects to design buildings for the school system.

Comparison Selection

This method of selecting an architect compares several different firms for possible employment. A school system uses this same type of selection procedure in hiring other professionals such as teachers, administrators and other staff. After a rigorous selection process, an architectural firm is selected based upon a comparison of the credentials of its employees.

Design Competition

This method of selecting an architect is based upon preliminary work that the architect has done. A school system selects firms to participate in the competition or may open the competition to all firms that want to participate. The educational specifications of the new building under consideration are developed and given to the architects who will be in the competition. The architects develop a preliminary design and several elevations—sketches of what the building will look like. The school board or a panel of educators evaluate the designs and chose one as the winner.

The architect who submitted the winning design then receives a commission to further develop the design. In this manner, the architect is chosen. The architect then proceeds in the normal manner to refine the design and bring the project to bid.

On the surface, this method looks extremely promising for the school system and ought to encourage the best architects to enter the competition. However, this is perhaps the worst way to select an architect as far as both school system and architect are concerned. The architect must put considerable resources into the design of the model that will be submitted. These resources are up front, and if the architect is not a winner, these resources might be lost. However, in an AIA competition, each of the submitting firms are compensated a fixed amount. These costs may not cover the expenses of the architects, but are factored into the total cost of the project to the school system. The chances of a particular architect winning depends on the number of architects entered into the competition. The design work of the architect cannot be used in any other project because the educational program will undoubtedly be different. The combination of high initial cost, the chances of not being selected and the waste of design effort if not chosen weigh heavily upon not entering a competition. Most architects will not enter such a contest for a school building commission unless there will be some benefit even if the commission is not obtained.

This method of selecting an architect is even more disastrous for the school system. If the competition is conducted according to rules of a design competition, the school staff cannot see or critique the design of the architect before it is submitted to the panel, and after the design is chosen, few changes can be made to the design because that was the basis of selection. The school system is then committed to the design.

One of the most crucial periods in the design stage is the conceptualizing of the building done by the architect early in the work when the school personnel should have extensive, direct input into the concept developed. The architect needs to have such input to be sure the design is being true to the educational specifications. Without this input, the architect is left to translate the specifications alone.

This is not a desirable situation for the school system because interaction with school staff is desperately needed in the initial stage of design. Further, the architect knows that an eye-catching elevation or sketch can often times sway a panel of judges and may design with that in mind. This, coupled with the fact that the design cannot be changed, makes this method less than desirable for both the architect and school system.

Selection Process

Assuming the school system will select an architect through the comparison method, several steps have to be taken to assure that an orderly process is used to make the selection. Several questions have to be answered by the school board in order to set parameters for the staff. These questions deal with the people involved, the degree of involvement, the criteria to be used, the materials to be evaluated, the method of evaluation and the final determination.

The school system administrative staff should recommend to the school board the process to be used in identifying, evaluating and selecting the architect. The process should be no more complicated than the school staff can administer properly, but it should be comprehensive. Those responsible for conducting the process should be identified.

In a large system, the office that has the responsibility for supervision of the architect should administer the process and involve appropriate personnel outside that office. This may be the Director of Architectural Services or Director of Architecture and Construction under the Assistant Superintendent for School Facilities.

In a medium-sized school system, the person or office responsible might be the Director of Buildings and Grounds under the Assistant Superintendent for Business Affairs.

In small school systems, the person responsible for administering this process might be an Assistant Superintendent or the Administrative Assistant to the Superintendent. It is not unheard of to have an outside Educational Consultant assist the school system in the architect selection process.

The process of selection should follow the board policies devoted to architect selection and to personnel selection, because much of what is done in the process is directly related to what a school system does when other professionals are employed. A review of the school board policies is the first order of business in developing the process.

The process developed should include who is to be involved, the manner in which material from the architect is to be evaluated, what visits are to be made, how selection criteria are developed, what information is to be requested from the candidates, various points of elimination of candidates, interview procedures, and the number of finalists. Once the staff has developed the process, it should be approved by the school board to serve as the official guide for the staff to conduct the selection process. The process should be published for staff purposes and given to each architect who is a prospective candidate for selection.

Personnel Involvement

The first question to be resolved is who to involve in the architect selection process. This applies to both school staff as well as people outside the school system. As stated above, one office or person in the school system should be responsible for conducting the process, keeping relevant documentation and insuring a timely completion. Staff members other than the responsible office should be brought into the selection process as needed.

In a large school system, several staff members in the office responsible for the project may be involved because of the number of potential candidate architectural firms. These people may conduct the entire process with little outside involvement. People in the School Facilities Department of the school system may be involved because they will be working with the architects. Members of the School Programming Department may work with the architect in review sessions during the design phase. The administration of the Facilities Department should be involved in at least the final stages of interviews before successful candidates are recommended to the school board. The school board may well want to interview the recommended candidate or candidates, if they want to make the final choice from among several recommendations.

Some school systems believe community members should be involved in selecting an architect. There are both pros and cons to this issue. Those who believe in community involvement feel that the community has a stake in the building and should help with the selection. This argument could well be used for any phase of the educational enterprise and thus, community members should be involved in selecting teachers, principals, superintendents, custodians, cafeteria workers, maintenance workers, textbooks, educational materials, busses, cleaning material, and on and on. The absurdity of this argument can be seen.

The real question on community involvement is whether or not community patrons can bring to the process some different insight than the school staff who will work with the firm, or even if these people have a compelling interest in this service. There is little doubt that few community members know what makes a good architect or what to look for in evaluating an architectural firm.

If such is the case, then perhaps involvement is more showcase than substance. If involvement of community patrons does not slow down the process or violate any employment confidentiality or protocol, then it would be permissible to involve them; otherwise, community patrons should not be involved. Actually, the involvement of community patrons might be at best a learning situation for them and a chance for them to be exposed to the processes used by the school system. Outside of that, the value of their contribution to the process is questionable.

Developing Criteria

Once the question of involvement is decided, the next task is to develop criteria for evaluating the architect. The leadership for this step is taken by the office responsible for the process. Developing criteria can involve many people both inside and outside the school system. If people outside of the school organization are used in this process, the office responsible within the school system usually organizes the effort through a series of meetings. These meetings often are held in the neighborhood of where the new school is to be built or in the school where an addition or renovation is to be done.

The central staff administrator will need to suggest possible criteria to initiate the process of criteria development. While discussing what the architect will do on this project, criteria can be developed as to what the community would like in the architect. From there, a logical extension of criteria would ensue. Following is a discussion of suggested criteria for choosing an architect. A local school system may add other criteria deemed important in their situation.

Registration and Professional Activities

All architects must be registered by the state in which they are working. Usually this registration is obtained by passing an examination following the completion of a degree from an approved university program. Registration is important, without it, an architect could not use the drawings that were done for a project. This is because architects must put their registration number on every drawing to indicate that it was done by a person approved by the state (Vickery, 1998).

Registration is granted on a state-by-state basis, and an architect from out of state must gain registration in the state in which work is to be done.

Architects can be recognized by their professional organization for outstanding work in their field by granting membership in the American Institute of Architects (AIA). These initials are used at the end of the name of the architect to indicate such membership, an indication that the profession deems the architects worthy of distinction. A further designation of outstanding work is election to the College of Fellows of the AIA (FAIA).

Other organizations to which architects belong enhance their stature. Some architects who design many school buildings or are at least interested in designing such structures belong to the Council of Educational Facility Planners International. This organization is composed of individuals in educational organizations interested in facility planning, architects interested in school facility design, private educational consultants, and professors who teach educational facility planning. Membership in this organization tells the school system that the architect is interested in designing school buildings and wants to keep abreast of the field.

Another standard that can be used under this criteria is that of design awards. Some architects submit schools they have designed to organizations that give awards for outstanding buildings. Organizations that sponsor such programs include the American Association of School Administrators, the National School Boards Association, the Council of Educational Facility Planners International, Association of Physical Plant Administrators, and the Association of School Business Officials International. Annually, these organizations recognize architects who have designed what they consider outstanding buildings. Architects are usually proud of these awards and list them in their achievements. School system personnel should evaluate these awards for what they are—recognition of good performance by the firm.

Experience

This criteria tells the school system much about the architect because the whole history of accomplishments of the firm is displayed in written form. A review of this list indicates how much work the firm has done and how much of it was done in school systems as compared to work outside of the field of education.

A firm may have designed only one school building in its history and that may have been several years or decades ago. This would be revealing to the school system that was looking for a firm with considerable educational experience.

This listing should indicate not only the kind of experience, but also the size of the projects that the firm has undertaken in the past. In addition, some projects entail considerable creative design work because of certain constraints of the site or situation. What the architect did to solve this problem can be recognized through the project lists and description. This criterion is very important in recognizing what the architect has done in the past and will indicate what the architect will do in the future.

Quality of Work

This is an extremely difficult criterion to evaluate because of the many factors that enter into it (Holcomb 1995). Every architect would like to design buildings using only first class material, but that is not possible because of budget constraints placed upon the architect in designing the building. In many instances, school boards or owners are interested only in initial costs and in keeping these costs down; therefore, the architect is constrained to meet these demands.

This was the case in many school buildings designed and constructed in the 1950s. School systems at that time were hard pressed to keep up with the growing population and, at the same time, to keep down the cost of buildings. As a result, many architects designed buildings that are not aesthetically pleasing, but even more importantly, are not holding up under use. However the architects who designed these building cannot be held accountable for the deterioration, the lack of quality was caused by the school boards and the school systems. The architects simply met their specifications.

The architect should tell the school system personnel the circumstances under which each building was designed so that the constraints can be understood. Architects should be able, however, to show examples of quality buildings that were designed over a period of time. School system personnel should look at examples of good quality buildings and, even, at some marginal quality buildings.

Staffing and Facilities

Architects usually indicate the staff available to them for projects. This gives the school system an idea of the strength of the firm to complete the project under consideration. For a large project, such as a middle or high school, a considerably larger staff is needed than for a small project. The size of the architectural staff is related to the number of projects or the size of the projects in the office under design. If a firm has a very small staff, they will need to expand to accommodate even a small elementary school building project. The number and kinds of professionals on the staff will tell the school system whether or not the architectural firm can perform the necessary design work.

The amount of space available to the firm is also a good indication of how the firm can accommodate an expanded staff to complete the design and engineering work demanded. There must be enough space to house an expanded staff unless the existing staff can complete the work, which might mean the firm is not fully employed at the present time. This might give some indication of the health of the firm.

Method of Operation

This refers to how a firm operates or interfaces with the client that is the school system. Designing a school facility is not exactly like any other design project. There are two reasons for this:

- There are many more approvals by offices and people within and outside of the school system.
- Presenting and defending ideas and concepts to a large number of individuals and groups.

An architect must feel comfortable in dealing with large numbers of individuals and groups and must be able to listen to what they say and at the same time not be overly influenced by their arguments.

Sometimes the ability to work under these conditions comes only through experience, and this is one reason some school systems insist that the architect they employ has had such experiences. This is not to say that an architect without such experience cannot perform nicely under these circumstances. Quite the contrary, for there are many architects who feel comfortable under these situations.

If an architect who is employed has not had experience in the school system, it is incumbent upon the school system to orient the architect to the system and provide whatever help is needed to allow the architect to perform successfully. In this manner, both the school system and the architect will achieve good results.

Interest in the Project

This is a subjective judgment at best, but there are many indicators that can be used to ascertain the degree of interest. Simply talking with the architect will inform the school personnel how interested the person is in the project. If the person talks about other projects to the exclusion of the proposed project, perhaps interest in the project may not be sustained throughout the length of the project.

On the other hand, a school administrator will be able to recognize the person who has considerable and genuine interest. A visit to the offices of the architect may also give school personnel an idea of how other employees feel about the proposed project. Obviously, the architectural staff should not think the proposed project a burden on top of an already busy schedule.

References

The references the architect gives are very important. The school system will want to speak to these people about whom the architect worked with on their staff and how well the architect completed the project. If the references contain former school system clients, the local school system should interview the people who worked with the architect and staff in designing a building. The interviews should cover not only how well the architect worked with the staff, but also whether or not the architect kept within the budget, the number of change orders, and the effectiveness of the building itself.

Some people may want to include creativity and imagination in the selection criteria. Such criteria are very difficult to evaluate in the first place. Secondly, judgments regarding creativity and imagination are extremely subjective. What seems to be creative and imaginative in a building to some people may not seem so in others, simply based upon individual likes and dislikes. There is no real way to evaluate creativity and imagination in a person. True, there are some measuring instruments that are administered to children and youngsters for instructional purposes, but similar evaluative instruments for adult architects do not exist. As a result, creativity and imagination might be low in selection criteria because of the lack of any agreeable method of measurement. On the other hand, some indices can show up in the work of the architect that might give a person a clue as to how creative and imaginative the person is.

If an architectural firm has a ready-made solution to the design problem a new building presents, this may indicate that the firm is not high on creativity and imagination and is relying on previous experience to solve a current problem. Perhaps creativity and imagination should refer more to a fresh approach to designing a building project rather than solving the problem with previous solutions. Creativity and imagination do not in school building projects refer to radical design or strange building configuration.

Such buildings may not be functional on the interior, which is of the highest importance to a good educational program. Educational buildings are used for many decades. The building, therefore, must look just as good 30 or 50 years in the future as it does today. The building must also work just as well in the future as it does in the present. Sound judgments on building design and configuration by the architect produce those kinds of buildings.

In some places, school systems use the fee an architect proposes to charge as a criteria for judging a firm. Such a criterion, if used at all, should be the last consideration and not bear the same weight as other items. In as much as the school system is the party requesting services, the school system can set the fee regardless of what the architectural firm offers; however, negotiations between the school board and architect should allow for a fee acceptable to both parties. Consideration of the fee in employing a firm leads to the practice of trying to bid for a commission. Such practices do not help the school system obtain the best architectural services but encourage practices that might lead to undercutting of services. School systems should offer a reasonable fee where the firm can make a sound profit without cutting services to survive a low fee contract.

Architectural Pool

The first task in the process of selection is to develop a pool of possible applicants. This can best be done by contacting the local, regional or state American Institute of Architects (AIA) chapter and requesting names of members who might be interested in receiving a commission for a school construction project (Vickery, 1998). The chapter will undoubtedly send a complete list of members with no definition as to field of specialty. This list will at least, however, be useful to the school system in making initial contact with interested firms. Architects are even listed in the Yellow Pages of the local telephone directory. In some cases, the advertisement there may provide some information on a firm. In some small communities that do not have access to large numbers of architects, the Yellow Pages may be a good source of architectural firms.

Larger school systems usually have a rather extensive listing of architects developed through inquiry by the firms rather than by the school system. Some school systems are interested in architects who have had experience or considerable work in designing educational facilities. There is very good reason for this criterion, and school systems may well make it the most important criterion for selection.

Once the list of potential candidates is developed, an initial letter is sent to each firm. The letter states that architectural services are needed for a project that is described. (See Appendix A) The letter goes on to state that if the firm is interested in being considered for the commission, certain material and data are to be sent to the school system for evaluation. An example of such a data-gathering instrument is included in Appendix A.

Once the school system has received the data and material from the architectural firm, they have to be evaluated. Someone who has some knowledge of architectural work can best do this evaluation. If the school system has an architect on the staff, that person might be the first one to evaluate the data and material. Other people on the central administrative staff might also evaluate this same data and material. The data requested by the school system deals with past performance of the firm, the capability of the firm to complete the proposed project, financial capability, and staff available to, or working in, the firm.

The material the architect submits in addition to the above usually consists of information about the firm, the number of projects completed, the type of projects, pictures and drawings of projects, and cost figures. When the firm has had experience in designing educational facilities, there will be mock-ups, elevations and drawings of the building as well as supporting data on type of program, square footage and costs. These are offered in an attempt to help the school system personnel see the type and kind of previous work done by the firm.

All of these data and material are the basis for making an evaluation of the firm for further consideration. When there is not a large number of firms to be considered, all of the firms that responded to the initial letter are interviewed. If a large number of firms submit materials, the next step is to reduce the number of firms into a group that can be adequately interviewed and visited. This is done by through an intermediate step of evaluating the data and material submitted by the architectural firms to reduce the total number of candidates.

An instrument can be developed and used to rank the firms in uniform manner by evaluating the material they have submitted. The instrument should take into consideration the size of the firm, number of engineers or availability of consulting engineers, years of experience, number of school projects designed, awards won by the firm, location of the firm, registration of the architects, costs of the school projects and the efficiency ratio of each project, and size of projects designed. Other items may be considered important by the school system and evaluated in addition.

If ten or more firms submit letters of interest and supporting material, the school board might have difficulty in interviewing that number of firms and adequately interpreting the results of those interviews. This would necessitate eliminating some of the firms in order to reach a final group of three to five firms that are of interest to the school board.

No ironclad rules exist for the number of architectural firms that can be interviewed. School boards have been known to interview all of the firms that submit letters of interest, in larger school systems, the press of time prevents the school board from interviewing many candidate firms. In this case, the staff must gather data and eliminate some of the firms in order to utilize best the time available to the school board to interview the most likely candidate firms. The administrative staff must carry on the process of elimination. In rare instances, a committee of the school board with administrative staff support may conduct the first evaluation to reduce the group to a manageable size.

A group of no more than five architectural firms is about the right size for a school board to interview for a single project. There are situations where a school system will be designing several school projects over the course of a few years or where several school projects are under the same bond issue, where the school board may employ several architectural firms at once. In those cases, a larger number of firms must be interviewed and the first level of evaluation empowered to select a larger number of firms than stated above.

Office and Site Visits

After the first round of elimination has taken place, the next step is to gather further data on the firms to present to the school board. This can best be done by visiting the offices of the firms and some of the buildings they designed. There are several reasons to visit the firms' offices.

The first is to ascertain the level of staff support and their surroundings. In spite of the fact that educators cannot adequately evaluate the offices of another profession, certain observations can be made that will tell something about the firm. Although these may be subjective judgments, they nevertheless are valid assessments of the firm. Items that may be observed include:

- Amount of space devoted to employees
- Kinds of space used by staff
- Number of employees that are currently working
- Types and number of projects on which the office is presently working

- Extent and kinds of technology employed in the design process
- How the staff feel about taking on another project
- Reaction of the staff to a prospective employer

Subjective judgments about these items are no different from other judgments made by professionals in determining the ability of a firm to satisfactorily complete a project. Some school systems require an architectural firm to have a local office if their headquarters is in a different city or state. This visitation then gives the school system an opportunity to see if that requirement is met. Most often a firm that has an office out of city or state will associate with a local firm so that the local staff and office can be used. This is usually a satisfactory arrangement for both firms and for the school system as there is a local contact that is known and can be reached.

The school system personnel will want to visit some of the buildings the architects designed to learn about the architectural work completed. One thing school personnel want to find out is how well the building has stood up over the years. School buildings are subject to relentless heavy usage by students. How well a building sustains such usage is of considerable interest to school personnel.

The users of the building should be interviewed to ascertain how the building fits the use. Caution must be observed here, however, because sometimes the usage is not what was intended. In other words, a room can be designed for 20 students and the principal assigns 25 or 30. Obviously, the room is overcrowded, but not as a result of the architect's design.

Likewise, a space can be designed for a certain activity and now a different activity is assigned there. The space cannot support the new activity because it was not designed for it. The fault is not in the architectural design but rather in the use of the space. Such conversions, however, give an indication of how the building can be modified, if indeed it can. Following visitations to these facilities, school staff can make judgments about these situations that will be to the benefit of the school system.

School Board Interview

Once the visits to the office and the various buildings recommended by the architect are made and the data gathered by the school system has been evaluated, the school staff usually makes a recommendation to the school board. Sometimes this recommendation consists of one firm, while in other instances there may be three to five firms that are included in the recommendation. In small school systems, the school board sometimes interviews all of the firms and then makes the selection. School boards in large systems cannot afford to spend that much time interviewing architects because of the press of other decisions. In these cases, the number of firms that may be interviewed would be around three, at most.

The interviews consist of a presentation by the members of the architectural firm to the school board to demonstrate their capability and experience. When more than one firm is interviewed, each firm is allotted a certain amount of time to make its presentation and respond to questions.

If questions are to be asked of the architectural firm, a pre-determined set of questions should be developed and asked by board members. In the interest of fairness, all firms should be asked the same questions and given time to respond. Following the interviews, the school board then decides which firm they will employ. This can be done formally or informally without a vote, but once the board decides upon a firm, they must vote to enter into a contract with the firm that is selected. A resolution is introduced and passed by the majority of the members to enter into such a contract.

This is a legal action the school board must take, and that action must also be recorded in the minutes of the meeting as a public record. This action gives the legal counsel of the board authority to prepare such a document and to execute it. In many cases, the contract may call for an initial payment to the architect of a token amount to seal the contract.

Architectural Contract

Architectural services are secured through a contract signed by a representative of the firm and the appropriate person to represent the school board. This legal document states precisely what services the architectural firm will give to the school system and the amount of money the architectural firm will receive for those services. As stated above, the school board must pass a resolution to enter into a contract with the architectural firm for a stated amount of money. The AIA has developed a prototype contract that can be used by the school system. The provisions of that document follow the usual services that are offered by architects. A delineation of responsibilities and liabilities is included in the contract so that each party will understand these areas.

A school system can develop its own contract through its legal counsel. Almost all large school systems develop their own contract so that provisions that are particular to the local school system or state can be incorporated into the document. Important safeguards for the school system can also be built into the contract that might not be in other contracts. Of particular interest might be the area of construction supervision. Appendix B contains a copy of a contract developed by a school system to secure architectural services.

The standard AIA contract states that periodic supervision will be given to the project by the Clerk-of-the-Works who is an employee of the architectural firm. In small school systems, this might be construed to mean daily or even 24-hour supervision whereas to the architect it means a biweekly visit or occasionally a weekly visit. When the school system has a contract written for it, such differences can be accounted for and adjusted accordingly. It is much more preferable for the school system to develop an indigenous contract that will cover specifics needed to be included.

The contract, regardless of what type used, will stipulate the method of payment to the architect, who is paid based upon an invoice stipulating the amount of work completed. During the design stage and into the bidding and construction monitoring phases, the architect is paid on a monthly schedule based upon the amount of work done. Payments usually reflect the following schedule of completed phases and represent a percentage of the total fee that has been paid:

- Schematic Design—15%
- Design Development—35%
- Contract Document Completion—75%
- Bidding Phase—80%
- Construction Phase—100%

By the time the architectural firm has completed the schematic design phase, 15 percent of the total amount of the fees payable will have been paid. Likewise, when the construction phase is completed, 100 percent of the fee will have been paid (Brubaker 1998).

Some school systems retain a small portion of the architectural fees for a year after the building is completed as a surety. If this practice is desired by the school system, the contract with the firm will have to stipulate this from the beginning.

The contractual relationship between the school board and the architectural firm is no different than any other relationship in which a commercial firm provides certain services to the school system. The architects and engineers of the firm are simply members of a larger team of professional experts who are working to plan, design and construct a building project. Architects and engineers are not decision-makers in the school system.

The school board retains the right to accept and reject any product developed by the architects, and the firm is employed at the pleasure of the school board. Architects must not be forced into the role of a decision-maker by the educators and school board members. The absence of clear and concise directions and leadership might make the architect believe some decisions must be made to keep the project going. Such absence of leadership on the part of the educators and school board members should not happen.

Time of Employing the Architect

The architect should be employed early in the planning process for a school project. Some school systems employ the architect before a site is selected so that the architect can provide some service in the actual selection process. These services are, however, beyond the usual conditions of the contract and must be paid by the school system. For a school system that does not have a great deal of expertise on the staff to deal with selecting a site, it might be a wise idea to employ the architect before that process begins. The architect might also provide some pre-design planning services to the school system, which is usually beyond the contract fee. If a school system needs some pre-design planning, the exact nature of the planning task needs to be analyzed to determine whether or not it is a task that can properly be done by an architect or by an educational planner. ■

chapterten

School Site Selection and Acquisition

SELECTING AND ACQUIRING AN ADEQUATE SCHOOL SITE IS ONE OF THE MOST DIFFICULT tasks a school system must do in planning a new school. Over the years, this task has become increasingly more tedious as a result of several factors over which the school system has little or no control.

Some of the factors stem from the geographic area in which the school system is located, others stem from of the evolution of the educational program. The natural increase in houses, industry and commercial enterprises tend to reduce the number of adequate sites available to the school system. With the increase in program demands by the state, local school systems find themselves needing larger sites upon which to locate a school. The end result is that there are fewer acceptable sites available from which the school system can choose.

Another factor is the rapidly increasing price of sites in almost every section of the country. Acreage has increased in price from 100 percent to 400 percent over the past two decades, effectively preventing the school system from competing for desirable sites. In effect, the school systems have been priced out of the real estate market in many areas. Real estate has also outpaced the rate of inflation for prices, often increasing as much as two to ten times the rate of inflation. School systems with limited funds to purchase sites can not keep up with the private real estate market.

Because of this situation, school systems have been forced to come up with some rather creative and different solutions to the location of school buildings and students. Some school systems have located schools in existing commercial buildings no longer needed for their original purpose. Converting these structures to house a school has been a very satisfactory solution to some difficult housing questions. Warehouse buildings, supermarkets, or other kinds of loft-type buildings have been converted to excellent school facilities.

One problem with such facilities, however, is that the existing structure is usually located where the students are not located, necessitating bussing of students into the facility. Sometimes the neighborhood in which the converted building is located is not in the most desirable location of the school system and other social problems exist or begin because of the school building site. Nevertheless, the conversion of existing structures to school facilities is an excellent idea.

Other solutions to obtaining a site have been to use existing public buildings. A good example is the Parkway School in Philadelphia. This organization rented a small commercial building for the headquarters and home station for the students. Classes were then held in various rooms and spaces in public and private buildings. Buildings such as museums, municipal courthouses, art institutes, insurance offices, and newspaper buildings, for example, had spaces where classes could be held. These spaces and rooms were located in a very compact geographic area so that students could walk from building to building. A flexible schedule was used to allow students to have several classes in one building so that they did not have to walk great distances between classes. Although the Parkway School no longer exists, the school was an excellent example of using the community as a classroom space. This idea, or at least modifications of it, could be used in many communities to house students and programs if a little imaginative thinking were used.

Another practical idea for obtaining a site for a school building is to use property already owned by the city or county government, parks department, or recreation department. Although the idea of sharing a site with two governmental units is not new, its application is not widespread. In many states this is a rather novel idea, but placing a school building in a park already owned by another governmental unit is a good application of this idea. Benefits accrue to the community in two ways. First, the school system does not have to pay the purchase price of a new site. Second, less overall land is taken away from the community upon which to locate two governmental functions.

Another problem in finding adequate sites for new school buildings is the political consideration of new sites. Each possible school site must in some way be considered or approved by the political power structure in the community. This fact has been well documented in a study of the large school systems in the country (Earthman, 1976). This does not necessarily mean that members of the various power structures must meet and approve each site. What this does mean, however, is that each site selected by the school board must not be intended for some other larger community purpose nor intended for another use by someone in the community's power structure. Most sites selected by school boards raise no general concern in the community as to the propriety of that use of the land, other than some community members who live near the selected site. But occasionally, there is a concern raised that the site could be better used for some other purpose.

The matter then boils down to how the members of the community in the power structure that is effected believe the site should be used. Generally, members of the various power structures become knowledgeable of the possible sites under consideration because of informal interaction with school board members. Consequently, if no concern is raised by some group or groups, the school board then believes it should go ahead with the consideration of the particular sites in question.

School boards are not politically powerless in this matter, and sometimes it is possible to gather the strength of a community to press successfully for a particular site when groups oppose that action. School boards can not always rely upon what political powers it may possess, but through compromises, solutions to site problems can be found.

To avoid the high cost of real estate, school systems need to plan for the future in selecting sites. Waiting until an area develops with new housing is not the time to purchase a site for a new school building. School systems need to be as forward thinking as the tract developer.

Traditionally, a school system waits until students are in evidence before planning for a new school building. This method leaves the school system reacting to situations and having to pay an inflated price for land.

A few school systems do plan for the future by purchasing land in geographic areas of possible growth long before the growth takes place. This could be called landbanking.

It is quite possible to identify and acquire sites for schools that will be used five to ten years in the future. This proactive planning can ensure the school system the best possible site for a school when the area does develop. Landbanked school sites that are not going to be used for a long period of time can be used in the interim for recreation. Park and recreation facilities can be constructed on the proposed school site and the community use these facilities. Planned correctly, these facilities would in no way hinder the construction of a new building when the appropriate time comes.

A system of landbanking future school sites requires a great deal of long range planning by the school system. Such a system also requires a commitment by the school board to finance such a plan. Although the total cost of sites in this plan would be much less, it would be necessary to raise sufficient funds to carry this out, and it might be difficult to convince lay people to support the plan.

Another problem encountered by school boards in trying to obtain sites for the future is the lack of appropriate legislation to control housing sub-development planning to insure sites for schools. Proper legislation can come from either the state or local government. The state legislation would be simply enabling legislation for the local government to pass restrictive ordinances requiring dedication of land for municipal services.

It is the local government that needs to pass appropriate ordinances restricting the growth of sub-developments so that schools are simply not inundated with new students. No one wants to control or hinder the growth of a community, but the unbridled growth that can take place in an area can cause considerable trouble with all levels of government, including the schools, in trying to provide services to new residences.

Some local governments enact ordinances that require housing developers to dedicate land for schools, as well as other municipal services, in every plan submitted for approval. This is a form of landbanking that helps the developer sell houses and enables the school system to save appropriate land for school purposes. Such ordinances can be enacted in almost every locality.

A different approach in controlling sub-development growth is taken by the State of Maryland. The Adequate Space Needs Act has provisions for partially controlling growth when public facilities are reaching a point of overcrowding. Under this Act, school systems notify the local government when certain school buildings are overcrowded. The school system certifies that the buildings can not accommodate any more students and that all available space in the building is being properly used. Based upon this certification, the local government notifies potential developers that their plans for a housing sub-development may be approved, but each building permit will be passed upon as it comes forward. This in essence controls all substantive planning by the developer until the school system can accommodate more students by either building new structures or redistricting for more space.

Each developer may get approval for a certain number of sites to be built upon, but each permit will be voted upon as it effects school population. The county board of supervisors will not approve permits if approval means the schools will be overcrowded by the children from the family that occupies the house on the site. There is a two-year provision for an approved permit, and if the builder does not exercise it within that time frame, the approval will expire. This moratorium on approval of permits may last until a new school building is constructed which may be three years. Since this situation prevents developers from proceeding with planning, this delay undoubtedly causes them considerable damage. The only recourse in this situation, therefore, is to turn to political solutions in an attempt to move the appropriate governmental unit to provide funds for construction of new schools.

Another problem associated with site selection is the need for the local school board to consider innovative approaches to housing educational programs. Legislation is needed in every state to allow school systems to try different approaches to meeting school building needs. The use of air rights over an existing site is one approach that could be investigated. Use of the air-rights over a site by a commercial firm could enable the school system to help pay for a new building. Multiple use of space on a school site or within an existing building is another approach to assisting school systems in financing building costs for new sites.

Site Acquisition

School systems may obtain a new site for a building in several ways. The most common methods are:

- Purchase from the owner
- A gift from a donor
- Exercising the power of eminent domain
- Receipt of surplus governmental property

The first method of obtaining a site is the most common way for all governmental agencies. Under this approach, the owner of a site is contacted for possible sale. When the school board decides to purchase the site, a resolution is passed stating that fact along with a contracted amount of money. Following this action, the legal counsel of the school board approaches the owner to complete the negotiations and consummate the sale. A contract is drawn up, signed and executed. A title is then obtained through the local governmental office that records deeds.

There are times when a piece of real estate is given to the local school board as a gift. The gift may be from a patron of the school system, a commercial firm or an estate. Regardless of the source of the gift, school boards may accept such offers. Sometimes the gifts come with conditions attached. Perhaps the giver stipulates that the land can be used only for a school building, and if a school building is not constructed on it, the property reverts back to the owner. There may be other conditions regarding use of the site or what can be placed on it. In such cases the school board must abide by the conditions if the gift is accepted. A school board does not have to accept a gift, and in some instances the school board would be wise to refuse the gift.

If the gift comes with no conditions, the school board may treat the offer of real estate as any other gift and use it as it sees fit to do: it may use the property for a school building or sell the property and use the proceeds for any program or activity in the school system. Sometimes real estate developers will offer the school system a parcel of land in a new housing development as a school site. Such gifts often carry a condition that a building has to be placed upon it. Then the school board must decide whether or not that site will fit into the overall capital improvement program. The timing of the receipt of a gift is out of the hands of the school board and many times does not fit the needs of the capital improvement program. In cases where the gift comes from an estate, legal entanglements can take considerable staff and legal counsel time for disposition of the real estate.

All local school systems are an extension of the state government. Because of this, every school system has the right of eminent domain. This simply means that the school system, through the school board, may condemn property for educational purposes. This is the legal act of taking the property of a citizen for public purposes, in this case, education, with just compensation for the property.

This legal right may seem rather easy and simple, but in actuality, this is the most difficult and emotional method of obtaining property. State highway departments use this method much more than school systems because of the large tracts of land necessary for highway construction. It is almost a routine practice for that department and seems to be accepted more generally than if a school system uses this method. This method of obtaining sites is rarely used by school systems and only in those cases where a particular site is needed and the owner is not willing to sell at what seems to be a fair offer by the school system.

To exercise this right, a school board must pass a resolution stating that this site is needed for educational purposes. The matter is brought before the local district court or usually the lowest court in the local government. The matter to be heard is the determination of the fair price for the property. Several methods can be used to determine this. The court may appoint two or three appraisers to determine a fair price. The court can then take which ever price it decides is proper. Or the court can ask each party to present estimates of the price, and the court again decides the final price. The reason the court is involved is to make certain the property owner receives a fair price for the property under consideration. The fair price set by the court may be higher than what the school system originally determined it to be. In that case, the school system has to pay the owner whatever price the court finally stipulates.

This is the chance the school system has to take when entering this procedure. In addition to the price of the land, there may be other costs associated with condemnation such as possible damages. These damages may be in the form of additional money to compensate a business for losses, costs of relocation, and payments to homeowners for purchase of homes of equal value. All of these may be in addition to the land costs. Thus, sometimes condemnation may be the most expensive method of acquiring a site. The school board must also gauge the possible emotional upset within the community for taking homes. Typically, the homes taken in a condemnation proceeding belong to owners who can least afford to move financially, socially, and emotionally.

The last way for a school system to obtain a site for a school would be for one other governmental unit to declare a site they owned to be surplus. This in effect is transferring a piece of property from one governmental unit to another. Such programs began shortly after World War II when the Federal Government began selling war furniture and equipment and even giving away war property and sites acquired previously. The selling of government property is very common and can range from typewriters and furniture to camps and even air bases. Most often real estate, rather than equipment or furniture, is declared surplus and available for transfer to another agency.

In these cases, the owner of the property notifies other governmental units that a certain piece of property is redundant. Following this, interested units can apply. The offerer determines which unit is to receive title to the property and the transfer is made. Surplus property usually has no cost attached to the receiver, other then supplying a fee simple title to the property.

Although there may be some exceptions, most land declared surplus by one government level is limited in its usefulness to the school system. In other words, the location of the property, the amount of land, or the characteristics of the land usually contribute to make the surplus property unsuitable for school use.

School Site Standards

Many states have mandatory standards for minimum acreage for school sites. States that do not have mandatory standards do recommend certain minimums for school sites. Each school system should know what the state requires as far as the minimum site is concerned and observe that in acquiring a site. More importantly, the school systems should ascertain the amount of land needed for a school site through analysis of the program that will be located there and then acquire a site to fit the program. The Council of Educational Facility Planners, International (1991) has developed some site standards as a result of careful study. These standards are:

- Elementary School   10 acres plus I acre for each 100 students
- Middle School   20 acres plus I acre for each 100 students
- High School   30 acres plus 1 acre for each 100 students

An elementary school of 500 students would require 15 acres using this formula. A high school of 1,200 students would require 42 acres.

These standards were developed through a study of the types of activities carried on by a student body in the particular type of school. The larger secondary school sites reflect the need for different playing fields such as soccer, softball, baseball, football and track. The elementary school site size reflects the type of outdoor physical education program that is common on that level. These standards were also developed under the presumption that land would be available for school purposes.

In urban areas such requirements would be impossible to meet. Indeed if such sites were even available, the price would be far beyond the financial capabilities of the school system. One school system located in a large urban area (Philadelphia 1973) developed the following minimum standards for their school sites with maximum number of students following an exhaustive study of the type of physical needs in the urban setting:

- Elementary School $2\frac{1}{2}$ acres   900 students
- Middle School   5 acres   1,500 students
- High School   10 acres   3,000 students

Of course, not every urban school is located on a site as large as these. In large cities, a five-acre tract of land could well demand a price of one to five million dollars per acre that is undoubtedly beyond the resources of the school system.

Existing urban school systems are very seldom located on a site as large as those recommended, and school buildings 30 years or older are almost never situated on a site that large. This could also apply to those school buildings located in the suburbs and rural areas as well. The need for more space to accommodate the modern physical education program has been a recent phenomenon in all school systems.

Site Selection Process

Selecting a site for a new school building is a volatile task because everyone wants a new building, but no one wants a school located next to their house or business. This is a natural feeling because of the amount of traffic that is normally around a school. Both pedestrian and vehicular traffic are problems a neighborhood must tolerate if a school building is located where students live. If students are bussed into the school, there is morning and afternoon traffic bringing students to and taking them from the building. In addition, students do not always use the sidewalks or paths to go directly home. Students wandering around the neighborhood present problems to some community people. In spite of this, a new school building and its occupants do not cause an intolerable amount of disturbance in the neighborhood, and the building serves as a focus for the entire community.

Some people claim a school building may lower property values in the immediate neighborhood. Such has not been the case. In fact, schools tend to hold the community together. Research has shown that the location of a school improved not only the value of the surrounding properties, but also the entire neighborhood; in fact, the school enhanced the economic health of the community. Grabe (1975) found this to be the case in a study of school sites in Michigan. The school building served as a central point of interest for the community because of the many activities, in addition to the day school, that took place there.

Very few school buildings are related to only one neighborhood. Rather, they are tied into several different ones that comprise the community. Only in the very dense city areas can a school relate to only one neighborhood. The school building should then relate to a service area composed of a variety of neighborhoods. This is especially true of high school buildings where the attendance area is very large.

The question of who to involve in the site selection process must be answered before the actual process is begun. Again, school board policies should be researched to determine the extent of involvement, particularly community involvement. Some school systems exclude community involvement as a matter of policy. In a survey of large school systems, the majority indicated the community was systematically excluded from the process of site selection (Earthman, 1976). The reason given was that parents and community groups could delay selection and acquisition of the site because of their objections to a particular site. Urban areas typically face the prospect of an inordinate amount of time being spent on acquiring a site; with parental objections, resolution of the question might be years from the date the site is needed. Such exclusion from the site selection process, however, might not be acceptable in a great number of school systems throughout the country. As stated above, the person responsible for leading the site selection process should refer to the school board policies for guidance in community involvement before initiating the process.

If the community is involved in this process, their role may well be that of a learner rather than anything else. Lay persons generally do not have a good grasp of the amount of land needed by a school for a modern educational program. Nor are they conversant with other criteria that should be applied in trying to select a site or even the selection process itself. This does not mean, however, that they serve as a rubber stamp for the school administration. Quite the contrary, for community people can help by lobbying for certain sites, identifying certain sites and even mediating between competing groups. Involvement in this process can also result in a group of people who are more knowledgeable about what kinds of sites are needed and the process that a school system goes through to obtain one. The bottom line for community involvement, however, is what the school board policies stipulate.

The process of selecting a site may seem like a simple task of identifying a piece of land by driving around the area and then presenting a recommendation to the school board. Such is simply not the case. In the first place, identification of potential sites is completed more scientifically than that. Identification of potential sites has input from a number of sources both inside and outside of the school system. The general area of the school system to be served by this site is identified through analysis of the projection of student population, transportation system, and the configuration of the county, district, township, or city. The resources of not only the school system, but also the city/county planning commission, and state highway department are used to locate potential sites.

The involvement and cooperation of other departments in the school system and other governmental agencies must be assured at the start of the process. Selecting the site necessitates many meetings with school system personnel, community leaders and local government officials. Obtaining some type of consensus through these meetings may result in the process lasting from six to eight months at the earliest and may extent to a year. The various steps identified in the selection process are:

- The site selection team is assembled by the superintendent
- The team meets with appropriate school department heads to initiate the project and begin to develop criteria
- Planning parameters of the search are established
- Meet with the local community and site team to establish the need for and obtain their input into developing criteria
- The site team meets with the local planning commission to talk about available sites and criteria
- The site team develops a list of potential sites
- Data on all potential sites is gathered
- Site selection team physically inspects all sites
- The site team meets with the community and lets them know the potential sites and how the criteria were applied
- The site team meets with appropriate school departments to bring them up to date on the process
- The site team meets with the local planning commission to seek approval of potential sites
- Recommendations are made to the superintendent who then makes recommendations to the school board
- The school board passes resolution to acquire the site after discussions.
- The legal counsel for the school board draws up a contract for the purchase of the site and negotiates with the owner
- The legal counsel examines the title, removes any liens, and produces a fee simple title for the school board (Earthman 1990)

In some of the larger school systems, this procedure is much more complicated and lengthy because of the increased number of people, departments and governmental agencies that are included in the process. Appendix E contains a flow chart of the site selection procedures of such a school system. This model of site selection relies heavily upon the involvement of various departments within the school system and agencies of the local government. Such a process may require at least 43 weeks of work to complete. Delays in public hearings or any other meeting may cause the procedure to extend to a year or more. In a large school system, it is not unusual to begin the site selection process two years in advance of the time of construction for the building.

Site Selection Criteria

Potential school sites are evaluated by the site selection team using criteria developed by them and adopted by the school board. In some cases these criteria are written into school board policies. However developed, the criteria are used to evaluate all of the potential sites in order to recommend the best site to the school board. Some of the criteria suggested may be:

- Proximity to centers of student population
- Adequate size and shape for the present and future enrollment
- Accessibility to the site
- Any existing traffic hazards and nearness to industrial areas
- Utility services available near the site
- Suitability of soil—percolation tests
- Price within range of the school system budget
- Contour of land to allow for drainage
- Consideration of urban/suburban planning
- Environment conducive for a school
- Aesthetic appeal of the site
- Favorable zoning regulations
- Close proximity to community resources
- Close proximity to safety facilities
- Suitable for construction
- Sufficient space for adequate parking
- The amount of usable land on the site
- Easements of any nature
- Sufficient free space to support anticipated educational program
- Safety of the site
- No geographical or topographic features which would present construction problems
- Recreational facilities and areas near the site
- Site development costs within the school budget
- Helps the desegregation program of the school system
- Using this site for a school does not remove desirable housing from the market

All of these criteria are important in evaluating a site, but in the final analysis, the total cost of the site may be the one criterion that determines whether or not the school system can obtain it. The cost to purchase the property from the owners is relatively simple to determine, but the total cost of the site should also include the cost of site development. It is necessary to calculate not only the initial cost but also the cost of land development and the cost of maintenance. Land development costs can be estimated in several ways. Professional landscape architects, building architects, and construction engineers can provide the school system with cost estimates for developing a particular site. In evaluating the development costs, estimates of the cost of the following tasks should be made by the appropriate landscape architect:

- Clearing and grubbing
- Demolition and removal
- Earthmoving
- Rock removal
- Underdrainage
- Electrical service
- Athletic and other facilities
- Storm drainage
- Water supply
- Sewage disposal
- Walks, drives and paving
- Sodding, topsoil and planting
- Fencing, gates and barriers

The total cost of these items, along with the cost to acquire the property, should give a reasonable estimate of the total cost of the site in question. A school system may wish to use other criterion to fit local conditions. The application of the above criteria to the site should constitute the evaluation procedure. Each of these items can be converted to a rating scale and a judgment then made on each item using that scale. The above items can also be converted to questions which might help the site selection team members apply the rating in a uniform manner.

Site Evaluation

Each site is evaluated by every member of the site selection team. A profile and total score is developed following inspection of the site. Site evaluation is a difficult job especially when many members are doing the task. The simplest method, however, is to use a standard rating scale developed by the school system with each member of the site team conducting an independent evaluation.

The initial judgment of each member of the team is recorded and compared to determine the degree of consensus. Since a high degree of consensus is desired on the final evaluation, disparity in results should be identified and discussed. After these discussions, consensus should be reached for each site and all the sites should be ranked ordered from the first to the last based upon the profile and total score. The site with the best evaluation should be the first recommendation to the school board.

Figure 10.1 shows an evaluation for a recommended site from a large city school system. The results of the evaluation can easily be seen and identified. This type of recommendation is presented to the school board following all of the staff evaluations. In this example, the city school system plans to put two secondary school buildings on one site to economize on the cost of two sites for the two schools. The evaluation form refers to the site standards for high schools used in this city, in this case the maximum acreage that is in keeping with densely populated urban areas.

While this process is occurring, the various power groups of the community should be appraised of the potential sites to insure acceptance by all segments of the community. Naturally, it would be a waste of time and effort not to acquire political acquiescence for a site long before it is presented to the school board as a recommended site.

Although school board members may not be members of all power groups, each member does have access to members who are high in the various power structures of the community and in that manner can obtain information. As a result, school board members can obtain a feel from the power groups concerning the advisability of acquiring a particular site for a school. In most cases, school board members do not have to go so far as to request a review of particular sites or even ask about the site; rather the absence of questions and expressed concern by members of the power groups indicates acceptance or at least acquiescence. In order to talk intelligently to power group members about potential school sites, school board members must be aware of the sites being seriously considered by the site selection team.

Figure 10.1
*Sample Site
Evaluation Report*

Washington County Public Schools—Washington City
Site Evaluation for Proposed High School

Description: The area bounded by Frankford Avenue, Hegerman Street (unopened) and a line parallel to and approximately 750 feet northeast of Stevenson Lane; parcel to be shared with proposed Vocational Skill Center.

Characteristics:

Size	24.3 acres (to be shared with Skill Center
Right of Way Affected	None
Physical Characteristics	Gently sloping, partly wooded, vacant, trianglar
Estimated Cost	$1,950,000
Availability	Unknown
Service Area	Well located to serve anticipated school population
Transportation	Busses 66 and 84 adjacent, Penn Central station .6 mile away
Community Facilities	City golf course and recreation center 2 mile away Industrial Park, Torresdale Industrial area within 1½ miles; proposed Prison Farm area 2 miles away
Relocation	None
Planning Comm Review	Approved, Open Session, May 4, 1999
Community Reaction	Acceptable

Advantages

Size	Excellent
Rights of Way Affected	None
Physical Characteristics	Very Good
Estimated Cost	Low
Service Area	Good

Disadvantages

Availability	Unknown
Transportation	Good
Community Facilities	Fair
Industrial Facilities	good
Relocation	None
Planning Comm Review	Approved, open Session, May 4, 1999
Community Reaction	Acceptable

Conclusions: At 24.3 acres, Site A could easily accommodate both the high school and the vocational skill center. The skill center would require approximately 4 to 5 acres, leaving about 20 acres for high school use—quite close to the School District maximum standard of 21.5 acres. Considerable benefits—operational, physical and financial—would be produced by this arrangement. Shared heating, air condition, cafeteria and other services, plus reduced site acquisition costs are examples. Site A is well located with respect to most of the major industrial area of the far northeast and offers excellent physical characteristics. The School Facilities Department of the School District recommends Site A to the school board.

Site Selection Resources

Several resources are available to the site selection team in identifying and evaluating potential sites for new schools. Most of these resources are located in the office of the local government, specifically in the city/county planning commission. There also are some useful resources in the tax assessor's office. The following resources can be useful in identifying possible school sites:

- Comprehensive plan of city/county
- Aerial photo maps
- Topographic maps
- Highway maps
- Sanborn maps

The comprehensive land plan of the geographic area served by the local government is maintained by the planning commission. No matter what level of government, such a map or plan is maintained in every locality. The map is the official document that shows all of the land and the applicable zoning. It also contains the projected use of land in the future. All of the present and future use of land is documented in this map. Some localities even project on this map where future public services such as fire stations, libraries, schools, recreation facilities, parks, and governmental offices will be located when that area is developed. At the same time, these maps show where vacant tracts of land in a particular development or area are situated that could be used for school purposes. The office of the planning commission should be the first resource that is used in the search for usable school sites.

The school site selection team may also want to use aerial photographs of the area in question to locate vacant tracts of land as possible sites. Such photographs are available from the local office of the United States Department of the Interior. This department of the Federal government periodically takes photographs of the entire country for their purposes and will sell copies of the photograph of the area in the school system.

These are really not maps in the true sense of the word, but are photographs of the earth that can be used as a map. These photographs are particularly useful in showing actual land conditions that may cause problems in situating a school. Actual roads and other topographic features can be detected from these photographs. Actual land use surrounding the potential site for the school can be determined. Also commercial firms can provide aerial photography service to the school system and can provide photographs of specific selected areas.

Topographic maps show the terrain and physical features of a geographic area and are useful not in finding potential sites so much as identifying physical features of an area under consideration. These maps show elevation and characteristics of the land. Topographic maps may be obtained from the state highway department, the federal government or any cartographic outlet.

The highway department of each state maintains a large selection of maps covering the entire state. Most of the maps are used for development of the transportation system; however, they can be useful in locating possible school sites. Maps showing present and future utility installations are valuable for determining availability of these services. Highway personnel are always pleased to work with school system personnel in site selection because of the heavy traffic impact schools have upon surrounding areas.

Sanborn maps are usually maintained by city departments of planning to show the actual dimensions of a structure on a site. These maps show the measurements of all structures on the site and the site itself. This is important in a densely populated area where schools are placed on extremely small sties. Such maps are not maintained for areas with large tracts of land or rural areas.

The above are but the most common resources that are available to the site selection team in trying to identify and evaluate possible sites. The Office of the Assessor will also contain data needed by the site selection team. In this office the owners of every tract of land are recorded, as well as the exact amount of land contained in a certain tract. These two pieces of data are extremely important for the school system.

Each piece of property in the governmental unit is listed in this office along with the assessed value of that property. If the state or county/city practice frequent re-appraisal of property, the current market value is then not hard to determine, which is very important for the school system. If the state does not reappraise property periodically, this piece of information is of very little use. Then it might be necessary to obtain the services of a land appraiser to determine the market price of the property in question, because the school system needs to know this information in order to negotiate with the owner for a possible sale. Additionally, the school system needs to know if the property is beyond the resources available for a site.

Site Title

Every school board needs to have a clear title to all property owned and operated by the school system. The title needs to be a fee simple title, meaning a title that is clear of any liens or assessments. Following the decision of the school board to purchase a piece of property, its legal counsel must negotiate the contract to purchase the tract. Then the legal counsel must examine the title in the county or city Recorder of Deeds office. If the title is clear with no liens or attachments, then a new fee simple title can be written for the school board for the school system.

The school board needs to hold the title to all property because no major construction can take place on the site if the school board does not legally own the property. In addition, in those states where financial aid is given local school systems for construction purposes, the state has to be sure the school system actually owns the land. Otherwise, whoever owns the property then owns the building constructed upon the site and that owner can make decisions about use and disposition of the building. Almost all states that give assistance for construction insist that the local school system own outright the property for which aid is given.

Site Use and Development

Proper use of the school site is extremely important to the community. The school system needs to so utilize the site that all educational and community needs are accommodated. To insure this, a plan of development needs to be promulgated. This plan is sometimes called a Master Site Plan. Specifications for this plan are developed by educators and approved by the school board, in much the same way educational specifications for the facility are developed at a later date. The architect uses these specifications to lay out and define areas on the site where different activities can be accommodated. A Master Site Plan is especially needed for those sites where more than one educational facility will be located in order to fully utilize the site and provide for all activities.

For those sites where only one school facility will be located, such as a high school, a site development plan should be made based upon the needs of the educational program. These specifications are usually contained in the set of educational specifications developed for the facility itself. The educational specifications should describe in detail the numbers and kinds of playing fields, courts and auxiliary spaces needed for the type of educational program at the facility.

Joint Use Sites

Quite frequently the school board and some other local jurisdiction such as the recreation department or library board may join in the use of a school site. There are several applications of this concept. The school board may be able to purchase a site larger than needed for the type and size school that will be placed there. This would then allow the other party to develop the site for a particular use. The recreation department might develop playing fields and erect equipment for their program after school hours that could be used by the school during the day.

The school board and other local jurisdictions could also purchase sites that are contiguous that go together to form a site large enough for both functions. This practice is generally more accepted because one jurisdiction usually is not able to fund the site purchase for the other jurisdiction. In addition, the school board must have a fee simple deed to the land upon which the school is located for loan purposes.

Joint purchases of a site needs considerable lead-time in order for each jurisdiction to budget sufficient funds and have those available at the time of purchase. This facilitates joint purchase of sites by two or more jurisdictions in that those funds can be budgeted in advance of actual need. Some counties utilize an advanced land acquisition policy to help identify possible joint use sites for future purchase. Such advanced notice serves the budgetary process very well. ■

chaptereleven

Developing Educational Specifications

MANY DIFFICULT DECISIONS MUST BE MADE IN PLANNING A SCHOOL FACILITY. ONE of the most difficult sets of decisions to make in this process is to define the type of program to be carried on in the new facility and to relate this program to building needs. Sometimes referred to as programming the school, this activity identifies the school's educational program and then relates these components to certain aspects of school planning such as the amount of space needed, relationship among spaces, furniture and equipment required, and various services and utilities needed. The completion of this task requires a person well versed in educational programs and methodology and at the same time knowledgeable of state requirements for space.

Educational specifications are a set of statements that describe to the architect the types and kinds of educational activities that will take place in the proposed building and relate these activities to school planning factors such as spaces, square footage, and relationships (Hawkins 1991). These statements are contained in a document that is used by the architect to design the building. Educational specifications should be clear, concise, and exact in what is requested in the building.

Needless to say, interpreting the needs of those who will use the completed facility is not an easy task. Developing these specifications demands a reasoned approach to school planning and a systematic procedure involving many people inside and outside the school system. The procedure enables people to have input into the new program that will become the basis for the architect's design.

It is no small task to write a set of educational specifications, and many times school systems do not devote sufficient time, energy and funds to complete a good job. There are several reasons why this occurs.

Perhaps the main reason for not developing a good set of educational specifications may be the lack of leadership on the part of the educators responsible for the task. When educators do not exercise leadership, a vacuum exists and there is always someone who is willing to step into the leadership vacuum and provide some direction to get the job done. The architect has a contract to complete a design project by a given date and needs certain specifications to complete the work. When these specifications are not forthcoming, the only thing that can be done is to complete the task that an educator should have completed. In such a situation, the architect feels compelled to provide that leadership.

Sometimes educators feel the task of writing educational specifications to be the responsibility of the architect because it has been done that way in the past. The custom of letting the architect complete the educational specifications is still practiced in some regions of the country. Sometimes there is a vague demarcation of responsibility in the mind of the educator and architect that results in the task being assumed by the architect. Again, some architects have a desire to provide extra services in exchange for a building commission and will try to write a set of educational specifications. Architects are the first to admit that they are not versed in the educational program to be offered and should not be the ones to write the educational specifications for the project.

Many times educators also hold the mistaken belief that the school system does not have the capacity or the staff to do the task and cannot afford to purchase outside assistance. The expenditure of staff time or funds to hire competent outside consultant service to develop a set of educational specifications is quite small compared to the amount of benefit the school system receives from well-planned facilities. In addition, the actual amount of money spent is a very small proportion of the total amount of funds spent on the project. Some educators feel they do not know how to guide the process of developing a set of educational specifications. All of these conditions underscore the point that educators need to exercise leadership in guiding the process of developing a good set of educational specifications. This leadership must be demonstrated by designating a member of the school staff to write the document or by obtaining the services of an educational consultant.

When a new building or an addition to an existing building is planned, many questions need to be answered. The answers to these questions are then written so that everyone will know what they are, and the questions will not have to be asked again and again. Out of the process of answering these questions will come a document that will serve as a planning tool for both the educator and architect (Holcomb 1995).

The following are typical questions relating to new facilities that need to be answered:

- How many students will the facility serve?
- What are the age groupings, backgrounds, needs and capabilities of the students who will occupy the facility?
- What subjects will be taught?
- What methods of teaching will be used?
- What type of educational technology will be used and where?
- How long will the school day be?
- How many students will eat lunch or breakfast?
- Will the program offer drama, music and sports?
- Will the community utilize the building?
- What kind of media center should the facility have?
- Will the program include science, mathematics and vocational subjects?

These are just a few of the questions that need to be answered in order for the architect to design a facility needed by the school system. The answers become the basis of a set of educational specifications.

At least two processes are in operation at all times in a classroom or instructional space. One concerns the activities a teacher goes through in teaching students. The other is the activities that a student engages in to learn something. Each of these processes is separate but complimentary. Describing these activities is important to the architect because this type of information allows the architect to then design the kind of environment that will support the activities.

For instance, if a kindergarten teacher wants a group of students to sit on the floor to engage in a reading activity, then the floor should have a soft covering. On the other hand, if the students will engage in an activity such as water painting or woodworking, a floor covering that can be easily cleaned should be specified. In addition, teachers need certain equipment, spaces and accoutrements in order to teach effectively. Only by clearly describing all of these types of activities, both teacher and student initiated, can the educator hope to successfully communicate facility needs to the architect.

Developmental Process

The preparation of the educational specifications for a school facility is clearly the responsibility of the school system, whether someone on the staff or an outside educational consultant actually prepares the document. The superintendent in a medium-sized school or the assistant superintendent for facilities in a larger system must assume this responsibility. But this responsibility is discharged by actually designating an office or person to take charge of the process.

In a large school system, someone from the school programming section of the school facilities department is usually designated with the responsibility. That person takes on the project as part of the work load. In some school systems where many school projects are planned simultaneously, there may be more than one school planner in that section. Projects are then assigned to individuals by either geographic area or by rotation. In medium or small school systems, a principal can be released from school assignment to complete the task, or a supervisor or other central staff person can assume the responsibility.

In addition to assigning responsibility, the school system must assign resources to complete the task. This may mean providing an office, secretarial, duplication, and communication services, travel funds and other resources. News of the task and the person responsible must be communicated throughout the school system so that everyone will know who will be working on the project.

Having one individual actually write the educational specifications is a wise idea because of the various input sources. One author can give the document sufficient focus and at the same time clearly state the needs of the users. This also centralizes responsibility for the document. The old adage that a committee cannot write a good report is undoubtedly true in this case. There will, however, be much committee input into the material of the document, but this will be through the interactive process.

As stated earlier, the process of developing a set of educational specifications was termed a fact-finding activity. In effect, the person writing the document must meet with many people to gain their input. How these meetings maybe organized and conducted is debatable, but some meetings should be on an individual basis. This would be particularly true of specialists such as people responsible for maintenance and operations, cafeteria, computer services and transportation. Meetings with parents and teachers may be group sessions. If the project is for a school replacement, there may be a series of meetings with parents and teachers.

The first group meeting should define the project and responsibilities of the planner. The staff and community are made aware of the scope of the project, if they do not already know it. Input maybe requested and obtained at the initial meeting and/or at subsequent meetings. The planner then tries to put together all of the identified needs of the potential users of the school facility. Some needs of the potential users may result from a desire to implement a new program or may arise because the school system is beginning a new program for all schools. In any event, all of the needs are sifted and put together within the confines of the financial budget for the school building.

Appendix F contains a flow chart for developing a set of educational specifications. This flow chart was developed for a rather large school system where many school projects are developed simultaneously. The flow chart is to be followed by a planner who is developing a set of educational specifications. All of the contact points in the large system are identified so that the planner will not omit one. In this situation, a school planner will complete 18 different tasks to complete the document and meet many more times with groups and individuals before the tasks are completed. In the school system where this chart is used, the school organization is subdivided into school districts with a district superintendent in charge. In this situation, there is a three-tiered organization, school building, district, and total school system, which must be brought together for closure on the specifications for a new building.

Obviously, there are general parameters for all school buildings that originate from the total school system (Herman and Herman 1995). These may be related to certain educational programs to be implemented, or they may arise from certain commonalties within the school system. For instance, school systems may specify that every school should contain certain elements such as a particular size of library, types of heating plants, standardized kitchens, or maybe grade organizations. Also, some program needs may be identified on the level beneath the total school system, when the school system is divided into sub-groups such as areas or districts.

Finally, some programmatic needs stem from the local school building organization, regardless of whether the project is a new school or a replacement. All of these needs must be merged into one program description with accompanying facility needs. After the final writing but prior to duplicating the document, the groups and individuals that had input may want to review the specifications for a last approval.

School Board Approval

The final approval for the educational specifications should be by the school board. It is important that the educational specifications be presented to the school board for its review and approval because the specifications will be used as the final arbiter for what will be in the building. School board approval represents policy in that changes in the educational specifications cannot be made by someone in the school system that thinks this or that should be included. Also school board approval of the set of educational specifications limits the size of the building to what can be accomplished through the budget.

Content of Educational Specifications

As stated above, the educational specifications contain answers to questions about the building so that the architect can design what is needed. The people who know the most about the educational program must supply the answers to all questions regarding the program that will be housed in the building. In the absence of any clearly written document, architects must guess or rely upon previous solutions to design problems.

No pre-determined subject areas must be included in the document, but general practice indicates that the following areas should be addressed:

- Educational situation and student body
- Description of the community to be served
- The site and site development
- Educational philosophy of the school system
- Educational program to be offered
- Educational trends in subject matter and methodology
- Space requirements in square footage
- Functional relationships of the facility
- Specialized facilities for vocational education, science, physical education, home arts, technology education, and music
- Indoor and outdoor recreational facilities
- Building communications and utility requirements
- Furniture and equipment
- Plant service area and facilities
- Parking and vehicular traffic
- Site and plant security
- Community use of the facility (Earthman 1976)

Other areas may be addressed, depending upon local circumstances, but the list is comprehensive enough to cover almost every area. Even though the educational specifications are clearly written, they need to be interpreted to the architect during the design stage.

The task in this phase of the planning process for school buildings is to describe the educational program that will take place in the new building and to specify the types and kinds of spaces needed to adequately house it. In order to do this, educators must show a great deal of leadership in developing the educational specifications that will be used by the architect. ■

chaptertwelve

Federal Regulations in Planning Educational Facilities

THE FEDERAL GOVERNMENT HAS NO DIRECT RESPONSIBILITY FOR PROVIDING AN education for children in this country and as a result no liability for funding the operation of the local school system. The Reserve Clause of the 10th Amendment to the United States Constitution states explicitly that services and responsibilities not mentioned in the Constitution are reserved for the states and therefore the sole responsibility of that level of government (Sergiovanni, Burlingame, Coombs, and Thurston 1987). In as much as the function of educating children and youth is not mentioned in the Constitution, this responsibility is reserved for the several states. This does not mean that the Federal Government has no interest in the education of the children and youth of the country, but the direct responsibility of this function does not rest with that branch of the government.

The Federal Government does have responsibility for the well being of all citizens of this country. Under this responsibility the Federal Government can and does provide a number of services to segments of the population or the entire population. The Constitutional provision under which this responsibility is discharged is known as the General Welfare Clause (Alexander and Alexander 1991). In essence, this clause states that Congress can pass any law that will provide for the general welfare of the citizens. The provisions under this clause have varied considerably over the centuries. As an example, Congress has provided educational benefits to returning veterans, food subsidies for the school lunch program, science equipment to local schools to better train scientists, and special instruction for children whose parents have low incomes. All of these programs are educational services to children and youth that were enacted by Congress as a result of this clause. Each of these provisions, however, must pass constitutional judicial review.

The result of these various legislative initiatives to provide services to children and youth forms a rather complicated partnership between the Federal Government and the local school system. All of the services in such legislation are provided under the supposition that the general welfare of the country is being served. At the same time, Congress, through such legislation, does require the local school system to provide certain programs and services. This in spite of the fact Congress has no responsibility for educating children and youth. These requirements also go so far as to mandate how the schools treat and protect certain groups and classes of people. The prime example of this is the Civil Rights Act (1964) where discrimination based upon race, color, or national origin is prohibited.

Such mandates are rather fundamental to the well being of the school system and to the country as a whole. They are also the manifestation of the concern the Federal Government, especially Congress, has for the general functioning of public school systems in a uniform manner throughout the country. The federal laws in which these mandates are imbedded are just one of many parts of the legal framework under which the public schools operate.

Federal laws along with state laws, state and federal court decisions, state department of education rules and regulations, school board policies all serve to guide the administration and operation of the public schools to insure equal educational opportunity to all children.

There are two main areas of federal legislation which effect the working of the public schools directly. The first area deals with those educational programs the Federal Government requires local public schools to offer because they are deemed important to the general welfare of the state (Guthrie 1991). The second area deals with the personal liberties guaranteed by the Federal Government. Examples of the former are listed above such as science programs, hot lunch services, and remedial instruction programs. A classic example of a law dealing with personal liberties mentioned above is the Civil Rights Act of 1964.

Special Legislation

There is also a special class of legislation, enacted by Congress that deals with the rights of persons with disabilities. These laws have had a profound impact upon how public schools are planned, designed, and operated. These laws were passed so that persons with disabilities would not be discriminated against and to guarantee them equal educational opportunities. These laws have had a profound effect upon the school building design, so much that they should be discussed in detail to provide guidance concerning what educators need to know about the requirements the school building must meet in order to provide equal access to educational programs.

The Civil Rights Act of 1964 made it illegal for individuals and organizations to discriminate against persons because of certain demographic conditions and factors. That legislation did not, however, make provision for protection against discrimination of persons with physical, mental, or emotional disabilities. It was not until the Americans with Disabilities Act of 1990 (ADA) was passed that it was illegal to discriminate against persons with disabilities. What previously might have been benign neglect in trying to accommodate students with disabilities became illegal following the enactment of this law. School systems might not have actively discriminated against students with disabilities, but the result was that in many instances these students were prevented from participating in certain events, receiving services, or taking advantage of certain educational opportunities. All of this constituted an actual denial of access to services and programs. Most of the instances of denial of access to services and programs resulted from restrictions of the physical environment in which the student was located.

Under the provisions of the Americans with Disabilities Act, school systems can not discriminate against persons with physical disabilities, therefore, the design and configuration of the school building becomes a very important component in trying to comply with ADA rules and regulations. For this reason, educators and architects must be familiar with the provisions of this legislation that deals with the physical structure of the school building.

There are other legislative acts that state specifically the rights of individuals with disability with regard to accessibility to programs, activities, and services and, therefore, seriously affect the design and configuration of the school building. Two acts that address accessibility of students are the Rehabilitation Act of 1973 and the Education for All Handicapped Children Act of 1975, and its amendments contained in the Individuals with Disabilities Education Act of 1975. These two major pieces of legislation, along with the Americans with Disabilities Act, constitute a tripartite legislative effort to deal with the rights of individuals with disabilities. These three acts have had a significant and progressive impact upon school facilities. From 1973 through 1975, each piece of legislation advanced the definition of what discrimination is and how school systems must respond to the needs of individuals with disabilities.

The Rehabilitation Act

The Rehabilitation Act of 1973 is a very far-reaching piece of legislation that greatly advanced the cause of disabled persons and impacted heavily upon school systems. Section 502 of the act deals with the elimination of architectural barriers in public facilities and Section 504 requires accessibility to educational programs by disabled students. Section 504 states the definition of accessibility.

No otherwise qualified handicapped individual—shall, solely by reason of his/her handicap, be excluded from the participation in, be denied the benefits of, or be subject to discrimination under any program or activity receiving federal financial assistance.

Almost every school system in the country receives some type of financial assistance from the Federal Government and consequently are covered by the provisions of this section of the act. This section guarantees students with disabilities access to all programs, activities, and services of the school regardless of the type of disability. The explication of the concept of accessibility is the controlling factor here. Accessibility is defined as having access to educational programs, services, and activities. Section 504 does not guarantee that all students must have access to all parts of the school building. On the contrary, if part of the building is inaccessible, the program, service, or activity can be moved to a spot in the building where a student with disabilities can participate. This is an important concept for both educator and architect, especially in renovated buildings. Not all parts of the building must necessarily be accessible to comply with the provisions of Section 504. This can mean a change of location for any or all programs in the curriculum of the school system. This can include programs and activities where special equipment or physical features are required for the students. A good example would be the art program that might be located on the second floor of a school building. If a disabled student wished to enroll in an art course and the second floor of the building could not be made accessible through installation of an elevator, the art laboratory would have to be moved to the first floor or some other part of the building that was accessible. The disabled student still might not be able to go to the second floor of the building, but the particular program would be brought to the student. In addition, the program, service, or activity that was moved must be equal to that which was offered previously. Naturally there are many conditions that must be addressed in the situation above, but accessibility can be addressed in several ways without making the building completely accessible.

Section 502 of the Rehabilitation Act required the elimination of physical and communication barriers in all public buildings where federal funds are used. This, of course, includes all public schools. Elimination of physical and communication barriers means some standards have to be developed against which architects and educators can measure accessibility. To accommodate and define what a barrier free environment means, standards have been developed. The American National Standards Institute (ANSI) developed specifications governing the design of facilities to accommodate persons with disabilities. The first set of specifications developed by ANSI was in 1961 and these have been periodically revised to accommodate provisions in new legislation. These specifications have been used since in the design of almost all school buildings.

Several governmental agencies and departments have, since the early legislation on disabled persons was passed, developed building specifications for certain classes of buildings. Four of these departments—Defense, Housing and Urban Development, General Services Agency, and the Postal Service—joined together to formulate the Uniform Federal Accessibility Standards (UFAS) to be used by these departments in designing buildings under their jurisdiction. These rules and regulations were later adopted by the Department of Education for use in designing buildings under that jurisdiction. The UFAS is considered by many as being more stringent than the ANSI standards. Other departments of the Federal Government have used UFAS as the basis for the re-writing of the specifications used to govern the construction of buildings. State and local governing jurisdictions and even private organizations that receive funds from the Federal Government can apply UFAS specifications to the design of buildings and thereby comply with the provisions of Section 504 of the Rehabilitation Act.

Education for All Handicapped Children Act

The Education for All Handicapped Children Act is now know as the Individuals with Disabilities Education Act. IDEA was passed and signed into law in 1975. Rules and regulations were published in the Federal Register in 1977. This act is considered a very far-reaching piece of legislation regarding the educational rights of students with disabilities. IDEA does not directly refer to physical facilities and does not impact buildings as much as other legislation, but the act does have a profound impact upon how such individuals are treated in the public schools. The most important provision of this act deals with the development of an Individualized Educational Program (IEP) for each student who has disabilities. IDEA provisions further address student assessment and evaluation, enactment of procedural safeguards for students and parents, and provision for an education in the least restrictive environment. The latter provision paved the way for more inclusive educational programs for students with disabilities and thus has some impact upon the accessibility of the school building.

The least restrictive environment has been defined as any physical location in the building where the student can learn effectively with the least possible restraint. Usually this means active association with other students, especially those without identified disabilities. For the most part, this usually means the regular classroom. There is also the proviso that the educational program must be of the same quality of instruction as other students in the school. Specifically, the least restrictive environment means the student with a disability would be in the regular classroom as much time as would be beneficial. This time limit would vary with each student. Some students might spend the entire school day in the regular classroom, but in some instances this time may be reduced proportionately for special instruction that could not take place within the regular classroom. One example of this might be where special equipment is needed for instruction and the equipment could not be located in the regular classroom. In all instances, the amount of time a student spends in the regular classroom is determined at the meeting where the Individual Education Program is developed.

In spite of the fact the least restrictive environment is an individual matter and defined individually for each student who has a disability, several implementation concepts regarding the housing of identified students with disabilities have been developed and implemented by school systems throughout the country. Like all educational concepts, the actual implementation of the concept is different from one school system to another. The idea of mainstreaming students with disabilities into the regular classroom was developed as an interpretation of the least restrictive environment. In subsequent legislation that interpretation was modified somewhat.

Americans with Disabilities Act
This act prohibits discrimination against individuals with various disabilities listed in the act. The ADA extends to all organizations the anti-discriminatory provisions of previous legislation such as the Civil Rights Act of 1964, the Rehabilitation Act of 1973, and the Individuals with Disabilities Education Act of 1975. In the Rehabilitation Act, organizations that received federal funds could not discriminate against disabled persons. This was later defined as being those programs that received federal funds. Title II of the ADA extends the anti-discrimination provisions to all activities of the school system, as well as all other governmental bodies regardless of the use of federal funds. This is the most far-

reaching of the series of legislation dealing with the rights of persons with disabilities. The ADA legislation is quite specific in requiring organizations, including public schools, to eliminate physical and communication barriers in buildings.

Specific provisions of the ADA which affect the physical environment include the following:

School systems:

- may not refuse to allow a person with a disability to participate in a service, program, or activity simply because the person has a disability
- must provide programs and services in an integrated setting, unless separate or different measures are necessary to ensure equal opportunities
- may impose safety requirements that are necessary for the safe operation of the program in questions, if they are based on actual risk and not on speculation
- are required to make reasonable modifications in policies, practices, and procedures that deny equal access to individuals with disabilities, unless a fundamental alteration in the program would result
- must furnish auxiliary aids and services when necessary to ensure effective communication, unless an undue burden or fundamental alteration would result (USDOJ, 1992)

In addition to the general provisions above, Title II of the ADA also has some provisions that address individual program access relating directly to building accessibility.

School systems:

- must ensure that individuals with disabilities are not excluded from services, programs, and activities because buildings are inaccessible
- need not remove physical barriers, such as stairs, in all existing buildings, as long as they make their programs accessible to individuals who are unable to use an inaccessible existing facility
- can provide the services, programs, and activities offered in the facility to individuals with disabilities through alternative methods, if physical barriers are not removed such as: relocating a service to an accessible facility, providing an aide or personal assistant to enable an individual with a disability to obtain service, providing benefits or services at an individual's home, or at an alternative accessible site
- may not carry an individual with a disability as a method of providing program access, except in "manifestly exceptional" circumstances

■ are not required to take any action that would result in a fundamental alternation in the nature of the service, program, or activity or cause undue financial and administrative burdens. However, public entities must take any other action, if available, that would not result in a fundamental alteration or undue burden but would ensure that individuals with disabilities receive the benefits or services (USDOJ, 1992)

These requirements may seem contradictory in that one section states that school systems must guarantee that individuals with disabilities are not excluded from services because the buildings are inaccessible, then in another section states the school system need not remove physical barriers. The key provision here is that buildings do not need to be modified providing the program, services, or activities are available in a location in the building that is accessible to students with disabilities. Further, school systems are not required to modify a building if such would cause an undue burden or financial hardship upon the school system.

Perhaps the one requirement that may have impact upon school facilities is the one that requires that programs and services must be offered in an integrated setting. This is a rather fundamental tenet of the ADA, that students with disabilities would be included in integrated programs. This has been interpreted to mean that students with disabilities should be included in all programs, activities, and services of the school. Another term that is used to describe this situation is immersion. Through immersion, students with disabilities are practically immersed into the entire life of the school. Immersion is an extension of mainstreaming used under the IDEA interpretation of least restrictive environment, but there is one important difference. That difference deals with the fact that teachers of special education go into the regular classroom to teach students with disabilities. The practical application of immersion is that students with disabilities are enrolled in the regular classroom consistent with their age group peers for all of their instructional activities. The antithesis of this is providing programs and services for students with disabilities that are different, in a separate program, or a separate location. This the ADA regulations prohibit explicitly, unless separate programs are necessary to ensure that the programs or services are equally effective for students with disabilities. This kind of separation has to be decided upon a case by case basis. The main impact of inclusion or immersion upon school facilities would be through increased numbers of students in the regular classrooms. The impact of increased numbers of students in the classroom should be minimal unless special equipment is needed in the classroom to be used by students with disabilities. The number of students with disabilities in the average school building is a very small percentage of the total student body and as a result distribution of these students throughout the school building would not cause space problems. Even in cases where the teacher of students with disabilities is in the regular classroom conducting lessons, space may not be a serious problem. There will undoubtedly be some instances where overcrowding would occur, but for the most part, overcrowding would not be a serious or widespread problem. Inclusion of the student with disabilities throughout the building may, however, require the modification of a existing building for accessibility.

Inclusion or immersion of students with disabilities into the regular classrooms and laboratories may have a positive impact in the planning of new school buildings. Many states require the standard classroom to contain a minimum of 720 square feet of space for 20-25 students. This amount of space is usually satisfactory for most high school classes, but the new demands of including not only students with disabilities and their teachers, but also increased computers in the classroom may cause the minimum classroom space to increase. Several states require 850 square feet of space in the standard classroom. This amount of space allows for an activity based instructional model. A classroom this size would better accommodate two teachers and additional computers than would the smaller size of 720 square feet. Regardless of the minimum state square foot requirement, local school systems should strongly consider increasing the size of the standard classroom to accommodate the increase in equipment and personnel now being deployed there.

Another provision of the ADA pertains to students with hearing, vision, or speech disabilities. The ADA mandates that schools must ensure effective communication in all aspects of the school life. To assist in this, the schools may be required to provide auxiliary aids which include such services or devices as qualified interpreters, assistive listening headsets, television captioning and decoders, telecommunications devices for deaf persons (TDD), video displays, readers, taped text, Braille materials, and large print materials. Most of this equipment and materials requires no adaption of the building other than the availability of sufficient electrical service and appropriate space for the equipment.

Provision for communicating with students with visual impairment may require some additional visual signage throughout the school, but little if any building adaptation. Provision for Braille labeling of all areas of the school building and visual warning systems to augment the bell system require little in the way of building adaptation, but the benefits to students with disabilities, as well as the student body as a whole, are innumerable. In addition, the internal and external telephone service should be such that students and employees with disabilities can use these devices effectively. This may well mean the lowering of telephone equipment to accommodate a person in a wheelchair or the provision of special communication equipment for the hearing disabled person. The provision for emergency services, including 911 numbers, for individuals with speech and hearing impairments need to be made. These provisions incur very little cost and should be included in the educational specifications for any new construction as well as any renovation, renewal, or modernization.

The law also stipulates that the removal of barriers should be readily achievable. The term, readily achievable, means the removal of the barrier can be easily accomplished and carried out with little difficulty or without great expense. The nature and cost of removing a barrier is the criteria to be used in making a decision regarding whether or not a project is readily achievable. The cost of removal, the ease or difficulty with which the project can be accomplished, and the overall financial resources of the school system come into play in making the final decision. But whether or not the project is deemed achievable does not relieve the school system from the responsibility of making programs, services, and activities accessible to students with disabilities. If a project is not judged to be feasible because of the above mentioned criteria, the school system must then use other means to make the program accessible. These means may be to bring the program, services, or activity to the student by moving it to a spot in the building that is accessible. In the matter of the school system, the intent is to accomplish the removal of the barrier, not necessarily to claim exemption because of the difficulty or cost of the removal.

The intent of the legislation is to make all programs, activities, and services accessible to all students. This means all institutions, including the public schools, must operate in such a manner that all programs are accessible. When this is not ordinarily possible, the school system must under take one or more of the following actions:
1. Remove the barriers to access in that facility,
2. Shift the location where the program, service, or activity is provided to an accessible site,
3. Provide the program, service, or activity in some alternative method like visits to the home,
4. Make alterations to existing facilities,
5. Construct new accessible facilities (Mayer 1982).

The provisions and requirements of the ADA have been operational since signing into law and the execution of the regulations. The legislation mandated a very swift timetable for compliance. Since January 26, 1992, all new construction and renovations to existing buildings started after that date have had to comply with ADA regulations. For existing buildings, the local school system was required to conduct a Self-Evaluation Plan by January 26, 1993 (Whisenant, 1993). For those buildings that needed alterations to comply with the law, a Transition Plan had to be adopted by July 26, 1992. Any identified deficiencies were to be corrected by January 26, 1995. It is doubtful that all needed physical alterations have been completed by that date. If such is the case, the option for the school system is to develop an Alternative Solution discussed above. Provisions for construction after the above dates are spelled out in the regulations.

1. New construction completed after January 26, 1993 must meet ADAAG standards [42 U.S.C. Sec 12183 (a)(1); 28 C.F.R. Sec 36.401], and
2. Alterations to existing structures made after January 26, 1992 must meet ADAAG standards (28 C.F.R. Sec 36.402).

Important Concepts

There are several important concepts in the ADA with which educators should be familiar. These terms or concepts deal mostly with a definition of how accessibility can be achieved in a building particularly to renovated structures.

Readily Achievable—refers to how easily a barrier can be removed in an existing building. Considerations regarding readily achievable are the nature of the barrier, the cost to remove it, the financial resources of the school system, and the type of operation.

Structurally Impracticable—refers to the unique characteristics of the site that might prevent accessibility. These characteristics might be a building located in a highly dense urban area, a building constructed on marshlands or over water requiring stilts (Battaglia, 1992).

Alternative Method—refers to the alternative method by which the programs, activities, or services of a school are made available to disabled persons when a barrier can not be readily removed.

Reasonable Modification—refers to the change in policies, procedures, and practices that permit a person with disabilities to participate in the program, services, and activities of the school. This is similar to Alternative Method of providing accessibility.

Undue Burden—this refers to an undue administrative or financial burden an alteration to a building might cost the school system to implement. Such alterations should not cause an undue or unbearable burden. This is a judgement call on the part of the school board that could very easily require judicial review. The school board must provide an alternative method of accessibility when an alteration to a building would cause an undue burden upon the school system.

These definitions serve to clarify important concepts regarding accessibility and achievement of accessibility in both new construction and renovation of existing structures. Educational planners and school administrators must be conversant with the meanings of the terms and how they can be implemented in order to properly advise school boards.

Costs to Implement Accessibility

In designing and constructing new school buildings, one might think the costs to making a school barrier free would be an enormous increase in the total cost of the project. The United States General Accounting Office suggests that fully implementing a barrier free environment in a new structure will add only approximately one-half of one percent to the total construction costs. On a $15 million school project, the total costs would amount to only $76,000 or the equivalent of less than four cents per square foot of space. Considering the total cost of the structure and the total benefits accrued by the school system in having a barrier free building, the costs are minimal.

On renovations and modernization to existing structures, the square footage costs are somewhat larger as might be expected, but still very small. The GAO estimates costs in making an existing building barrier free would amount to between one-half and three percent of the total costs. If a renovation project would cost $3 million, additional accessible costs would increase the project from $15,000 to $90,000. This range of costs is an insignificant amount considering the total cost of the project.

In a normal capital project, whether it is new construction or a renovation, the costs will not be prohibitive. Any cost-benefit analysis will more than indicate the desirability of making the environment barrier free. There are, however, some instances where building modification on an existing building might prove to be too costly for implementation. When this occurs, some alternative method of making the program, activity, or service accessible to students with disabilities must be implemented. The decision whether or not a capital project can be implemented ultimately rests with the school board, but that decision must be based upon data from the architect. In working with the educational planners of the school system, the architect can be valuable in providing input into an alternative method of accessibility. The viability of the alternative method, however, is a decision of the school board based upon a recommendation of the educational planners and school administration.

Educator Responsibility

As with any legislative enactment, the major question regarding the role of the educator in implementing its provisions revolve around the amount of information that is needed to effectively comply. In other words, how much of the provisions must the educator know in order to function legally and effectively. In the case of the ADA and other legislative acts dealing with special education, the educator must know what policies and practices to implement to comply with the regulations. In the IDEA legislation, there are a number of practices regarding the implementation of the individual education program that must be in place for compliance. Regarding the ADA and accessibility of buildings, the educator must know the important concepts and terms of the legislation sufficient to either take action to implement or to guard against certain practices. In the case of the latter, there are some very precise statements in the regulations regarding accessibility that must be guarded against. One such practice is that concerning physically carrying students with disabilities to programs or services. Such actions are specifically prohibited and the school administrator must establish practices so that such does not occur. Knowing what actions to take and those not to take is extremely important in complying with federal regulations.

The ADA and accompanying regulations refer to several sources of technical specifications that are crucial to the planning and designing of a school building. These specifications are quite precise in detailing certain aspects of the building such as how wide a door should be, the height of a water fountain or sink, the slope of a ramp, the number of stalls for disabled persons in a restroom, and even acceptable raised signage. All of these technical specifications are extremely important in order for the design professional to achieve a barrier free environment in the building. Specific knowledge of these technical specifications is not a requirement of the school administrator or school board, however, they must know of the existence of these specifications, the sources, and how they impact a school building.

There are several managerial functions that are required of the school administrator to insure the school system is complying with ADA regulations regarding facilities. The first of these managerial functions is exercised through the employment of the architect. When the school system employees an architect, the school board and administrators must make certain the architect and staff are very familiar with the regulations of ADA and the requirement of technical specifications as they relate to public schools. This is usually determined during the interview by asking the architect about previous building design projects. The school board and administrators will also desire to know about where the architect gained knowledge of the provisions of the law.

Another managerial function that must be exercised revolves around the review of architectural plans. In reviewing plans for new construction, the educational planner and school administrator must make certain the plans conform to the requirement of a barrier free environment. This can be done by a careful study of the plans regarding the circulation of the building. The review process should include a detailed study of how students and teachers circulate throughout the building, as well as an analysis of the physical and educational needs of various disabled students. One very simple method is by using the architectural drawings to practice walking through the building from entrance to exit using a variety of student schedules of classes. If it can be found, through tracing paths a student would normally take to complete a daily schedule, that students and teachers do not have any barriers, then the plans can be assumed to be barrier free. Such review sessions are crucial to the success of a building project.

In renovation and modernization projects, the architectural review process is exactly the same as for new construction. Student and teacher circulation patterns need to be employed to determine degree of accessibility in the renovated facility. The subject of the review being an existing facility, however, is different. In a new building, a barrier free environment can be implemented with no physical constraint. In renovation and modernization projects, completion of a barrier free environment may not be entirely possible in all situations because of existing structural limitations. In such cases, an alternative method of accessibility for disabled students and teachers must be developed. The school administrator, educational planner, and architect must work together to seek alternative solutions to any unresolvable barrier problems.

The second part of a barrier free environment deals with communication. ADA stipulates that public schools must, in addition to eliminating physical barriers, eliminate communication barriers. Providing alternative methods of notifying individuals of places and events does this. This is a requirement in both new construction and renovated structures. Ensuring barrier free communication is a little more difficult than ensuring physical barrier free environments, especially when reviewing architectural plans. It is not possible to trace communication routes like the way a student would travel to the library or some other facility in the building. In these situations, school administrators and educational planners must inquire of the architect the types of signage and oral communication that will be employed in the new or renovated building. These simple questions are the means for guaranteeing that communication barriers have been eliminated.

The school administrator must employ certain managerial functions to guarantee complete accessibility to school programs, activities, and services. These functions include the following:

1. Know and understand the general provisions of the law as stated in this chapter,
2. Know the timetable and schedule for when accessibility is required under provisions of the law,
3. Be able to identify and recommend to the school board competent architects and engineers knowledgeable about the provisions of the ADA and supporting codes,
4. Understand what a barrier is and how to recognize one when reviewing an architectural drawing and in evaluating an existing building,
5. Be able to intelligently read architectural drawings and plans to determine possible barriers and situations where persons with disabilities would have difficulty,
6. Be prepared to raise the appropriate questions to the architect to help ascertain accessibility (Earthman, 1994).

The school administrator and educational planner are key players in helping the school board comply with the provisions of ADA in ensuring accessibility by students with disabilities to all of the programs, activities, and services of the school system.

Architect Responsibility

Architects are employed to design spaces, whether in a new or renovated structure, that will accommodate a specified educational program and the students who will be engaged in that program. This is a very important responsibility that requires considerable knowledge and skill. Educators are responsible for determining the type of program, number of students, and the required spaces in order for the architect to design these spaces. In doing this task, the architect must then use all of the expertise in the firm to create a desirable and responsible building that conforms to all of the legal requirements and regulations.

Architects are required to be knowledgeable of and conversant with all building codes and regulations to which a school facility must conform. There are several different codes in operation each layering upon the other. There are federal, state, and local building codes to which a school building is subject. The general rule is that the school building must conform to the strictest building code regardless of which level. As a general rule, the local building code is the strictest code and as a result, school buildings must conform to these. The architect must be knowledgeable about these codes and how to apply them. School facilities must never be subject to the lesser of building codes.

Some states require state approval of all capital projects in a local school system. This review process may or may not involve state building code reviews, however, the architect must be aware of this. In addition, the state fire marshal may be required to review school building projects for compliance with state code, this may be in addition to other reviews on the local level. Approval of the school building project is usually required by the local fire marshal, in as much as the local authority is the one which issues a building permit. The architect needs to be aware of the various review processes, regardless of the level, in order to move expeditiously the project forward to construction.

School building projects need to conform to various codes and standards for compliance. Some of the more important standards are ANSI, ADAAG, UFAS, and ATBCB.

(ANSI) American National Standards Institute—guidelines promulgated by a private organization covering general building standards including disabled access. Used in many schools, but is considered by some as not as stringent as other standards.

(ADAAG) Americans with Disabilities Act Architectural Guidelines—standards developed by the Department of Justice consistent with minimum guidelines developed by the Architectural and Transportation Barriers Compliance Board. To be used by architects in designing schools (Tucker and Goldstein 1993).

(UFAS) Uniform Federal Accessibility Standards—standards developed by four standard-setting federal departments and agencies for use in enforcing existing rules requiring nondiscrimination on the basis of disability. A very detailed set of standards that clarifies which standards apply in what situations (West, 1991).

(ATBCB) Architectural and Transportation Barriers Compliance Board—a set of recommendations for supplements to the existing UFAS that would apply to environments used by children. Contained in Recommendations for Accessibility Standards for Children's Environments (U.S. ATBCB, 1992).

All of the above sets of standards can be used in designing a school building project, whether new construction or renovation of existing space. Public schools may be designed using either UFAS or ADAAG because of the specific reference to application of the ADA. Architects are very familiar with all of these sets of standards and knowledgeable about when they apply. Educators should be cognizant of these different sets of standards and then ascertain from the architect that standards are applicable and which are being used for the project.

Sources of Assistance

There are many offices that can be of assistance to the local school system in finding out more about architectural standards and how they affect local school building projects. The sources most used are:

Americans with Disabilities Act Information Line—(202) 514-0301. Answers general questions about the ADA law.

Architectural and Transportation Barriers Compliance Board—(202) 653-7848. Information about accessibility guidelines for ADA.

ERIC Clearinghouse on Disabilities and Gifted Education—(800) 328-0272. Provides general information about disability programs. ▪

Monitoring the Design Phase

AFTER THE EDUCATIONAL SPECIFICATIONS HAVE BEEN APPROVED BY THE SCHOOL BOARD, the architect is officially given the document to begin design work. This document becomes the program the architect uses to design the building and should be studied by the staff of the architectural firm in preparation for a kick-off meeting to get the design project started. Architectural firm representatives who will be working on the project and appropriate school personnel will attend the meeting. At this initial meeting, parameters of the project are given, questions about any phase of the project are answered by the school staff, communication lines are discussed, and the design schedule is approved. The conclusion of this meeting indicates the beginning of the design phase.

Design Team

The people in the architectural firm who will be responsible for the design of the building form a working team. This group of individuals will work with the project to the end and will be termed the Design Team. This team is headed by the project architect and supported by other individuals. In rare instances, more than one architect may be on the team, but usually one-architect is the head, responsible for determining the basic concept of the building, giving direction to the team, and making final decisions on the design. The project architect also assumes responsibility for designing the building within the school system's budget. This last responsibility is very important because many of the decisions made in the design stage depend upon how that decision affects the final cost of the building. In essence, this person minds the purse strings so the project stays within budget.

The project architect is assisted by others both within and outside of the architectural firm to provide engineering expertise. If the architectural firm is very small, experts from other companies may collaborate with the project architect to form a Design Team to complete the project. In a larger firm, such expertise is employed on the staff. These support personnel usually follow the traditional disciplines associated with the building industry. An engineer is needed for the design of the basic structural work of the building. In addition, engineering expertise is needed for the other basic building systems such as the HVAC systems, plumbing and electricity. This group serves as the basic component of the Design Team.

The Design Team may also be augmented by other experts in related fields from time to time. The design of a special area in the building may require added expertise. For instance, if a theatre is to be designed in a school, the Design Team may call upon the services of a theatre consultant or an acoustical engineer for design advice. Someone well versed in the design of kitchens may be called upon to help with the design of that portion of the building. Likewise, expertise in the field of landscaping, library science, and gymnasium may assist when needed.

Design Review Team

To assist the Design Team, the school system should appoint a Design Review Team consisting of the school personnel who are responsible for managing the design phase of the project. Specifically, this team is responsible for monitoring the work of the Design Team, assisting in the interpretation of the educational specifications, and giving approval to all parts of the design of the building (Earthman 1994). This team is the counterpart of the Design Team and represents the owner, which is the school board.

The Design Review Team should be composed of a small group of individuals who will form the core and will stay with the project to the end of the design phase. The head of this group should be the staff member who wrote the educational specifications for the design project. In a large school system, this may be someone in the school facilities department on the director or supervisor level and may be designated an educational planner or school planner. In a smaller school system, the person maybe a principal relieved of responsibilities to complete this planning project. If the school system employed an educational consultant to write the specifications, that person may well be the head of the Design Review Team.

Regardless of the designation, the person who actually wrote the specifications should provide direction for the Design Review Team. The second person on that team should be from the cabinet, council, or team of the superintendent. This person should be able to make decisions about the design work and have that decision hold without constant review by the superintendent or school board. Indeed, that person should have the full confidence of the superintendent and school board to make everyday decisions without the need for review.

The third Design Review Team member should be a principal of a school building in the school system. A principal should know the workings of a school and how a school organization operates. In this manner the principal should be able to anticipate the consequences of certain designs as far as student movement, access, program demands, and school organization requirements are concerned.

The basic core of the Design Review Team should be expanded at certain times to include other expertise in the school system. Expertise in selected areas such as maintenance and operations, cafeterias, libraries, vocational education laboratories, and gymnasium might be needed when these sections of the building are under study. Directors, supervisors or teachers of these subjects and areas could be brought into the Design Review Team at the appropriate time.

This group of secondary support personnel will eventually approve the design of that portion of the building for which they have either responsibility or expertise. For instance, the person in charge of libraries for the school system should be the one who eventually approves the layout of that area of the school. This applies to all other parts of the building.

The Design Review Team may expand from the basic unit when necessary and then contract to the three-member unit as the need may exist. It is not necessary for all persons in the school system to be involved in all phases of design review because they have neither the interest nor the expertise to provide sound advise.

The interface relationship between the Design Team and the Design Review Team is shown in Figure 13.1.

The Design Review Team closely monitors the design of the building from start to finish, reviewing all of the work of the architect for acceptance. The review sessions usually begin with a presentation by the architect and then a question-and-answer period by the Design Review Team. Sometimes there are questions the architect has of the Design Review Team because a clarification is needed in the educational specifications. A resolution is made at the presentation by either approving what has been presented or by the architect agreeing to study the problem further and come back with a different solution.

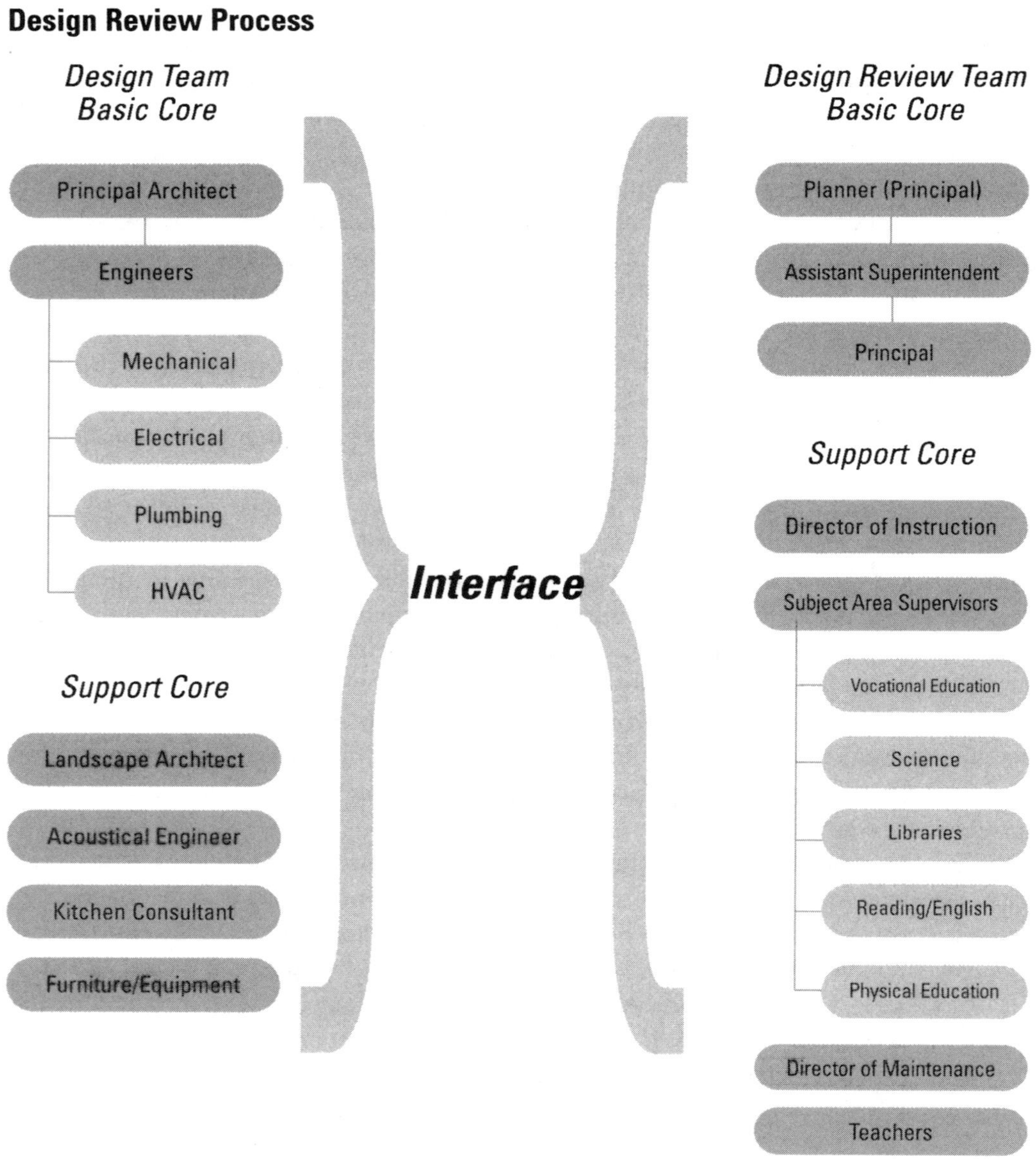

Design Review Process

*Design Team
Basic Core*

```
Principal Architect
        │
    Engineers
        ├── Mechanical
        ├── Electrical
        ├── Plumbing
        └── HVAC
```

Support Core

```
Landscape Architect
Acoustical Engineer
Kitchen Consultant
Furniture/Equipment
```

Interface

*Design Review Team
Basic Core*

```
Planner (Principal)
        │
Assistant Superintendent
        │
    Principal
```

Support Core

```
Director of Instruction
Subject Area Supervisors
        ├── Vocational Education
        ├── Science
        ├── Libraries
        ├── Reading/English
        └── Physical Education
Director of Maintenance
Teachers
```

Figure 13.1
*Relationship
between the Design
Team and the Design
Review Team*

These review sessions occur very frequently during the middle of the design phase. In fact, the Design Review Team should not let more than two weeks pass without a review of some type. The sessions include examining architectural drawings of various parts of the building. Generally, the drawings that are used in this review are ⅛-inch scale, but occasionally when a detail is to be studied, a ¼-inch drawing will be used.

Developing the Design

There needs to be a very close working relationship between the Design Team and the Design Review Team in this stage of development to guarantee fidelity to the educational specifications and to produce a functional building. Many questions need to be answered for the architect in this phase, and the school personnel, through the Design Review Team, should be available at all times.

The architect usually begins this phase by locating the building on the site. After a thorough study of the site and the requirements of the educational program for open space, the architect will suggest a specific location for the building, taking into consideration the location of utilities, traffic patterns, parking needs, as well as the contour and aesthetics of the site. The building's location will be the first big decision to be approved.

The second decision will have to do with the concept the architect is trying to implement through the building design. The architect will develop a concept of the building keeping in mind the scale of the neighborhood, the environment, type of surrounding architecture, certain site factors, the educational program, level of school, and even the idea of what a school is and the image the architect would like to project. All of these things comprise the architect's ideas in conceptualizing the school building. Within the concept, the architect has to fit all of the various components of the building that are needed to enable the educational program to function. The architect may develop more than one concept for study purposes, but only one idea is chosen to be further developed. The architect and Design Review Team agree upon the concept that allows further development.

After these initial decisions have been made, the architect begins work on the schematic drawings. The schematic design is the point where the basic configuration of the building is determined. The architect seeks to define the concept internally by locating the various components of the school building. The relationship between these components has been defined very exactly in the educational specifications, and the architect follows these directions in expanding the concept. Circulation of students, material and supplies within the building are also concerns at this stage of development. The architect works to develop efficient lines of circulation within and outside the building. All of these design problems are addressed at this stage of development. Approval points on all of the work done in this phase take place at design review meetings where both the Design Team and Design Review Team meet to review the drawings. The series of weekly reviews and approvals lead to the completion of the schematic drawings.

When the Design Team has completed the work in this stage, the drawings are formally presented to the school board. This consists of a review of the program and the actual design approved by the school staff. The school board should formally approve the schematic design of the architect. This can be done by resolution or by informal consensus of the school board. This approval is important because it gives the architect the signal to proceed into the next stage of design work.

The schematic design is also a milestone in the development of the design. At this point, the exterior of the building is set and should not be changed. The architect has reconciled the square footage in the building with the budget allocation for the building and, therefore, should be reasonably assured that the size of the building will not change after this approval. To change either the basic design of the building or to add or subtract from the size after this point in time, would be cause for a re-design which would cost the school board extra payments to the architect. Needless to say, in order to ensure the design is what they want, the Design Review Team should work very closely with the Design Team. After school board approval, the Design Team is able to start the design development.

The design development stage takes the longest amount of time because of the amount of exacting work needed to be completed by the Design Team. Each segment of the building must be drawn to provide drawings from which the building can be constructed. Here again, weekly meetings between the Design Team and the Design Review Team are required to keep the project on schedule.

During this period of design work, many of the specialists on the school system staff are brought into the design process to review that portion of the building for which they have responsibility. Also during this stage, these specialists will eventually sign off on the drawings indicating approval of the design. During this period, the furniture and equipment needed in the building is specified either by the school staff or by the architect. In very small school systems, the architect may take on this responsibility as a separate contract to assist the school system. In most other school systems, the school staff should write the specifications, conduct the bidding and secure the loose furniture and equipment needed in the new building. This act saves the school system considerable funds in additional architectural fees.

During this stage, the technical writers produce a document describing all of the building materials that will be used to construct the building. This document is termed the technical specifications, and the final architectural drawings then serve as the contract documents from which bids are developed by contractors. The specifications in this document must be approved by the school staff if they did not write them. With the completion of the design and the technical specifications, the design development stage ends and the public bidding phase begins.

Evaluating Architectural Designs

In evaluating the work of the architect and the Design Team, school system personnel are placed in the position of having to review the work of a profession for which they have not had any training. The educators must decide if the design meets the need of the organization that they are representing. This can be done successfully only if the people doing the review are well versed in the type of program that will be offered in the building. This is the first requirement in order to review successfully architectural plans.

The time frame for completing the design work for a new building varies depending upon the type of building involved, the size of the structure, the location, the availability of school staff to review designs, and the amount of staff the architect is able to employ on the project. Generally speaking, the design of a medium-sized elementary school should take approximately six to nine months, depending upon how much time the architect can devote to the project. On a large high school project, the design stage could well consume the better part of 12 to 18 months. In planning for the opening of a new building, the school staff should anticipate these lengths of time for proper design work. There is a point when the design work can be pushed so fast that mistakes in reviewing the plans can take place. Therefore, this possibility must be avoided at all costs. The proper and timely development of a good design for the new building is the first order of business.

Design Review

As described in the last section, educators are required to evaluate the work of a different profession, one for which they have not had any formal training. This presents a dilemma for those school staff who actually approve design work.

These people will be required to read and interpret architectural drawings in order to approve of the design and most school personnel have not been trained to do this. In fact, it is extremely rare for an educator to possess such background. Such expertise usually comes from experience in actually reviewing plans and not from any systematic study.

Actually reviewing plans is the best way to become familiar with architectural drawings. In addition, asking questions and listening to explanations is a good method of learning. Even if a question sounds simplistic, it should be asked because that person is representing the owner of the new building, the school board. Design professionals are very expert in being able to answer questions and are more than willing to do that. The responsibility for asking the question, however, rests with the school staff.

The basic question is what to look for when reviewing plans. One approach is to try to anticipate problems that may arise when a large number of youngsters are in the building trying to find classrooms and doing the work they are supposed to be doing. The Design Review Team members must be able to ask these questions to see if the plan works. If a principal is a member of the Design Review Team, that person can add valuable experience in looking at the proposed building. Another way is to take a typical schedule of a student in the school and follow the schedule as the student would during an average day. Circulation patterns can be studied, relationships between building components can be evaluated, and student-grouping problems can be identified in this manner.

The basis for evaluation of any design is the set of educational specifications prepared for that particular building. This is the document that is to be used in evaluating every aspect of the building. All of the descriptions given in that document must be found in the design of the building before approval can be granted. Questions generated from these descriptions can guide the design review sessions. The following list contains general questions that may be useful in evaluating architectural designs. These are but some of the questions members of the Design Review Team should raise at any review session.

1. *Traffic patterns*
   a. Is the building barrier-free?
   b. How do students enter a building, get to their lockers and classes?
   c. Are there any hallways or intersections that might cause student traffic congestion?
   d. Are the hallways sufficiently large to accommodate the numbers of students?

e. Is there a well-identified main entrance with reception lobby to help community users?
f. Do the hallways serve all areas with ease?
g. Is the circulation system compact enough to allow students to get from one area to another in the given amount of time between classes?
h. Is the traffic flow from one building component to another efficient?
i. Will areas not open all the time be located so that they can be closed off when not in use?

2. *Relationships between components of the facility*
   a. Are the proper relationships between subject areas observed?
   b. Are the general relationships of the building efficient?
   c. Are the noise areas separated from other areas?
   d. Are necessary relationships to outside facilities observed?
   e. Are community spaces clustered together?

3. *Numbers and types of instructional, administrative and activity spaces*
   a. Are there the number of teaching spaces called for in the educational specifications?
   b. Are these spaces the right kind?
   c. Are these spaces in the needed relationship to each other?
   d. Are there the right kind and number of administrative spaces?
   e. Are there the right kind and number of guidance/health spaces?

4. *Size and shape of spaces*
   a. Was the ratio of 75 percent instructional and 25 percent non-instructional space observed throughout the plans?
   b. Is each space sized correctly?
   c. Are the teaching spaces the shape that will enhance the program?
   d. Is there sufficient space to do what is necessary in the teaching program?
   e. Are there any odd or irregular spaces being assigned as administrative space?
   f. Has sufficient storage been provided in all administrative and instructional spaces?
   g. Are there any triangular, oval, angular, or other similar spaces being assigned as teaching spaces?
   h. Is there any wasted or non-assigned space?

5. *Utility service*
   a. What type of energy source is being used?
   b. Is there sufficient utility service to each area presently and in case of expansion of the building?

c. Are there electricity, natural gas and water outlets where necessary?

d. How many electric outlets are there in the instructional spaces?

e. Are utilities zoned so that portions of the building can be heated and lighted independently?

f. Are there water and electrical services where custodians need them?

g. Is the building energy efficient?

6. *Potential supervision problem areas*

a. Are there any areas that may present a supervision problem?

b. Can students get onto the roof area?

c. Are there blind spots where students cannot be observed?

d. Are there places where trash can build up to present an eyesore?

e. Are there nooks, crevices, or indentions in the building that would allow undesirable hiding by people?

f. Are the restrooms free of problem areas and design features, such as low ceiling heights?

g. Are locker areas easily supervised? (Earthman, 1990).

The Design Review Team must also raise questions about other aspects of the building such as types of building materials used in the structure and especially wall finishes. This last is important because of heavy student usage that would generate maintenance problems later in the life of the building. In addition, the Design Review Team might want to raise questions about initial costs, maintenance costs, lifetime operating costs, energy conservation and other design features. All of these matters are within the purview of the Design Review Team.

Keeping the Project Within the Budget

With all building projects, a major problem that must be faced is keeping the scope of the project within the given budget. This is true for each building project completed by the school system. The original budget for the project was established at the time of approval of the capital improvement program. Each year the project is in the program, the cost estimates are projected to account for inflation. In this manner, the project costs are considered current. When the design of the project is started, presumably the budget is current and the architect can feel reasonably sure there are sufficient funds to complete the project.

During the design stage, the architect periodically prepares cost estimates for the school system to determine if the budget is sufficient for the project. The architect continues this process all through the design stage until the project is put out for bid. All of this is to ensure that the school system has enough funds to complete the project. In a time of steep inflation, reserve funds may have to be set aside to complete the project.

There are several points at which control over the project is mandated to ensure the funds will be available to complete work. The first point of control is in the development of the educational specifications. Tight control over the allocation of space to each program area is necessary to ensure that the scope of the project will not exceed the funds and at the same time sufficient space is given to allow a program to properly function. The person developing the educational specifications must keep the project within the space allocated by the budget and not allow unreasonable requests to expand the project beyond what is available.

The second point of control is during the design stage. Many times requests for more space seem reasonable, but in trying to accommodate a program the entire project is expanded to exceed appropriated funds. During the design stage, the educational specifications must be rigorously followed so that the scope of the building will not expand and thus exceed the available funds.

Another factor that impacts upon the total cost of the project is the materials that will be used in the building. The higher the quality of materials in the building, the higher the per-square-foot cost and subsequently the entire building project. The original capital improvement budget cost estimate should allow for high quality materials to be used in the building to reduce maintenance costs later in the life of the building. Changes in the quality of materials may have an adverse effect upon the total cost of the project.

When there are differences between cost estimates of the building at any stage and the budgeted amount, something has to be done to reconcile the difference. There are only two ways to accommodate a cost difference. Either more funds must be allocated to the project, or the project itself must be reduced in some fashion. When additional funds can be obtained from other projects or reserve funds, these can be applied. In some states, however, such fund re-allocation is not possible.

If the building is being constructed under a set-sum bond issue, there may not be any reserve funds. Most school systems even under a set-sum bond will establish a contingency fund of approximately 5 percent to cover such emergencies. When such financing is not possible, the scope of the project must be reduced.

There are two ways to reduce the scope of the project if more funding is not possible. One way is to reduce the size of the entire building either by reducing segments of the building or by reducing sizes of classrooms. In both instances, a less desirable building will result. The second way to reduce the scope of the project is to reduce the quality of materials that go into the building.

In reality, this latter method of reducing costs simply shifts costs to a later time in the life of the building. Reduced quality of material will undoubtedly increase the maintenance costs of the building over its lifetime, therefore, it should be avoided at all costs.

Uniform Building Codes

The design and construction of all public buildings is governed by the uniform building codes of the state. These codes are adopted to protect the health and safety of the occupants of the building. The codes govern the type and kinds of material used in the building, the application of the material, space allocations, sanitary provisions and other legal matters. Buildings must conform to these codes before a building permit is issued. Administering the uniform building code occurs on the local level because that is where the permit to construct the building is issued.

Architects and engineers must be particularly aware and knowledgeable about all codes that govern school design and construction. Local building inspectors review the plans for conformity to codes and, when such is the case, issue a permit. Members of the Design Review Team do not have to be as familiar with these codes as the design professionals, but they should know the source of the codes, how they are administered, and where they can obtain authoritative information about code conformity. In cases where there may be a doubt as to the conformity of any design, school personnel can obtain assistance from the state as an impartial party. The first inquiry for assistance should be made at the office of the state fire marshal. In some states, the department of education can assist the local school system in applying building codes to specific designs.

Steps of Approval

There are many approval steps in the design of a building. These can be both inside and outside the school system. There are both formal and informal approval steps. The most important formal approval of a design is at the schematic stage where the school board formally receives a presentation of the project and then approves the design for further development. Further approvals by the school board are not necessary, and in many instances would slow the architect's work. At the schematic stage, the building exterior is set and will not change; as a result, further approvals are redundant.

Informal approval steps occur at every design review meeting. At the end of each meeting, the documented approvals should be shared between architect and Design Review Team. This keeps the record straight and provides the architect with immediate feedback of decisions. These approval sessions continue throughout the design development stage of the project until the final working or contract documents are finished.

In some instances, local governmental offices or commissions may require approval of the project. It is not unusual for the local art commission to have approval supervision over public works projects. When this occurs, the architect or school staff person must apply for a presentation and seek approval at that time. The architect must know of and anticipate these regulations.

In many states, some office or department may require approval of the building project. This is especially true if the state provides any funding for capital expenditures. Each state has specific requirements for the approval process and the architect should become familiar with the requirements. The school staff should make sure the architect is cognizant of these requirements so that the project is not delayed unnecessarily.

Computer Assisted Design Development

The computer has become a great assistance in the design of buildings. All architects use a computer in their work of designing a building. This process is called computer-aided design development (CADD). Use of the computer provides the architect with a great deal of power and speed in designing a building (Brubaker 1998). The particular system that is used may require square footage limits, preset relationships, circulation requirements, and many other conditions determined by the architect. Using CADD, a series of drawings are developed for consideration by the architect and owner. These drawings can be reproduced on hard copy for further study.

Using CADD can save the architect considerable time in just drawing alone. The computer can produce in a very short period of time what would have taken a technician or architect several days to produce. In addition, changes to any design can be made almost instantaneously and the results evaluated on the spot. Several variations of a drawing can be considered within a short period of time to allow for comparison. Needless to say, the rapidity of this kind of design development permits greater options for the architect and owner. In addition to the capability of producing drawings at a high speed, the computer allows the architect to view the drawings from more than one dimension. Computers provide a three-dimensional display so that the architect can see through a design that is being developed. When designing a multi-story building, relationships between different sections of the building are difficult to determine on a one-plane drawing. With CADD, two floors of a building can be juxtaposed and viewed from different angles. In this manner, creative design relationships can be created that meet the requirements of the educational specifications.

Development of the contract documents, final drawings and technical specifications, can be completed with a higher degree of accuracy and speed with CADD. These documents are used in bidding the project and must reflect precisely the work to be done and the materials to be used in constructing the building. Cost estimates are also more readily available by using the computer (Brubaker, 1998).

Along with the benefit of faster design work by the architect, there are some cautions that must be observed. The normal design review meetings should not be changed in any manner because of the rapidity in producing architectural drawings, except to have the review sessions closer together. Sometimes when a process is accelerated, approval points may tend to be eliminated or reduced which would not be to the advantage of the school system. The increase in speed of obtaining design drawings from an architect should in no way eliminate the thoughtful and thorough review of each plan to insure fidelity to the educational specifications. ▩

chapter fourteen

Bidding the Construction Project

THE BIDDING PROCESS FOR A CONSTRUCTION PROJECT IN THE GOVERNMENTAL SECTOR is a complicated system of determining which firm or company will be able to complete the work at the best competitive price. This system of procurement is seen as a very equitable way for all qualified firms to have a chance at being selected to provide services and at the same time for the governmental agency to obtain work at the lowest possible price. It is definitely a fair and advantageous system for procuring goods and services for all concerned. Not to use a bidding system in procuring goods and services is to invite practices that are not in the best interest of the school system and may violate ethical and legal norms.

There are many misconceptions regarding the bidding process; therefore, anyone involved in the bidding process should be familiar with the legal requirements of both the state and local school system. Most states require the local school system to have some sort of procurement provision in the school board policies to govern the acquisition of goods and services. Whether or not the state mandates such a provision, the local school system should protect itself by establishing such procedures.

The school board policies regarding bidding procedures should address what goods and services are to be bid and the size of these projects or amounts. Usually some dollar figure is specified in these policies above which all projects must be publicly bid. The bidding procedure for items and projects below this set amount is usually handled differently, such as receiving telephone bids or some similar informal method. The procurement policies should also address advertising, opening, pricing, awarding, rejecting and withdrawing bids. In addition, the policies must have provisions for bonding and qualifying bidders.

Although most people generally assume all bids are sealed, such may not be the case. The policies should state which types of bids need to be sealed and which do not need to be sealed. Bids for small items usually do not need to be offered in a sealed container, bidding on a project which involves a great deal of money, such as construction proceeds, needs the formality of being offered in a sealed envelope.

A quick review of the school board policies will indicate if these areas are covered. If, by some chance, they are not, the school board should enact such policies before any bid is publicly tendered. Local school system personnel should also be very familiar with state legal provisions governing the bidding procedure that might impinge upon local policy so that there is no conflict.

Bidding Documents

In the final stages of the design process, the architect produces documents that are called the bidding documents or contract documents. These are a set of architectural drawings and technical specifications.

The set of architectural drawings contain at least four different sets of plans of the building to be constructed. The different sets follow the usual disciplines involved in the design process. There is one set dealing with the structural and mechanical design of the building, another set detailing all of the electrical service in the building, another containing the plumbing and drainage systems, and the final set describing the heating, ventilation, and air conditioning (HVAC) system.

These four sets of drawings are needed by the various engineering disciplines to determine the work to be done. There may be other sets of drawings depending upon the complexity of the building. For instance, there may be a separate set of drawings detailing the communication system in the building or alternative structures which might be bid separately. Additionally, there may be drawings for special areas in the structure such as a television studio, a stage area or a locker area.

In any event, this set or group of drawings is called working drawings, final drawings, or contract drawings, all describing the same thing. The architect is responsible for preparing and signing all drawings to be used by the school system in the bid process.

The architect is also responsible for preparing a document called the technical specifications, which describes all of the material to be used in the construction of the building and the amount that will be needed. This description is quite detailed. The size and quantity of nails, bricks, and wood, the mix of concrete, the slope of the roof, and the quality of workmanship in the building are all described very precisely. This document is needed by the contractor to determine the bid price to offer the school system. Accountants in the office of the contractor can determine the price of materials very accurately from this document.

The description of the building in this document also enables the estimator to determine the cost of the work force in the project. All of this forms the basis of the bid that is submitted. Of course, the competitive nature of the bidding process means the estimator for the contractor must be rather precise to enable the contractor to have a good chance of being awarded the bid. These documents then become the items upon which bids are prepared by contractors.

Pre-qualification of Bidders

A school system can request that potential bidders pre-qualify before they submit a bid on a construction project. This means that the school system desires firms to have certain qualifications before their bid is considered.

Although the surety bond is a way of pre-qualifying, in that the company has been appraised by a bonding company, usually pre-qualification means something more definitive. Pre-qualification can refer to any type of demand made by the school system. For instance, pre-qualification can refer to type and amount of experience, number and types of employees, financial security and even location of offices.

The City of Philadelphia developed a pre-qualification based upon the number of minority persons employed by the firm. Firms wishing to conduct business with the city had to have a certain percentage of employees of a minority race on the payroll before they could successfully bid on projects. Potential bidders had to submit a list of their employees with minorities identified with their sealed bid. In this manner, firms would qualify themselves prior to the bid opening. Firms, which could not qualify by having the proper number of minority employees, would not have their bid opened.

School systems may place pre-qualifications upon potential bidders so long as the pre-qualification has a relationship to the ability of the bidder to perform work. All firms submitting bids to federal, state and local governmental agencies, federal, state, and local, must agree before the bid to abide by the rules and regulations concerning affirmative action and equal employment opportunities. Agreement to the employment practices as derived from the Civil Rights Act of 1964 and subsequent revisions can be considered pre-qualification of potential bidders. Almost all bid advertisements now carry the stipulation that successful bidders must agree to these practices.

Procedure for Bidding

The method of conducting a bidding is rather simple and straightforward; however, it must be carried out in a manner that observes all legal requirements.

The first requirement is to publicly advertise the bid. The school system is responsible for placing a legal advertisement. This consists of placing an advertisement in the legal newspaper of the locality. Usually a newspaper located within the jurisdiction of the school system or one that at least serves the general population of the school system is chosen by the school board as the legal outlet for advertising bids.

The advertisement must state in quite precise terms all of the conditions relative to receiving bids. This includes when the bidding will take place, where materials for making a bid can be obtained, the deadline for when bids will be received, who to contact for more information and how a firm can be qualified. The advertisement must also specify how bidders should submit their pricing, such as lump sum, cost plus per centrum, or fee basis. All three pricing arrangements are legal in school systems, but the method to be used must be stated in both the legal document, which is the technical specifications, and the advertisement.

The school board policies governing the procurement of goods and services must be observed in this advertisement in as much as it is a legal notification of action by the school board. Figure 14.1 shows a typical newspaper advertisement that a school system would place. Such an advertisement must be run in the newspaper for a certain number of days before the deadline for receiving bids.

Advertisement of the bid offer is not limited to the legal outlet of the school board. Advertisement of the bid is also made in various trade journals. These outlets may be architectural and construction industry journals such as F.W. Dodge and Cost Management Data Group publications. These publications notify their readership of opportunities for bidding on projects that may not be advertised in their local paper.

In small school systems located in rural or isolated areas, advertising in more widely circulated newspapers than the local legal newspaper is very likely. Legal requirements demand advertising in the official newspaper, but good administrative practices demand as wide a distribution of the advertisement as is possible to obtain a good number of bidders. In some circumstances, the architect may actually contact firms to encourage them to submit a bid. This may stimulate competition resulting in better bids for the school system.

When the deadline for submitting bids arrives, the school system must conduct a public opening of all bids. This is done at the time and place stipulated in the bid advertisement. Usually representatives of the purchasing department of the school system conduct the meeting and open the bids. Representatives of firms that have submitted bids usually attend.

As each bid is open, the submitted price is announced and put on a board for all to see. When all bids have been opened, the school system personnel must prepare a recommendation to the school board.

The architect attends this meeting and advises the school personnel on the adequacy of the bids. This advice may be a recommendation for action on any and all bids, such as which to accept or reject. When the bid price is over the budgeted amount, the architect may advise the school personnel on ways to reduce the project to come within the budgeted amount or to negotiate with the lowest bidder to reduce the bid price. The school system personnel must, of course, make the final recommendation to the school board, but the architect has direct input into that action.

The final recommendation by the school system staff is presented at an official school board meeting. That body then considers the staff recommendation and takes appropriate action. Such action may be to vote to enter into a contract or to reject any and all bids.

Lowest Responsible and Responsive Bidder

Almost all procurement provisions of public governmental bodies stipulate that the lowest responsible and responsive bidder be awarded the contract. This is a very common interpretation of the result of competitive bidding. Defining the lowest bidder is a very easy task that can be decided simply by looking at the offered prices. Defining the most responsible and responsive bidder is a little more difficult.

Responsiveness can generally be determined if the bidder submits a competitive bid, at least a bid that could be considered competitive with other bids. Responsiveness can also be defined as submitting a bid that meets the needs of the school system in the scope of the work and the established time line. The important point is that the firm can be considered a viable company to do the work.

Responsible bidder may be more difficult to define in that it involves subjective judgment. A responsible bidder is a firm that can obtain the necessary bonding such as the surety bond and subsequent performance bond. The quality of being responsible may also hinge on previous experience with either the school system or another public body. If the firm has a good history of completing proj-

Figure 14.1
Bid Advertisement

ADVERTISEMENT

The Fairfield School Board will receive sealed Bids for a new Kings Mill Elementary School, Kings Mill, Virginia, State Project 11 -25A. One story, bearing wall, brick exterior, Elementary School, approximate area 45,850 sq. ft. includes associated sitework, roads, grading, paving, billfolds, etc. Kitchen equipment is in the Construction Contract. An early sitework package has been awarded and work is under way.

Location: Kings Mill, Virginia All Bids must be on a lump sum basis, including specified allowances. Bids will be received until 2:00 p.m. local prevailing time, July 12, 2000, at Fairfield County School Board Room, 108 Main Street. All interested parties are invited to attend. Bids will be opened publicly and read aloud. Bidding Documents (Drawings and Project Manuals) may be obtained or examined at the Architect's Office:

Smith and Smith, Inc., 86 Prospect Avenue, Fairfield, VA 24011. Other locations where Bidding Documents may be examined are: Dodge Plan Rooms at: Roanoke, VA; Richmond, VA; Dodge Scan.

1. One set of Bidding Documents consists of one Project Manual, and a complete set of Drawings, plus all Addenda issued prior to receipt of Bids. Addenda will automatically be issued to all parties on record of receiving Bidding Documents.

2. Bidding Documents deposit will be $100 per set. The number of sets available with full deposit refund shall be limited to two sets for General Contract Bidders and one set for mechanical and electrical subcontract bidders. Additional

sets and sets to other interested parties are available with a 50% deposit refund.

3. Deposits will be refunded as described above for complete sets of documents returned in good condition within ten days after Bid opening.

A pre-bid conference will be held at the construction site on Tuesday, June 28, 1988, at 2:00 PM.

Each Prime Contract Bidder must deposit, with his Bid, security in the form of a Bid Bond, as described in the Instructions to Bidders, Withdrawal of bids due to error must conform to the provisions of Section 1 1-54A(a) of the Code of Virginia. The successful Prime Contract Bidder will be required to furnish and pay for satisfactory Performance and Payment Bonds as described in the Instructions to Bidders.

The attention of each Bidder is directed to Title 54 of Chapter 7, Code of Virginia, pertaining to registration. All Bids shall remain valid for a period of 60 days after the scheduled closing time for receipt of Bids. Bid Bonds will be forfeited for Bids withdrawn prior to the end of this period. The Owner intends to award a single lump sum contract to the lowest responsible Bidder meeting the requirements of the Instructions to Bidders and this Advertisement for Bids providing the Bid amount falls within the amount of funds available. If lowest bid exceeds available funds, the Owner may enter into negotiations with the lowest responsible bidder to lower the bid within the available funds, using the following procedure.

1. The Owner and Architect shall notify the first lowest responsible bidder, within 10 days following the bids opening, that negotiations will be entered

into. An itemized price and quantity breakdown of the bid shall be furnished to the Owner and Architect by the bidder within 10 days.

2. The Owner and Architect shall prepare a revised scope of work that will be given to the first lowest responsible bidder for revision of his bid.

3. It the first lowest bidder's revised bid is within the available funds, a contract will be awarded.

4. If the first lowest bidder's revised bid is not within the available funds, negotiations will be entered into with the second lowest responsible bidder using the same procedures outlined above.

5. If the second lowest bidder's revised bid is not within available funds, negotiations may be continued with each subsequent lowest bidder until a satisfactory bid is obtained.

Bidders and subcontractors of this work will be required to comply with the provisions of Executive Orders 11246 and 11375, which prohibit discrimination in employment regarding race, creed, color, sex or national origin. Bidders must certify that they do not and will not maintain or provide for their employees any facilities that are segregated on the basis of race, color, creed or national origin. The requirements for Bidders and Contractors under these Executive Orders are explained in the Specifications. The Owner reserves the right to reject any or all bids and to award Contract to other than the lowest Bidder, if, in his opinion, such action would ensure better performance and a higher level of function, quality and value.

ects on time and to the satisfaction of the owner, this is a good surrogate for that quality and can be judged accordingly. This is especially true if the previous employer is the school system.

Conversely, a history of poor performance might be a good indicator of non-responsible action. School systems can disqualify the lowest bidder if, in the judgment of the school staff and school board, previous performance was not adequate. There can be a great deal of latitude on the part of the school system in interpreting both responsible and responsive bidder, but it usually centers around financial stability and previous performance of the company in question.

Rejection of Bids

One common misconception is that the school board may not reject the lowest bidder. This is not true for schools systems, or any governmental unit. School boards may reject any and all bids depending upon the circumstances. If all bids are above the budgeted amount, the school board may reject all bids, even the lowest bid. If the school board does not identify a firm as responsible and responsive even if it is the lowest bidder, the offer can be rejected.

When all of the bids are above the budget, the school system is obviously placed in the position of rejecting bids. Following this action, the school planners and architect need to downsize the project or find additional funding. Most often, the latter alternative is not available and the project must be reduced. This is regrettable because reductions made at this time often result in severe distortions of parts of the building or loss of space that is needed for the educational program. Reductions that take place at this point in time are desperation moves that often do not have the benefit of thoughtful examination. They will hurt the operation of the plant for a good many years in the future.

If a reduction in the scope of the project has to take place at the bid stage, there may have to be a re-design. Depending upon the reason the project came in above the budget, this re-design may incur additional design fees. If, however, the project was excessive because of architectural work, these fees would not be assessed against the school system. Most often projects draw bids over budget because of economic and inflationary factors, rather than anything the school staff or architect did or did not do. If the project adheres to the boundaries of square footage and cost of materials specified, excessive reductions at this stage usually do not have to be made.

During the design stage, the architect periodically estimates the cost of the project by applying the latest square foot costs to the school being designed. In this manner, the architect keeps the school system informed of the anticipated project cost. Once the budget is set for that project, it is incumbent upon the architect to keep the design within that price range.

Several things impinge upon that action. First the programming of the project should be within the amount of funding set in the Capital Improvement Budget. The school staff is responsible for determining the total square feet of space in the building on which the square foot cost is based. In other words, the building is budgeted for a certain amount based on the number of square feet in the building times the square foot costs for that space. Square foot costs are based on market conditions. If these factors are controlled, then the chance of the building costing above the budget are reduced greatly. But the quality of materials specified by the architect should also fit the budget.

If all of these are controlled, the building should fit within the budget. If any of these factors is not studiously controlled, the building may draw bids above the budgeted amount and force the school board and architect to take drastic action to reduce the cost of the project.

Bidding Furniture and Equipment

A new building or other major project will need desks, chairs, moveable storage cabinets, physical education equipment, audio visual equipment and similar items. This is called loose furniture and equipment and is not considered a part of the building structure. Loose furniture and equipment are funded separately from construction and, in most cases, bid separately from the building.

The task of writing specifications for the capital project usually falls to the school system staff. In medium and large school systems, there is an office or person responsible for writing specifications for all the new furniture and equipment that will be used in the building. In these cases, the school system may also conduct the bidding procedure for these items.

In small school systems, the architect may be employed to write the specifications and include these items in the contract for the design of the building. This means an added fee to the architect, sometimes as much as five percent of the bid price of the furniture and equipment. Although this may seem like a small charge for this type of work, the school system could do the task itself at a savings to the school board. Of course, this task cannot be added to the daily tasks a person is already doing. A staff member must be released from current responsibilities. Even then, savings can accrue to the school system by taking responsibility for writing the specifications.

Bonding

When a contracting firm submits a bid to the school system, a good faith bond must also be submitted. This bond is called a surety bond because it guarantees that the bid is presented in good faith and is backed by a willingness to accept a contract if the bid is accepted. This surety bond tells the school system the bid price is a bona fide offer to do the work specified in the advertisement. The surety bond will serve to indemnify the school system in the unlikely case the successful contractor does not carry through to signing a contact to complete the work. If this happened, the bond amount would be paid by the bonding company to the school system. The surety bond is usually five to ten percent of the total bid price and the precise amount is stipulated in the bid advertisement. A bonding or insurance company issues the surety bond submitted by the contractor following an evaluation of the credit worthiness of the company.

Once a construction firm is offered a contract by the school system and signs the document, the surety bond is returned. However, the successful bidder must produce, at the time of signing, a performance bond payable to the school system. The performance bond is equal to 100 percent of the contract price and guarantees the contractor will complete the work identified in the contract.

Where the surety bond guarantees the earnestness of the bid, the performance bond guarantees the work will be completed by the contractor, This is a big difference in the relationship between bidder and school system and contractor and school system. In the former, the bidder indicates that the price is firm and the company stands behind the bid. The performance bond guarantees completion of work and will indemnify the school system in case the work is not completed.

Caution must be exercised in interpreting what the performance bond will do. Some people might think the price of the construction will be paid to the school system if the contractor fails to complete the work. This is not exactly correct. The performance bond will indemnify the school system only to the extent of losses sustained in not getting the work completed because of failure of the contractor or in the event of demise of the company. The performance bond serves as a safety net for the school system only to the extent of losses.

The Contract

The contract signed by the successful bidder and the school board is a standard legal document that stipulates the work to be done. The contract makes direct reference to the contract documents that are the set of architectural drawings and technical specifications. In essence, the contract states that the contractor will build the facility detailed in these documents adhering to the quality and quantity specified in the documents.

Usually the school system's legal counsel prepares the contract in accordance with state law. Appendix C contains a sample copy of an agreement between a contractor and school board. But, there are general conditions that are in all contracts dealing with the construction of a building. These conditions usually state that the contract documents consist of the agreement, the conditions of the contract, the drawings, specifications and all addenda issued prior to and all modifications issued after execution of the agreement. Specific sections in the agreement deal with the scope of the work, time of commencement and substantial completion, final payment, miscellaneous provisions, contract sum and progress payments. Any special conditions that require additional work on the part of the contractor or that the contractor must be aware of are listed in the contract. ▪

chapter fifteen

Managing the Construction Phase

AFTER THE SUCCESSFUL BIDDER IS IDENTIFIED AND THE SCHOOL BOARD VOTES TO ACCEPT the bid, a contract is executed with the winning firm to complete the building project. At this point, the school board returns the surety bond of not only the successful bidder but also of the other firms that submitted bids. The successful bidder then must deposit a performance bond with the school board for 100 percent of the agreed upon construction price. In addition, the firm must also give the school board a payment bond which guarantees all payments to workers, suppliers and vendors so that liens cannot be placed against the completed building. Following this, the contractor mobilizes the work force and proceeds with the construction, usually within ten days. All necessary building permits, applications for utilities on the site, and any easements are obtained before construction begins.

Supervising the Project

A construction project is a very expensive effort by the school system. In some cases a new school building is the largest expenditure of funds a school makes over a short period of time. As such, supervising the expenditure of public funds is an important responsibility of the school system. Some school boards do not realize the importance of direct oversight in a construction project. The tremendous amount of public funds involved in such a project and the responsibility for supervising all expenditure of funds should certainly demand close supervision of all construction projects.

Every contract with an architect has a clause stipulating that the firm will provide some site supervision by the clerk-of-the-works. Careful reading of the clause, however, will reveal that the amount of supervision to be provided is minimal. The supervision of a construction project by an architectural firm is not intended to be a continuous process. The contract will probably call for only periodic supervision visits that could be once every week or once a month. Generally, the actual number of visits the architectural firm employees will make, and their frequency, is not stated. School boards should not, under any circumstances, rely solely upon the visits of the architectural firm to provide the necessary supervision the district should be giving to the project.

The difference in perception between the school board and the architectural firm on the amount of supervision the architect should give a construction project differs greatly and is thus an area of constant dispute. Commonly, the school board thinks the architectural firm representative will provide daily supervision of the construction project. The school board does not realize the architectural clerk-of-the-works has many projects that require supervision simultaneously; therefore, the project of the school board must wait supervision until time is available, just as all other projects do.

Daily supervision is not only beyond the responsibility of the architect, it is beyond its scope. Architectural supervision is more to provide the architectural firm with data on the progress of the project, rather than providing the school board with up-to-date progress reports. If the school board wishes the architectural firm to provide daily supervision, or supervision above what is normally given through the contract, the architectural firm will charge a fee in addition to the fee charged the school board to design the building. Purchasing such supervision is costly because overhead must be factored into the overall supervision fee charged the school board.

The school board is better advised to provide its own daily supervision for every construction project by employing someone to be the construction supervisor of the project. This way, the school board has an employee at the site to provide supervision of the project at all times. This school board employee should be charged with keeping the project on schedule and within the budget, and with ensuring good quality workmanship. The supervision provided by this employee should be in addition to the supervision by the architectural firm.

The school board can easily recoup the expense of this employee if the project is kept to schedule or through proper administration of change orders necessitated by the project. The importance of having a school system employee on the site at all times can not be over emphasized because judicious administration and prudent supervision of this very expensive project guarantees a quality product within available resources.

The person employed as the construction supervisor should be very knowledgeable about all phases of the construction industry and have experience in the field. The person should be able to discern quality workmanship and be able to show leadership in a group situation to protect the investment of the school board. A person with these qualities is not difficult to find even in a very small community.

In a large school system, the construction supervisor should report directly to the director of architectural and construction services, or, in smaller districts, to the person who is leading the school planning effort. In extremely small school systems, this may mean that the construction supervisor reports directly to the assistant superintendent for business or even to the superintendent of schools. Regardless of whom the construction supervisor reports to, there should be written monthly (or bi-monthly) reports to the school board on the construction project's progress. The school administration may require other reporting times when the construction supervisor should submit reports.

As the representative of the school board, the construction supervisor usually conducts weekly job site meetings with representatives of the architectural firm and the contractor to determine the project's progress. This is when time schedule problems are settled. Questions regarding management of time by the contractor, types of materials used or substituted, quality of workmanship and any other items may come up at these weekly meetings. Weekly meetings help keep a project on schedule more than infrequent meetings. Regularly scheduled meetings also allow the construction supervisor to anticipate problems that could arise from specific work or as the contractor begins different phases of the building's construction. By anticipating such problems, many can be solved before they occur. A complete job description for the construction supervisor is contained in Appendix G. Regardless of any other service provided by an outside firm, the school system should always employ a construction supervisor to guarantee that the interests of the school system are being protected.

Construction Management

Construction management services are offered by commercial firms to assist the school system in project delivery using modern management techniques. Construction Management is defined by the industry as a comprehensive array of services spanning all phases of the design and construction process. The Construction Manager may be a member of the school system staff or be selected on the basis of professional qualifications and experience from among firms and consultants offering services. Construction Management services are compensated based on a negotiated fee for the scope of services rendered.

There are two basic contractual formats for delivering Construction Management services from which all others are derived. One format is termed CM-Agency format. This arrangement is where the CM firm provides services to the school system who holds the construction contracts for the work. The other format is called CM-GMP where the firm provides services to the owner and prior to commencement of construction guarantees the price of the project. Under this arrangement, the Construction Management firm generally holds the construction contracts and assumes the risks and obligations of a general contractor.

Although this is a standard definition, there are many variations depending upon the firm and the situation. Construction management may be simply overseeing the construction phase similar to what the school system's employee, the Construction Supervisor, would do. Construction management may also mean supervising and providing all services to the school system from the beginning of the design stage until the school building is occupied. Some firms even advertise they have the capacity to write educational specifications.

Construction management firms can provide supervision of many of the planning, designing and supervising functions of a capital improvement project. At the same time, the firm can provide a certain amount of continuity over a large segment of the school system's planning process. While providing that service, there are some that feel that construction management duplicates services the school system is or should be providing already. In addition, purchasing such services from an outside commercial firm might tend to divorce the planning process from the school staff and their planning process, thus becoming something that others do for the school system. Needless to say, there is plenty written about the separation of planning efforts within the school system.

In spite of this fact, construction management firms contend that they work in conjunction with the school system efforts. In fact, most contracts ensure the independence of the planning and execution of the design and construction of the school building from the school staff.

There might be other problems that need to be addressed when using a construction management firm to design and construct a school. These involve:

- Legal constraints and requirements of the bid process
- Lack of continuing staff involvement in all phases of design and construction

- Design changes made but not documented in final drawings
- Additional supervision costs

State law requires every school system to publicly ask for sealed bids for major construction projects. Construction management might be construed, by some educators, as a way of avoiding that process because the management firm conducts the bidding effort. Depending on the locale, it may not be legal to do this. If a school system wants to use a commercial firm for construction management, the school board should ask the state legal counsel for an opinion on the legality of the process.

During both the design and construction processes, many decisions are made. Unless the school staff is directly involved in these decisions, the resulting building may not be what was wanted, or needed. The propensity of this occurring is probably greater under a construction management contract than if the school system directly supervises the project. Changes in the building are inherent in construction, and since design often proceeds simultaneously with construction, plan review is greatly complicated. This may be untenable for the school staff who need to review plans.

Most school systems have neither the experience nor the staff needed to make the technical decisions to be resolved each day as the owner. Some educators feel the construction manager is, in essence, a general contractor relieved of all payment and performance bonded responsibilities. Some school systems have found that to preserve the time schedule, design decisions were made by the construction manager without involving the school system staff. This results in changed drawings, sometimes without proper documentation. When this happens, the school system could easily end up with drawings that are not necessarily accurate. If a construction management firm is used, school systems should stipulate in the contract that "as-built" drawings be provided by the Construction Management firm at the conclusion of the project.

Last, the school system must employ someone to provide an interface with the construction management firm. If this person is in addition to the regular staff, the annual salary of this person is an added cost to the school system and must be averaged into the total cost for construction management. Some school systems find they cannot save by employing a commercial firm to perform construction management, when they can provide such supervision and management themselves by employing another staff member. If a construction management firm is employed for any kind of services, the school system should also provide for construction site supervision by a school board employee to guarantee the success of the project.

As with all types and kinds of professional services, it is suggested that the school system make its first task the precise definition of what level of service is needed. The school system should decide, after careful examination, what services are needed and the cost of these services. Following that, a satisfactory contract can be executed.

Managing Change Orders

Even with the best developed architectural plans, changes in the project are inevitable. Such changes may occur during the construction phase, after the contract has been signed. For example, site conditions such as hidden rock may mandate changes in the design, or certain materials are not available and different materials must be used. When changes are requested and processed, they are called change orders, which are simply orders to change the contract between the school board and the contractor. When change orders are approved, the contract is modified.

Change orders may be initiated in two ways: from the owner (which is the school board) or the contractor. When the school board originates a change, it is usually the result of omissions from either the educational specifications or the architectural drawings. Change orders originating with the contractor are usually the result of certain field conditions such as difficulty with the site or change in materials.

Once the request is identified, it passes to the architect to determine what modifications, if any, need to be made to the drawings given to the contractor. Once the contractor receives the request, it is priced and forwarded to the construction supervisor. After the construction supervisor reviews it, the order is forwarded to the proper superior and then to the school board for final approval.

Considerable negotiations go on about the change order and its cost before it arrives at the school board meeting. It is during this process that the construction supervisor protects the interest of the school system in the process. Following approval, the contractor is officially notified to complete the work.

Change orders require either the crediting or debiting of funds for the extra work involved. If something is deleted from the project, a credit is due to the school board from the contractor and the contract amount is reduced. If something is added, the contract cost is increased.

The work and materials called for in the change order are not publicly bid because the hired contractor is the firm that is doing the work and the change is in the contract in effect. Because the change order is not publicly bid, prices are often higher than on the open market. Thus, the fewer the change orders, the better it is for the school board.

A certain number of change orders are always needed, and some should be expected in the normal course of the project. If the number of change orders is excessive, the total price of the project may exceed the budget. Some school boards establish a contingency fund in the capital improvement budget to handle such cases.

Excessive change orders may indicate that the architectural drawings were not in sufficient detail or that the materials requested were not readily available. In either case, these problems are the responsibility of the architect. Excessive requests by school staff may mean that the educational specifications were not specific enough. In any event, the school staff should analyze the origin and reason for change orders and seek to remedy the situation for the next project. The number of change orders in a project may well be a criterion in determining the employment of an architect or contractor for another project.

School Board/Contractor Relationships

There are many types and kinds of contractual relationships in which the school board and contractor can engage when a building is to be constructed. The usual method of securing construction services is to publicly bid a project and then sign a contract with one contractor to complete the work. There are variations in this method that school boards and administrators should know.

Figure 15.1
Continuum of Contract Types Available to School Boards

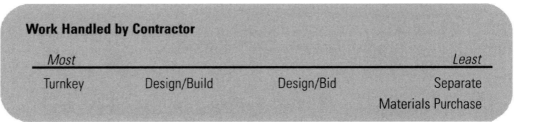

Work Handled by Contractor

Most			*Least*
Turnkey	Design/Build	Design/Bid	Separate Materials Purchase

All contractual relations between a school system and commercial firms are governed by state law and local policies. This often limits the type of relationships that school boards can legally enter. For example, some states mandate four separate contracts be entered into for the different systems of a public building; one for the structure; one for the electrical system; one for the plumbing and sewer system; and one for the heating, ventilating, and air conditioning (HVAC) system. A single contract covering all construction disciplines is prohibited. In other states, a district may employ a prime contractor that then subcontracts electric, plumbing/sewer, and HVAC systems. Under this arrangement, the prime contractor may supply the work on the structure of the building and coordination of the other three subcontractors.

Contract Options

There are four different contractual relationships that can be considered by the school board. Figure 15.1 shows the contract type and what the contractor is expected to do under the contract.

Turnkey—In the turnkey contract, the contractor does everything. The contractor writes the educational specifications, designs the building, constructs it and equips it and after this gives the key to the owner. For office and apartment buildings, this might work out very nicely. For educational facilities where the educator is the one who writes the program for the building, this is not a very judicious way to go about building a school.

Separate Materials Purchase—On the other end of the scale is the contract where separate material and services are purchased under a series of contracts to different firms. The four-contract provision above would fit into this contractual relationship. The school system would have to provide for the coordination of the project. Many school systems operate under this method of procurement of goods and services.

Between these extremes are two other methods of securing services:

Design/Bid Method—The design/bid contract is where the school board employs a separate company to do the design work and then publicly bids the project with a different company securing that contract.

Design/Build Method—In the design/build contract the school board enters into a contract with one company to provide both design and construction services. Under this contractual relationship, public bidding is not possible, so most school systems are prohibited by law from using this method. There is some possible danger, beyond the legal question, and a school system is cautioned regarding this type of contract.

Design decisions must be reviewed by the school system staff regardless of the method used to contract for construction services. The design review process can not be hurried or shortened without compromises that would not be beneficial to the educational program. Sometimes, in an effort to get the project under construction, the architects from the firm contracted to design/build the school will make design decisions without school system input. This is not a good situation for the school system. Unless adequate time safeguards are built into the contract with the design/build firm, there is a danger of short circuiting the review process. This and the requirement for public bidding prevents many school systems from using this method of contracting.

Contract Payment Options

The contract payment continuum (Figure 15.2) shows the different methods of making payment to a contractor.

Bid Fixed Price—This is the most common method a school system may use. A contractor makes a bid to complete the project, submitting one price. If this bid is accepted, the contractor is paid that amount over the course of the project. Some negotiating for price adjustments may occur when exceptional situations arise, such as rapid increases in prices of lumber or other building materials, but this is not expected over the life of the contract and the school system can hold to the original price.

Negotiated Fixed Price—There are some circumstances where it might be beneficial to the school system to negotiate with possible contractors for a set price. This is called competitive negotiations, but the final price is fixed for the life of the contract.

Figure 15.2
Continuum of Contracts Payment Methods Available to School Boards

Firmness of Price			
Most			*Least*
Bid	Negotiated Fixed Price	Target Price	Cost Plus Payment

Target Price—A contractor sets a target price that the school system will pay. The contractor tries to meet that target using whatever methods possible to keep the final price within a range. This method is very seldom used by school systems.

Cost Plus Payment—The contractor charges the school system for the cost of the materials and labor that go into the building plus a certain percentage for profit and overhead. This method is seldom used by school systems, but when it is used, it is when public bidding is not demanded.

The last two methods of contract payment or fixing the price of the contract can be completed under a bidding arrangement. Potential contractors can submit a bid on each one with the school system selecting the one it feels is the best and lowest and award a contract. In some states, these may not be legal arrangements for public school systems. Legal opinion should be secured to determine if these are feasible.

Acceptance of the Building

When the school building is substantially complete, the builder notifies the school board in writing that the structure is completed and ready for occupancy. Upon receipt of this notice, the school board meets at the new building to complete an inspection tour. The school staff involved in this project, the architect, and representatives of the contracting firm officially tour the building to determine if the building is indeed substantially complete.

Upon finding the building substantially complete, the school board passes a resolution accepting the building. This is an important step for both the school board and the contractor because the liability for the building is then assumed by the school board, and the contractor is relieved of liability. In addition, the utilities and associated costs are transferred to the school board. The building is then officially added to the inventory of the school system and becomes the official responsibility of the school board.

Even though the school board has accepted the building as being substantially complete, many small items are undoubtedly missing, need repair or completion. All of these items are put on a list to complete called a punch list. The punch list is an official listing of the items that need to be finished before the building is complete. These items may be as insignificant as a missing switch plate or light bulb or a major item such as air conditioning machinery. Nevertheless, the school board will permit the staff and students to occupy the new structure and use it accordingly.

The contractor usually has a year from the date of acceptance of the building to complete the items on the punch list. School boards usually withhold a small portion of the contract to ensure all the items are finished. When all of the items on the punch list are completed to the satisfaction of the school board and the architect, the school board makes the final payment to the contractor and the building is considered complete. ▨

chapter**sixteen**

Orientation and Evaluation

FOLLOWING THE ACCEPTANCE OF THE BUILDING BY THE SCHOOL BOARD, THE NEW staff and administration need to be oriented to the structure. Even if staff members were involved in the planning the building, they need to be oriented as to how the building will work. They will want to find out how the architect interpreted their programming needs and how this is reflected in design features.

No matter how well designed, the success of the building depends to a great extent upon the perceptions of the teaching staff. If the architect has captured in brick and mortar the words used to describe the building features that are needed, the staff will be able to conduct the type of program desired. The architect may not have designed a specific feature the way some of the staff perceived it, but if the feature allows the staff to do the job, the building will not impede their work.

Thus, the specific features and their operation need to be identified and explained during the orientation. The specific purpose of the orientation process are:

- For the staff to become familiar with the building and how to use it to facilitate the educational program,
- For students to find their way around the building and the specific features they will use in learning,
- For the custodial staff to become familiar with all of the systems of the building and how to operate them efficiently, and
- For the community to recognize and appreciate the building as a resource that can be used by all residents.

An office or person within the school system should be placed in charge of the orientation for each new school building or major construction project. There should be a broad base of involvement by all school system departments. In addition, the committee that plans the orientation should include a representative from the office of the architect, teaching staff and the principal of the building. In some school systems, the principal of the new facility is the person placed in charge. In other settings, a person in the central administration heads the planning. The building principal should most certainly have a strong role in the planning. Most of the orientation activities need to be completed before the entire student body occupies the building.

Roles in the Orientation Process

Even with just one building orientation, many roles must be fulfilled. Roles people play in an orientation include:

School Board
1. Makes all policy decisions regarding the project;
2. Approves the people involved;
3. Determines and approves how much staff time will be freed for the orientation program;
4. Authorizes reports;
5. Decides the name of the building;
6. Decides whether signs are in order and what they should contain;
7. Establishes the wording of dedication plaques and programs;
8. Accepts the building on behalf of their constituents, and says the official words of thanks to those who participated;
9. Approves expenses associated with the orientation program.

Administrator
1. Helps get people involved;
2. Sets up the communication system;
3. Designates or recommends the person placed in charge of the orientation;
4. Assists and arranges for continuing reporting;
5. Arranges ways in which those unique needs discovered through the use of the building can be met.

Teachers
1. Help to orient others;
2. Visit the building under construction;

3. Play an important role in the communication process as they receive and transmit information;
4. Actively participate in the tasks of occupancy;
5. Stay alert to new needs that may arise as the building is used.

Students
1. Help explain the building and the program features to parents;
2. Help write reports of what is going on;
3. Aid the communications process by taking questions to the authorities and carrying the replies back;
4. Help prepare simple floor plan maps and instructions;
5. Serve as tour guides of the building.

The Architect
1. Explains certain technical aspects of the construction to gain acceptance of certain features of the building;
2. Plays a vital role during the occupancy of the building.

The Public
1. Attends meetings; asks questions; gives opinions;
2. Assists with the public dedication program

The form the orientation takes varies considerably, but the architect should have an opportunity to explain the building as designed. The architect will need drawings of the building to point out specific features and answer the questions that usually arise about the circulation patterns of both students and materials. Safety features need to be discussed with both the staff and the students. These features can be explained by the architect and engineering staff. The communication system of the building is usually complex enough to require explanation by the architect.

The above presentation and question period should take place at the first general meeting of the faculty and staff. This should be the kick-off activity of this group's orientation. Usually the principal or person who is in charge of the orientation conducts the meeting and makes the necessary introductions to the faculty and staff. The superintendent might also wish to be present and speak to the group. Time should be left during the meeting for the architect to thoroughly explain the building and answer all questions.

After the general meeting, the architect should lead the staff on a tour of the entire building, pointing out selected design features. The tour should also include the outdoor spaces devoted to the school program. All unique features both inside and outside should be pointed out and explained. This tour also provides the staff with an opportunity to ask questions about features when the architect or engineer is available. By the end of the tour, the staff should have a good knowledge of the extent of the building and features in all parts of the structure.

These activities should enable the staff to conduct an orientation for the student body. Students will need to know circulation patterns and where certain sections of the building are located, such as the gym, cafeteria, library, and office. The teaching staff will have to explain the safety features of the building and assist the students in the first few fire and evacuation drills. There will be many orientation sessions for the students during the first few weeks of occupancy. Some orientation activities may well extend through the first year. Of course, incoming students will have to be oriented in a similar fashion. In succeeding years, the orientation for new students may become a responsibility of the student organization.

Community Orientation

The completion of the building is probably well known throughout the community, but the orientation of the community is a very important part of the entire orientation process. After the building is in operation and the staff has become fairly familiar with its features, a public orientation should be held.

This should be an open meeting with all individuals in the community invited. This invitation should include people who do not have children in the school as well as students' parents. An invitation to attend should be communicated in every way possible such as through radio, television, and the newspapers. Students can also deliver invitations to those who do not have direct contact with the school.

This event should be a large community celebration of the completion of a distinctive community resource. It should be advertised as a special event in the life of the community, regardless of the grade level of the school building. This event should also commemorate closure to a process of planning in which the entire community and school staff participated. Even if a person or segment of the community did not participate in the planning, this closure should be recognized.

The community orientation should be coupled with the formal dedication of the building and symbolic transfer of the keys of the building to the principal and a community representative. The dedication should not be a religious ceremony, but a public gathering where the school board dedicates the building to the community for its use. This symbolic gesture, along with the transfer of the keys, tells the community the building belongs to them, not only to the school system. Students should participate in the ceremony in a number of ways. Groups of students can sing songs, read poetry or other appropriate selections, play instruments, dance, or do other performances in celebration of the event.

Following this formal activity, the people attending should be taken on a building tour. Students, in particular, should assist in this activity, for by doing so, they gain pride in the building and enhance their feeling of ownership. Printed material such as programs, floor plans, fire escape routes, history of the school, and specifications of the building are usually made available during this event.

Post-Occupancy Evaluation

Once the building is completed and occupied, it is time to evaluate the outcome of the entire planning effort. It is easy to overlook this evaluation because the building is occupied and working well. It must be remembered that some information can be obtained only at certain times. Post-occupancy evaluation is one such time where certain data is needed and can be obtained in only a short period of time. The building will stand for many years and can be evaluated at anytime, but people tend to forget the process that was used to plan the building.

Two things should be evaluated at the completion of a school building planning effort: the process that was used to plan the building; and the product of the planning process, the building itself.

Product Evaluation

The product of the planning effort is the physical structure that was completed. The evaluation of the product covers the adequacy of the building for the type of program to be carried on, how the building operates, the cost of the building, and whether or not the school system acquired what it needs at the best price.

The cost of the facility can be determined in several ways with differing results, depending upon the measurement used. Typical measurements such as square foot rates, cost per square foot of space, costs per pupil, square feet of space per pupil, construction time, number and cost of change orders, cost/benefit ratios, and even life-cycle costing are used in determining the cost of buildings. These are all very important cost comparisons when evaluating the building. Historical comparison between projects also produces excellent results. Comparing costs between school systems is rather difficult and limited because the quality of material used in the various buildings is never exactly known or specified.

All of these measurements will assist in making decisions on other projects, but the evaluation of the product should not be limited to cost comparisons.

The finished product should be evaluated using the educational specifications written for the project. The person who guided the program planning effort and wrote the educational specifications should do this evaluation. This is not an easy task and, if done properly, is time consuming. The evaluator should go through each room and space in the building and check off the items contained in the specifications to determine if the school system got what it needed. The evaluator should also look at relationships of the various parts of the building to one another to see if what was asked in the educational specifications was observed. In this way, the educational specifications serves as a building appraisal instrument.

Through this evaluation process, the school system can determine how effective the architect was in interpreting the educational specifications and also how successful the design review team was in monitoring the architect's design.

The users of the facility should also be included in the data gathering effort for they have an important contribution to make regarding how well the facility works. Through interviews, successful design features in the building can be identified, as well as less successful ones. What one wants to find out here is how well the building is serving the people who are using it.

Interviews or locally developed survey instruments can be developed for this purpose. An interview protocol can be developed to elicit the standardized information desired. Data obtained through this exercise should be used in future educational specifications developed for similar capital projects. Some of the data may well serve to correct deficiencies in the new building through the capital improvement program.

Process Evaluation

The effort expended in planning a building is sufficiently important to be evaluated. The school staff and community representatives expend considerable time and effort in planning the school. As such, the school system should determine if the process was a success. Evaluating the process will provide the school system administration with data to use to improve the process. The people involved in the process would also like to have a chance to tell the administration their ideas on the success of the effort. A copy of an evaluation form is shown in Appendix H.

The evaluation of the process should be done immediately after the school building is occupied while people can remember how they were involved and to what purpose. The longer this evaluation is put off, the less reliable the data will be. Individuals will be more ready to respond if they are surveyed while the new school is still an important item in the community and before other aspects of community life take their attention.

No pre-determined, proven protocol exists for gathering this type of data, nor is there any standardized instrument. Rather, the school system should determine the purpose of the evaluation and develop a local evaluation instrument specifically for the school system and the planning process used. This evaluation should determine if the people involved in the planning process felt their contribution was significant and if the school system obtained the desired school building as a result of the planning.

Many items may be asked, but it is important to find out if the school building is what they believe it should be and if they believe it will work. The survey should also ask whether or not, as a result of their involvement, they would want to be involved in the planning process again. This type of question often shows how successful the individuals feel the process was.

Appendix H contains an evaluation instrument used by a school system to measure perceptions on just one part of the entire planning process: the development of educational specifications. This survey was administered to a committee of school staff and community representatives who assisted a consultant in writing a set of educational specifications for the school system. The results were given to the school board to appraise the planning process.

In this particular School District, community involvement was particularly important and this survey enabled the school board to assess their success. If it is important to involve people, both community and school staff, then it is important to determine the success of the effort.

Another aspect of evaluation is the efficacy of the planning model. Many steps should be taken in the planning process to complete a capital improvement project, such as a new building, an addition, or a major renovation. These steps are the responsibility of the school staff, and it is important to determine how effective the organization was in completing all steps.

School systems which have a number of substantial capital improvement projects going on simultaneously, need to monitor the work of a sizable staff charged with guiding the entire process. By using a checklist like the one shown in Appendix I, data on the effectiveness of the organization can be obtained. This is a very simple instrument, but it does cover important aspects of organizational planning.

Data Use

The natural question is how this data is used. Evaluating the planning process will help determine organizational effectiveness in managing a process, in particular the facility planning process. The process evaluation will enable the school board and administration to streamline the process in future efforts and improve on effectiveness, or to maintain the effectiveness as measured. The other evaluation process deals with the product, namely, the school building. This provides information about the success of various architectural features that were program-driven such as flexible walls between classrooms or certain area relationships desired.

The educational specifications are the basis of the evaluative instrument and, as such, the building should serve that program. Good or marginal architectural features of the building resulting from these educational specifications can be identified. This information should be worked back into the capital improvement program and into subsequent educational specifications.

If a mistake was made in a new building, that mistake should not be made in subsequent buildings; the school staff should learn from each building planned and constructed. Conversely, an architectural feature that works very nicely might well be incorporated in subsequent buildings. Only by evaluating the product of the planning process will the school system be able to make these kinds of judgments.

Evaluation Periods

The purpose of the evaluation effort determines when and how often it is carried out. Obviously, the process evaluation should be conducted immediately after the building is occupied because of the recency of the planning effort. This is a one-time evaluation and can be done only then.

The product evaluation should be conducted in several stages. The first evaluation should be conducted immediately after the building is occupied to determine the fidelity of the design to the educational specifications. In other words, how well did the design team and the design review team adhere to what was contained in the educational specifications?

This is an important evaluation because not only is the building evaluated, but so is the ability of the architectural firm to interpret educational specifications. This appraisal may well play a part in determining further employment of that particular firm. This evaluation also reflects how well the design review team monitored the design phase. This evaluation would show if a finer tuned design process is needed.

In addition to the immediate evaluation, an appraisal should be conducted within one year of the acceptance of the building by the school board. According to some, this evaluation should take place within 11 months—before the one-year warranties and guarantees expire. This would be a prudent evaluation to determine premature wearing of parts.

Following this evaluation, the building should be scheduled for periodic evaluations associated with the development of the long range plan of the school system. These evaluations should occur regularly until the 20th year of life of the building.

Then a very substantial evaluation should take place. This 20-year evaluation should include not only the adequacy of the building to accommodate the educational program offered, but all of the building systems. Systems comprising the building's internal structure should be seriously examined by architects and engineers. Replacing certain parts of the building at this time would not be out of order.

Many times the roof has a 20-year guarantee and would need to be evaluated, if this has not already been done. Other parts and systems of the building need to be critically examined and appropriate engineering tests conducted. Usually, a complete renovation is needed to bring the building up to the standards of the rest of the buildings in the school system.

In addition to these evaluations, the principal of the school should conduct an annual evaluation to determine maintenance needs that have occurred during the year. Although a formal evaluation instrument is probably not needed, the principal may develop a checklist to assist in appraising every part of the building. Data from these evaluations should be fed directly into the maintenance schedule of the school system for completion.

The school board needs to determine the evaluation program for school facilities in concert with its long range planning effort. The purpose of evaluation, data-gathering instruments, responsible staff, and process all need the attention of the school board if adequate data is to be generated so that the school board can make decisions about housing students. ▪

chapter**seventeen**

Planning for Technology

TECHNOLOGY BECAME A DRIVING FORCE IN EDUCATION WITH THE MINIATURIZATION of various electronic devices and machines and the rapid development of education-specific software. Since that time both the utilitarian benefits of technology and the reduced cost of hardware and software have presented the schools with an opportunity to expand educational opportunity for all students. At the same time, implementation of technology into all school buildings, new and renovated, has become a major issue for educators and school board members. The implementation of sophisticated technology is no longer a hit-or-miss proposition where the largest problem is deciding which brand of computer to purchase. A whole industry has been generated, devoted solely to the application of technology to the educational process and the subsequent impact upon school buildings. Educators and other decision makers must now deal with the problem of how to incorporate appropriate technology into the educational program.

School Readiness

One might be tempted to think that implementing technology into school buildings is a very routine and commonplace activity because technology has been in the public mind for quite some time. One might also be tempted to believe that every school child in the country is completely computer literate and has access to all of the latest electronic and digital devices and gadgets that are used to support learning. Unfortunately, neither assumption is entirely correct for two major reasons.

First, the growing complexity, versatility, and speed of electronic communication has kept the industry in a constant state of flux. New advances in all aspects of electronic communication are being made almost daily. New sources of data become electronically available to students in rapid order. It is difficult for the average educator to keep current with the present state of development of the industry. For every new building that is constructed or an existing building renovated, the educator is faced with many decisions regarding the implementation of a system that will serve the student population not only now, but also in the future. The rapid change in the industry means that educators must continuously seek assistance in obtaining information to help in making decisions regarding technology implementation.

The second reason technology implementation is a continuing serious concern for educators is the poor state of school building conditions across the country. A report of the U.S. General Accounting Office (GAO) on public school buildings indicated that 46 percent of the existing buildings do not have sufficient electrical service to adequately accommodate computers in the classrooms (1995). In addition, the report cited 52 percent of the schools reported they did not have access to a computer network. These data show that many public schools are far from having access to a decent technology assistance program. To administrators and school board members in these school systems, trying to implement a technology program is a very real issue. Even in school systems that have a rather good level of technology implementation, continuous updating of hardware and software is a challenge because of financial constraints.

Educator Needs

The present book deals almost exclusively with the planning processes that educators and school board members must initiate, guide, supervise, and evaluate in order to complete any capital improvement project, whether it is a new school building or a renovated school building. These identified processes all contribute to the completion of the total project. Each in turn must be completed to the satisfaction of all concerned before progress can be recorded. Each chapter in this book discusses and examines in detail the responsibility educators and school board members must exercise to make certain each process is completed satisfactorily.

On the matter of using technology to enhance and support the educational program, the type of guidance educators and school board members need is in identifying the right questions to be asked and then helping them find the right sources of expert information and assistance. This is the greatest benefit this chapter can impart to those engaged in planning a capital improvement project.

Because of this intent, the book does not necessarily deal with prescriptions as to what a school building could or should contain, how it should be configured, what kinds of spaces should be in the building or even the type of hardware that best serves an educational program. Many books on school facilities show good examples of the latest trend in school construction, the most innovative approach to a specialized area within the building, and the latest furniture and equipment. These sources of information are excellent in permitting educators, school board members, and community members to expand their ideas of what the school they are planning should be like. The National Clearinghouse for Educational Facilities (NCEF) in Washington, D.C. is a very good source of books and material discussing these building needs. The NCEF can be reached through the Internet at www.edfacilities.org.

Communication Growth

The growth and development of electronic communication systems within the last ten years has been phenomenal. Today through technological assistance, almost instantaneous communication with any person or data source in the world is possible. This has had a profound influence upon the schools and how they operate. This development has also greatly influenced the school buildings in which the students are housed.

The sophistication of technological equipment available today has generated a growing body of specific knowledge relating to application. This body of knowledge centers on the installation and proper use of both hardware and software. Along with equipment expertise, there is also a growing body of knowledge relating to how students learn using all types of technology. The latter, however, has not proceeded as rapidly as the development of more sophisticated equipment. Development of new hardware and practical application of existing equipment has outrun thoughtful consideration of how all of the technology available on the market can be harnessed and used for effective and efficient learning by students. Part of this lag is the difficulty in conducting research involving human subjects, especially students in the public schools. The development lag between hardware development and human application is not unique to electronic technology available for the public schools. However, the lag does present some critical problems for educators and school board members who are responsible for technology implementation in any capital improvement project. How the building will be configured and designed for new technology is not an easy decision to make.

Pressing Questions

What are some of the questions educators should initially raise and think about in considering technology application in a new building or newly renovated building? Listed below are some of the major considerations administrators, teachers, and school board members must address to successfully implement a program of technological assistance to the teaching and learning processes.

1. What and how do students learn best with the use of electronic assistance?
2. What kinds of hardware and software products are needed to implement the kind of teaching/learning strategy the school system desires?
3. How will the technological systems in the new building, or newly renovated building, fit in with the rest of the school system?
4. How can equality in technology application be assured for every student on a school system-wide basis?
5. Does the school system have the expertise to plan and design the technology program?
6. If not, what kind of outside assistance is needed to insure an effective technology installation and where is this assistance obtained?

All of the above questions must be addressed before a sensible application of technology is implemented. The questions listed can be answered only through a self-appraisal and study of the needs of the school system, done by the appropriate people in the local school system, with the assistance of whatever technological advice available. This may mean an outside consultant is employed to assist the staff in delineating their needs. This appraisal or examination should take place long before any plans are developed for the building itself.

Durost (1994) has posed similar questions that can help in planning for the purchase of specific technical equipment.

1. What are students doing that could be enhanced by technology?
2. What could students do with more advanced technology that they can not do now?
3. Which software best accomplishes the required tasks?
4. Which computer will run that software most effectively?
5. What peripherals (printer, mouse, CD-ROM, and so on) are needed?

In addition to the above questions, there are some special issues and considerations that must be accounted for in the implementation of technology.

Special Issues

Among the myriad questions and issues that surround the acquisition and implementation of a technology plan, four need the serious attention of school administrators and school board members. These four issues deal more with implementation than with the kinds and types of equipment that will eventually be acquired. Decisions need to be made and actions taken in plenty of time before the completion of a capital improvement project to have these issues in place.

Staff Preparation—Regardless of the kinds of equipment and systems that are purchased for a new or renovated school building, the entire school staff needs training in the proper use of the systems employed long before the school is ready for occupancy. The training should include not only explanations on how the equipment works, but also how the technology application fits into the overall educational program of the school. The training should include discussions on how technology influences student learning. In addition, such training might also be in the form of examining recent learning theories devoted to discussions on how children learn. All of this should take place long before the staff moves into the building. The technology consultant the school system employs to assist in the design of the technology system should have a part in the training program, as should experts in learning theory.

Technology Support—Along with proper training, each person in the school who will be working with the technology system should have the necessary technical support to maintain the equipment in working order. Occasionally school boards many not understand the need for such a staff to keep the system functional at all times. Equipment that is not functional at all times does not represent prudent management of resources. Sometimes these staff support personnel can be located within a school building, which is the ideal situation. Every local school system with more than one building, however, will probably need to have a system-wide cadre on call to the staff in each building. The size of the technology support staff will largely be determined by the sophistication of the system employed and the number of buildings to be served. The consultant who advises the school system on the technology system should also advise on the size and complexity of the support staff.

Equal Availability—This issue deals with the equal treatment of all students in the school system. Every student needs to have the same accessibility to hardware and software as all other students. This includes the number and kinds of equipment as well as the types of programs and activities utilized. Certainly, there needs to be some form of meeting individual educational needs through technology, but the central administration needs to assure that every student in the system has equal access to technology equipment and programs that are in the school system. When a new school building is opened with rather sophisticated equipment and programs, these same kinds of programs and equipment need to be available to students attending school in older buildings, even if this means a special renewal program of upgrading for all existing school buildings.

Uniformity of Technology Application—The technology application of a local school system should be uniform for the most efficient use of equipment and programs. The school system should develop technical specifications regarding the kinds and types of electronic equipment that will be used in every school in the system. These specifications should assist the staff in individual school buildings relative to the kinds of systems that can be purchased. Many times the parent-teacher association provides funds for the purchase of computers, cameras, laptops, and other finite equipment. The equipment purchased through such plans and schemes needs to be compatible with what the school system purchases. This is especially true if the computers in the school system are networked for more efficient use of programs. In addition to the compatibility of equipment, a system-wide approach to technology implementation also enhances and simplifies the warehousing of computer parts for repair purposes. Compatibility of equipment also allows better repair expertise to be developed in the technical support team. This permits the support staff to develop a great deal of expertise in keeping all equipment functional because they do not have to repair and maintain a variety of equipment.

Basic Considerations

There are some basic considerations educators need to address before any technology system can be designed for implementation. These considerations deal with some decisions that need to be made early in the project.

Computer Displacement—A single computer in the classroom requires the same amount of space as one student. As a result of placement of one computer, the student capacity of the classroom is diminished by one student space. Most states compute the capacity of the classroom unit on a per pupil square foot basis. This basis can be from 30 to 36 square feet per pupil in a classroom, which includes space for the pupil to sit and for necessary circulation. If the capacity of a classroom is set at 25, the total classroom area could be from 750 to 900 square feet, depending upon the square foot allocation. If a computer is placed in the classroom, then either the total classroom space has to be increased or one less pupil can be placed there. The unfortunate part of this formula is that it is extremely difficult to increase the overall size of the classroom because of a number of problems mainly centered around financial considerations. The problem becomes even more acute when four or five computers are introduced into the classroom. This would result in an effective reduction of 20-25 percent of the student capacity. Nonetheless, the die seems to be cast that computers are needed in every classroom. In new buildings the possibility of creating larger classrooms to accommodate pupils and computers has some possibility, if addressed long before the design of the building is started. When an existing building is renovated or renewed, the opportunity to increase the size of the classroom space is very limited. The most plausible solution to this dilemma is to reduce the number of pupils in each of the classrooms. This effectively reduces the total capacity of the school building. This is a very good solution, if the school system can accommodate the reduced seating capacity of the building.

Sometimes decision makers fail to keep the above problem in mind when planning a capital improvement project. As a result, classroom space is planned and designed based upon the old formula of 25 pupils per classroom multiplied by either 30 or 35 square feet of space without allowance for computers. If computers are subsequently placed in the classroom, an overcrowded condition will prevail. The size of the classroom as well as the number of computers to be installed needs to be spelled out in the educational specifications during the planning stage. The specifications then need to allow for an increase in the size of the classroom or the reduced student capacity if the square foot allocation is not increased. In either event, the appropriate space for students and technology equipment is accounted for in the instructional space.

Rudimentary Classroom Needs—Every classroom, laboratory, and instructional space in the building needs to have the basic provisions of receiving and sending voice, video, and data signals throughout the building and outside of the building. This means that all of these spaces will have appropriate wiring for internal communication and at least one or more outside telephone jacks. This applies even if the school system does not plan to purchase sufficient hardware for full implementation in the immediate future.

Students need to be able to access the Internet, receive and send voice and electronic mail, electronically obtain and analyze data, and participate in closed-circuit television activities and programs for an adequate education. Without this capability, students can not be adequately prepared for a world of technology use. The knowledge boundaries of the classroom extend far beyond the four walls of the school building and the physical means for extending it need to be made available to all students.

In addition to the electronic means for communication, the proper sized student furniture should be available at all locations. Sometimes little thought is given to the sizes of students who will use equipment while seated. Research findings regarding the proper height for a computer keyboard and monitor, the distance a person should be from the screen, and the types of desks for productive work should be used in designing all electronic stations.

Networking Computers—Decisions regarding the networking of computers in a building need to be made early in the planning stage. Individual buildings can be networked internally and also networked to a system that includes all buildings in the school system. Many school systems network a selected number of building computers to the school system-wide network for more efficient use of programs. There are some convincing arguments for establishing a Local Area Network (LAN). By networking a computer laboratory, the teacher can have a number of students working on the same program, whereas, if the software is available only individually, more than one student might not be able to use simultaneously. In addition, with a LAN more than one school building can use the same software product at the same time. The main disadvantage to networking is that when the LAN is down programs are not available. In addition, providing software products on a LAN might be a little more costly initially. The decision on the degree of networking, how the LAN will be configured, and program availability is usually a system-wide decision based upon educational program needs and available resources. Not all computers in an individual school building need to be networked, however there should be some kind of LAN operating in the school system with access by students in all local buildings.

Computer Laboratories

Many school systems make a point of having at least one computer laboratory in every school building. The usual application is for approximately 25-30 individual computers to be located in one room to be used as a laboratory for instructional purposes. Both computer literacy and keyboarding can be effectively taught in such a laboratory setting. These are the basic skills and knowledge for which a large number of computers are needed. Other instructional activities can normally take place in a laboratory under the supervision of a teacher. In some cases, students are permitted to use the computer laboratory on an individual basis when it is not used by a class.

Some educators argue that if computers are located in the classroom there is little or no need for computer labs. This may be an economic argument in that schools might not be able to afford computers in both laboratories and classrooms. Regrettably, some school systems may have to make a decision to place computers in either the classroom or the laboratory, but not both. This is indeed unfortunate because computers are needed in both locations for different purposes. As stated above some very basic skills and knowledge can be taught efficiently to a group of students in a computer laboratory, whereas this would be virtually impossible in a classroom with a limited number of computers. In addition, teachers can use software products for the entire class when each student has access to a computer. This does not negate the need for a small number of computers within the classroom. Computers in these areas can be used individually by students who need either reinforcement or enrichment. In addition, a small group of students can use the computers to solve a problem or create an experiment. A teacher can prescribe specific software packages to fit the needs of individual students or a select group of students and can then directly supervise the work. In the classroom, teachers can give students immediate assistance and clarification. Computers in the classroom can best serve individuals and small groups of students for different instructional purposes than a computer laboratory.

The either/or argument for computers in the laboratory or classroom is a "straw man" argument that should not be raised, even if a school system is strapped for funds to implement a technology program. Of course, the very reason for using computers to support an educational program should be the basis for decisions regarding how many to purchase and where to locate them. A school system should purchase as much equipment and software as possible, and always work towards full implementation through future purchases.

Technology Futures

At the present time, almost all electronic communication available in schools requires some sort of wiring. Knowledgeable people in this field tell us that in the future wireless communication will be available, even to the schools. The only question seems to be when this will happen. The rapid increase in speed, quality and versatility of electronic communication within the past five years may be a good indicator of when wireless communication will be commonplace.

Nevertheless, until such time as wireless communication is actually in place, schools will need to configure a wiring plan to accommodate all of the electronic communication needs of their student body. Even schools that are now on the drawing boards will need to be wired for communication. Wireless communication, of course, will greatly facilitate updating older, existing buildings that are not presently wired for modern technology applications and where re-wiring is a serious problem.

The personal computer may well give way to laptop computers for significant student use. The laptop computer can be carried around by a student and plugged into data sources located throughout the school building. In fact, some newer schools have data outlets and electrical service in areas such as the student commons area and the library for specific use by students. Several small schools have provided every student with a laptop computer as a means of enhancing their studying. In this way, students can study on an individual basis. One such application was in a rather small school where a very large number of students scored below the national median on achievement tests, the thought being that students would be able to learn more effectively if they had their own computer. This might be an unusual application because large schools might not have the financial resources to provide each student with such equipment. Unless school buildings have suitable data outlets, such application might be extremely limited.

This example does point to what some educators have maintained, that every student in the school should have an individual laptop for use. As desirable as this may be, the local school system must weigh the cost benefit of this expenditure of funds with other applications for enhancing the educational opportunities for all students. The laptop computer has already made an important appearance in the schools of today and this presence will increase in the near future. The impact technology has upon the learning process of students will increase as new and better electronic hardware and software become available in the future. ▪

chapter eighteen

Critical Issues in School Facility Planning: A Look To The Future

AS THE COUNTRY BEGINS THE 21ST CENTURY, THE PUBLIC SCHOOL SYSTEM HAS REACHED perhaps the highest level of efficiency and effectiveness since the beginning of the United States. Having said that, however, one must also realize that public schools do not always meet the expectations of the various client groups who interact with the educational establishment. The public school system has a long way to go before the majority of citizens feel comfortable with how the schools work. Nevertheless, considering the purpose of the public schools and the number of children and youth enrolled, the country is well served by the system of public schools currently in existence. However, this does not mean that the public schools do not face challenges in the future.

In the early part of the last decade of the 20th Century, President George W. Bush and the National Governors Association adopted a set of goals toward which public schools should work, leading to the next century. These goals eventually were cast into the Goals 2000: Educate America Act (1994). These were a set of rather modest, but important goals dealing with the performance of the public schools. In December of 1998, the National Education Goals panel presented a report on the accomplishment of the states toward meeting the goals. They gave the public schools a marginal success score. According to the commission, the public schools had made valiant efforts toward the goals, and in the process had made considerable headway in improving the performance of the schools. Yet the panel stated "The nation as a whole is not likely to meet the ambitious education goals set for 2000." (APR, 1998). Public education in the country apparently still has a way to go to meet these goals. In the process, the schools face many challenges and have problems with which to deal in trying to meet Goals 2000. This is not unusual because the public schools have always had problems and challenges with which to deal throughout the history of the country.

Political Decision-Making

School facility planning, like every other part of the educational enterprise, has many critical issues or problems germane to housing students in adequate buildings. Some of these problems seemingly have no rational answer, in spite of the fact that there is plenty of data to provide solutions. Many problems relating to the planning, construction and maintenance of school buildings suitable for students have a political aspect. What individuals believe is important in life usually governs the decisions they make, and in some instances these decisions may fly in the face of empirical evidence. The application of empirical evidence to arrive at a decision must first of all pass political and philosophical muster before it is used. This has been the case in the field of education since the inception of the country. Political and philosophical beliefs of individuals in authority influence public decisions regarding all aspects of how schools operate. This is especially true regarding capital expenditures for any major building project.

The intensity of politicization of decisions has increased over the past decade as resources have become more limited. It is expected that political and philosophical beliefs will increasingly influence decisions regarding when and where schools are constructed, as well as how much funding will be available. School administrators will want to use strong empirical evidence on the benefits of good school buildings to the education of students to mount an effective case for building needs.

School Facility Equity

One very pressing problem relating to school buildings is that of providing equitable buildings throughout the local school system, as well as the state at large. Everyone knows that equitable school facilities should be provided to all students by the state and local school board, yet such has not happened in a large majority of the states in the nation. The fact that students in one part of a local school system should have the same access to safe and modern facilities as do students in every other part of the school system is indeed a vital part of the American educational scene. A poignant example of the inequity of school facilities can be found in some large cities where students in the inner city attend school in buildings that are not safe to inhabit, while students in the outer portions of the city, or in the suburbs, attend school in buildings that are safe and modern. A similar inequity scenario is duly played out in some of the rural or isolated regions of each state.

Perhaps the absence of an application of providing equitable educational facilities in every part of the school system or country relates more to the political process inherent in the allocation of funds than anything else. The reason for such political action may be as mundane as the desire on the part of the governing body to keep taxes at a low level. Such action might also relate to decisions regarding priorities of spending public funds for various projects beside school buildings. Sometimes educators find that decision makers firmly believe a good education can be obtained in any kind of a physical environment, regardless of condition.

State Litigation

There has not been significant legal action to force states or local jurisdictions to equalize school facilities, even though the principle of equal treatment is fundamental to public education in the United States. Many states have experienced litigation to rectify inequitable operational funding plans. Most of these suits and subsequent court decisions have not extended directly to the equity of educational facilities. Two states, Arizona and West Virginia, have had to address this issue through the force of a judicial decision rendering the state funding program for school facilities unconstitutional (Pauley v. Bailey; Roosevelt Elementary School District No. 66 v. Bishop). These court decisions are promising and more such actions undoubtedly will occur in the future.

Technology

Another critical issue school systems are facing relating to school buildings is the provision for access to the latest technology. Everyone agrees each student enrolled in the public schools should have such access to the most advanced technology applications, yet many schools do not have even the most basic or elementary parts of a good technology system in operation. To prove this assertion, one has only to visit school buildings to witness the lack of decent technology applications. Recently, a superintendent in a medium sized school system admitted the school system did not have access to e-mail. As basic as that access is, one can imagine how extensive are other applications of technology in this school system. Although this example may sound rather strange, this is not an isolated case. Quite the contrary, technological equipment and educational application are readily available on the open market, but are not being used to the extent of availability in the majority of school systems. This is not because of reticence on the part of the professional educators, but perhaps because of the lack of dedication of funds to implement a viable program. The difference between technology availability in the commercial sector and actual application of technology in the classroom is very wide and constitutes a critical issue. How can the schools adequately prepare users of technology or workers for the new technology world, unless the most advanced applications of hardware and software are available to every student in the public schools?

Planning Process

Within the past decade, many school systems throughout the country have implemented strategic planning efforts as a process to give direction to the school system. There has been considerable success with this process in both addressing community needs and by involving the community. Yet the success of strategic planning in the public school sector has not achieved the intended results and perhaps needs to be expanded to provide for a more comprehensive internal planning effort. The local school system is a very complicated and complex organism, and there are a great number of planning efforts that proceed concurrently within the organization of the school system that are not integrated into a total planning effort such as a strategic plan. For instance, the planning for capital improvement projects often is not directly related to the overall strategic planning efforts of the school system. In many cases local school systems plan for a new building to accommodate growth or the renovation of an existing building without that process having any relationship to the strategic planning of the rest of the school system. Planning for a new school or a renovation in that case becomes an isolated event in the history of the school system. The planning for any capital improvement project, whether a new building or a renovation project, must result directly from the major school system planning effort that determines how the educational program will evolve and develop over the next segment of time. How can the building fit the needs of the educational programs and students unless planning for the building goes hand-in-hand within the overall planning of the school system?

Planning of this nature is called "integrated planning." Comprehensive planning of the school system incorporates the needs of housing students, based upon an examination of: 1) the educational program, 2) the number of students to be served, 3) the condition of the school building inventory, and 4) financial costs. Lack of clear identification of school system goals, the complexity of the organization, and communication that is oftentimes fragmented, all hinder the implementation of a planning process that should be integrated and comprehensive. Each local school system must work to marry the individual planning efforts within the organization to the overall strategic planning effort of the school system in order to achieve stated goals with the limited resources available.

Existing Buildings

Perhaps the most pressing problem or critical issue facing each local school system is the inability to keep the present inventory of school buildings in a safe and usable condition. This is not a recent occurrence or a new problem, but is probably the most crucial in that it affects so many school children. More than 14 million students, according to a GAO report, attend school in buildings that are below standards or even considered dangerous (1995). Educators and governmental officials have been aware of the need to save and upgrade the infrastructure of local government for a long time. A study completed by the American Association of School Administrators (AASA, 1983) identified the need for infrastructure repairs for all parts of the local jurisdiction. In a subsequent report, the Educational Writers Association (EWA) identified the need for public school building repair and maintenance to be $41 billion (1989). This figure has since been increased by inflation for the intervening period of time. In the most recent study on building needs, the GAO (1996) projected the monetary need to bring all public school buildings up to standard at $112 billion. Of this amount, more than $11 billion is needed in the next three years to bring the buildings into compliance with federal mandates to make all programs accessible to students and to remove certain hazardous materials.

As staggering as this reported amount of public funds might be, it is first of all an estimate of the total amount based upon a survey of 10,000 school buildings out of a possible population of more than 80,000. The actual cost may be higher than that stated in the report. This amount of funds continues to grow due to inflationary pressures and as a result of the continued aging of the inventory of school buildings in every locality.

The EWA reported that more than 50 percent of all school buildings used today were built during the 1950's and 1960's, a time of rapid growth of the student population. Most of these schools were constructed rapidly and made of inferior materials because quality building materials were not readily available during the decades immediately following World War II. School buildings constructed at that time had a life expectancy of approximately 30 years at the most. As a result, these school buildings have not stood the test of student use over the years. As these structures approach the fifty year period of life, school boards across the country will be faced with the decision of what to do with these aging buildings, some of which may not be worthwhile to renovate. Consequently, the critical issue of keeping the school building inventory in good condition is a growing problem.

Building Condition and Student Achievement

The almost overwhelming need for upgrading existing school buildings and the extremely limited resources available makes it even more important to insure that any funds spent on school buildings are spent wisely. Although there will be a variety of criteria used by the various states and communities to determine priority, perhaps educators and school board members should look at the findings of research as to where the funds should be spent for the greatest good of the students.

School board members and educators have a responsibility to make certain all students are housed in safe and modern facilities because of their custodial responsibility and moral accountability for students. These professional burdens extend beyond the letter of the law. Educators and school board members must create the best possible environment for the most productive learning of students. This implies that every student will be in a school building that will promote good learning.

The literature is replete with studies that show that air conditioned classrooms are a very large factor in facilitating effective student learning. Likewise, research findings indicate that classrooms where there are windows, the roof does not leak, the heat is controlled, educational and scientific equipment is available and working, the building is invitingly painted and kept clean, and the students are not overcrowded goes a long way to improve student learning.

Recent research findings have shed some light on the relationship between student learning and the condition of the physical environment in which the student is located. Research completed by Edwards (1992), Cash (1993), Hines

(1995), Earthman, Cash, and Van Berkum (1996), and Phillips (1997) explores the relationship between the variables of student achievement, student behavior, and building condition. All of these researchers found there was a positive relationship between the condition of the school building and the achievement of students. In each study, the researcher found from 5 to 17 percentile rank differences between the achievement scores of students in buildings in poor condition and students in above standard buildings. In other words, students in above standard buildings had higher mean scores on achievement tests than students in poor buildings. The findings of these five researchers corroborate previous studies as described by McGuffey (1982). The percentile rank differences found in the above studies represent the variance the school building could account for in the learning of the student. The total amount of variance accounted for by all school-related factors, at best, is very small compared with the influence parents, home and community have on the student, therefore, whatever the variance accounted for by the building takes on increased importance. A 5 to 17 percentile rank difference in student scores may at first seem rather insignificant, but it can mean a great deal to the administrator who is trying to raise all student achievement scores. These research findings could well mean that the expenditure of funds to improve the condition of the building might result in increased student learning. The suggested relationship between the two variables might be tenuous, but it is rather significant to every educator. A building principal or administrator would be remiss not to take advantage of any possibility to improve the learning of students; improving the building condition is one such way to directly impact student learning.

Federal Funding for School Buildings

The findings of these researchers become even more important when one considers the urgency the federal government has recently placed upon improving the condition of school buildings throughout the country. In 1994 the U.S. Congress passed the Improving America's Schools Act that provided federal funds to improve the condition of public school buildings (P. L. 103-382). In a later budget request to fund the act, $100 million was allocated. This budget request was not funded and as a result, no federal relief was provided to local school systems. Then again in 1997, the president sent to Congress proposed legislation to help communities and states rebuild public schools. This proposed legislation entitled "Partnership to Rebuild America's Schools Act of 1997," requested $5 billion in federal funds over the next four years to help upgrade old schools and build new schools (S. 456). The proposed act called initially for $2.45 billion in federal tax credits to help the states fund increased school construction and renovation. One way of doing this will be to permit the leveraging of additional local and state spending on school construction and renovation. The legislation would focus on incremental spending by local school systems. In this manner, the federal funds could be leveraged so that the total amount spent on school construction in the states would increase. In addition, the state and local governmental unit would have the flexibility to determine which construction activity would be deemed the highest priority and thereby receive federal funds.

Educational Program Location

Several decades ago, Alvin Tofler made the prediction that in the future, more and more students would be educated at home rather than in the school building (1980). He implied that because of the availability of computers, students would no longer need a school building in which to learn. He predicated this statement on the supposition that technology would make a dramatic change in how and where students would learn. He specifically thought the computer would become readily available to all students and that there would be suitable educational programs available through varied technological sources to provide a complete education without having to go to a school building. Obviously this prediction has not yet come about, in spite of the vast improvement in the computer and in the availability of them to everyone. Perhaps the biggest flaw in the prediction was in ignoring both the nature of children and youth and the tenets of many reputable learning theories.

Even if all students, regardless of age, could have a computer at their disposal, the prediction would not come about because of the socializing nature of children. Students of all ages want and need to be together for socialization purposes. Even if the opportunity was given to students to be out of school, they would find it necessary to congregate for these purposes. Equally important, however, is the fact that technology can not fill all the educational needs of students. There are some things students can learn very efficiently and effectively by means of technology. Other more esoteric concepts and meanings of education can be taught better through the aid of a teacher and the group process.

The idea that students would not have to go to a school building to receive their education gave rise to the idea that the country would not have to build or maintain school buildings in the future. As with most generalized predictions, this idea was short lived. Local communities still need to maintain school buildings for their students and will for the foreseeable future. There are some aspects of the issue of where students learn that are important to educators and school board members.

The alternative school program has grown considerably over the past three decades, so much so, that almost every school system has at least one program. In the beginning of this movement, students were many times housed in buildings that might be termed marginal. Most of the early high school alternative programs served students who were either in trouble with the authorities or had difficulty being in the regular education program. Existing commercial structures and older school buildings were almost routinely converted for these programs. As a result, the building sometimes did not exactly fit the type of program. Now that alternative programs are very accepted by the educational establishment, new buildings are being planned and constructed to house these programs. The stigma of alternative programs has been removed because the benefit of alternative educational programs for various ages of students has been recognized. Alternative educational programs and the buildings that house the students are seen as a viable means for meeting the needs of more students. More consideration and attention is now given to the type of building these programs and students need. This change has resulted in some exemplary school buildings to house students in alternative education programs.

Another ramification of the idea that students do not need to be in the school building can be seen in the various programs designed to have the students use more community resources to supplement their education. These practices have been used in vocational programs for many decades, but the recent growth of the internship and similar outreach programs has allowed students great opportunity to use community resources, even outside of vocational education preparatory programs, to augment their education.

Size of School Buildings

All of the above mentioned ideas and extensions of the educational program have not resulted in the need for fewer educational buildings. Quite the contrary, school systems have felt the need to expand their building inventory to meet a growing need for more space within which to educate students. The increase in size of buildings has resulted in many cases from educational program changes.

The most important impact upon the size of school buildings in the past three decades has been felt from implementation of special education programs to serve a larger population of students. Even with a program of complete inclusion of special education students in regular education classrooms, there is a need for certain spaces in a building for special functions. School buildings need to contain specialized laboratories, small classrooms, diagnostic areas, training rooms, conference rooms, and a variety of offices for specialists to adequately serve the special education program needs. These areas, of course, increase the overall gross square footage of a school building. This increase must be factored into the total per pupil square footage allocation for a building.

Another factor that increases the overall size of a building is the implementation of a technology program. Computer laboratories have long been introduced into new buildings or created out of existing space. These laboratories are usually the size of at least three or four general purpose classrooms which again increases the square footage of the building. Perhaps the most important consideration of introducing technology is seen when computers are installed in classrooms. One computer takes up the space equal to one student. As a result, for every computer placed in a classroom, the student capacity is lowered by one student. When four or five computers are placed in a classroom, the capacity is reduced by that number of students. The question then becomes whether the school system lowers the student capacity of the classroom, or builds a larger classroom to accommodate the computers. Unfortunately, in too many instances neither alternative is implemented and the classroom is then overcrowded. In planning a new building or in renovating an existing building, the administrators and school board need to consider proper implementation of computers in the individual classroom and make appropriate space or pupil allowances.

A different ramification of the space issue revolves around the increasing number of adults who are now housed in all levels of school buildings. Most school systems have implemented a program of employing aides to teachers, whether or not they service special education or regular education students. It is not unusual to find two adults working with students in a single classroom designed for a specified number of students. Many classrooms are simply not designed to accommodate the activity of two adults working with various groups of students or with individual students.

A great number of schools also conduct a strong volunteer program where adults from the community come into the schools to assist with various aspects of the educational program. Whether these activities include supervising students in the cafeteria, on the play grounds, or in the library, space is needed for these individuals. Most volunteer programs include adults working in the classroom in a tutoring or assisting role. It is very unusual to find space in the building during the school day to allow these adult volunteers to have a place to relax or sit when not on duty. Although schools do not see it as their responsibility to provide a space for volunteers to either complete some paper work or meet with a student outside of the classroom, the need is there for most beneficial use of the time of the volunteer.

The increased emphasis on the physical wellbeing and development of students has impacted the size of space devoted to physical education. This, plus the desire of the adult community to have a space in the school to conduct wellness and physical exercise programs have placed a new demand for additional space for these activities. A typical elementary school physical education program needs a space of only 3,000-4,000 square feet of space. With the demand for more community use of the physical education space, school systems are constructing regulation sized gymnasia in all elementary schools. The size of a regulation gym ranges from 8,000-10,000 square feet of space. Thus increasing the overall per pupil square feet allocation and subsequent total cost of the building. This application, however, is a good example of shared use of facilities between school system needs and community desires.

All of these programs are extremely beneficial to the work of the school organization, yet, each program requires space for the people to function efficiently and effectively. These requirements have increased the need for space in the building and have increased the overall square footage of buildings. As the demand for more services increases and the number of individuals involved in the educational process increases, the size of school buildings will also increase.

Summary

There are several reasons for the push for federal funds for local school systems to upgrade facilities. Perhaps the major reason is the critical issue of the inability of local school systems to adequately fund the needed upgrading of existing buildings and the construction of new facilities. Most local school systems do not have the financial ability to go into debt to fund such improvement projects. In some states the bonding capacity of the local school system is constitutionally set and results in fiscal ability too low to produce the needed revenues to upgrade the facilities. In other states, local school systems are already to the debt limit. In addition certain debt limit measures apply in some states to the effect that local school systems do not have the means, in most cases, to raise the needed funds to complete the upgrade of facilities. To adequately fund the needed upgrades would be legally impossible because of debt limits. Some agency, other than the local school system, must assist with the massive upgrade of school facilities and that agency must be either the state or federal government. Some states have the ability to provide assistance to the locality, but do not have the mechanism to do it. Other states feel that the localities should shoulder this responsibility. This difference in philosophy then places a heavy financial burden on the locality to address the need. In the absence of a response to a public need on the part of either the locality or state, the federal government must then step in to resolve the need.

So many of the critical issues relating to school facilities identified above revolve around the question of how we should fund public education. The real issue is not whether or not we have the financial ability to fund the needs so much as whether or not there is the will to fund them. This may sound rather fatalistic, but it is true that we invest our money in things or efforts we consider important. The nation does have the means to provide an appropriate and healthy learning environment for all children in every location in the country. With the federal government and almost every state showing a budget surplus, the country does have the means to upgrade all school facilities by simply using these excess funds. However, the country needs to consider what is the most important thing in which we wish to invest. There is no better way to influence the future of our country than to invest in our students and thereby positively influence the next generation. ▪

Washington County Schools
100 Elm Street
Washington City, VA 22031-2045

May 1, 2000

William Jones, AIA
Jones and Jones Architects, Inc.
303 Elm Street
Washington City, VA 22031

Dear Mr. Jones:

The Washington County School system is planning to construct a new elementary school building to serve 500 elementary school students in the northern quadrant of the county. The new school will be constructed on a 25 acre site located at the corner of Harding Road and Spruce Avenue in the Deercroft area. The school is to be ready for student occupancy by September 1, 2003. The school system staff is currently developing the educational specifications that will be the basis for the architect designing the new building.

The school system is desirous of contracting for architectural services to design the facility. If your firm is interested in being considered for such a commission, I would like to invite you to send me data relative to the experience and qualifications of your staff. Any other information that would enable our staff to adequately evaluate your firm should be included. Please send your material to the Architectural Selection Committee, School Facilities Department at the school system address. All submitted material and photographs will be returned to you after the selection process.

All information submitted will be reviewed by an architectural selection committee composed of school personnel. Following this review, three architectural firms will be selected from the pool of applicants for interview. The school board will interview these firms and then select one firm for the commission.

If you have any questions regarding this letter or any other phase of the selection procedure, please call me. I look forward to working with you.

Sincerely,
Thomas S. Barrett
Superintendent

Washington County Schools
100 Elm Street
Washington City, Virginia 22031-2045

July 1, 2000

William Jones, AIA
Jones and Jones Architects, Inc.
303 Elm Street
Washington City, VA 22031

Dear Mr. Jones:

Your firm has been selected to present a formal oral presentation to the Architectural Selection Committee and the School Board for designing a new elementary school.

Your presentation will take place on Wednesday, July 20, 2000 at 10:30 AM in the Board Room of the school administration building on 100 Elm Street. Your presentation will be limited to 20 minutes and facilities to present slides and overhead transparencies will be available.

The presentation shall include but not be limited to:

1. Your management approach to meeting the design requirements of the project.
2. The personnel to be assigned to the project during the design phase and construction phase.
3. The engineering consultants to be used in the design of the project.
4. Your firm's approach and commitment to have the project ready for bidding on schedule and within the assigned budget.
5. The experience and qualifications of your firm in similar projects.

If you have any questions, please call me. We look forward to working with your firm.

Sincerely,

Anthony Phillips
Director
School Facilities

AGREEMENT: made this first day of July in the year of Two Thousand.

BETWEEN the Owner: Washington County Public Schools

and the Architect: Jones and Jones, Architects, Inc.

For the following Project: New High School
Maple Road and Hamilton Drive
Washington City, Virginia

The Owner and the Architect agree as set forth below:
1. The architect shall provide professional services for the Project in accordance with the Terms and conditions of this Agreement.
2. The Owner shall compensate the Architect, in accordance with the Terms and Conditions of this Agreement:

A. FOR BASIC SERVICES, as described in Item I. Basic compensation shall be computed as a PERCENTAGE OF CONSTRUCTION COST defined in Item IV.
The sum of $1,347,500.00   percent (5 1/2%) Based on a fixed limit construction cost of Twenty-four Million, Five hundred thousand and no/100 Dollars   ($24,500,000.00).

TERMS AND CONDITIONS OF AGREEMENT BETWEEN OWNER AND ARCHITECT

I. Basic Services
1. The architect's Basic Services consist of the six phases described below and include normal civil, structural, mechanical, and electrical engineering services. The Owner's General Design Requirements shall be considered a part of this contract. See Item XI, Other Conditions or Services.
2. Prior to beginning the Schematic Design Phase, the Architect shall provide a progress schedule based on the Owner's overall project schedule.
A. Schematic Design Phase
1. The Architect working with the Owner, school staff, and community shall develop the program based on the general scope of work contained in the Educational Specifications and furnished to the Architect by the Owner.
2. Based on the mutually agreed upon program, the Architect shall prepare Schematic Design Studies consisting of drawings and other documents illustrating the scale and relationship of

Project Components for approval by the Owner. These plans will be presented to the school staff and community as required prior to proceeding with Design Development Drawings.

3. The Architect shall submit to the Owner a Statement of Probable Construction Cost based on current area, volume or other unit costs.

4. The Architect shall provide to the Owner four sets of the Schematic Design Package for review and comments.

5. The Schematic Design Package shall be presented to the School Board for their approval.

B. Design Development Phase

1. The Architect shall prepare from the approved Schematic Design Studies, for approval by the Owner, the Design Development Documents consisting of drawings and other documents to fix and describe the size and character of the entire Project as to civil, structural, mechanical, and electrical systems, materials and such other essentials as may be appropriate.

2. The Architect and consultants shall be required to make extensive field surveys as necessary to determine all conditions that will affect new work, including but not limited to areas above ceilings electrical panel spare capacity, etc.

3. The Architect shall submit to the Owner a further Statement of Probable Construction Cost.

4. The Architect shall provide to the Owner four sets of the Design Development Package for review and comments.

5. The Architect shall submit the Preliminary Design Plans to the Virginia State Department of Education for approval after the Design Development is approved by the Owner.

C. Construction Documents Phase

1. The Architect shall prepare from the approved Design Development Documents, for approval by the Owner, drawings and specifications setting forth in detail the requirements for the construction of the entire project. The Architect and consultants shall use the Owner provided educational and technical specifications that if modified, will require the Owner's approval.

2. The Architect shall provide the Owner Construction Document review sets at the 30% completion, 60% completion, and 100% completion stages with updated cost estimates.

3. The Architect shall provide to the Owner four review sets at the end of each Construction Document Phase.

4. The Owner will file the required documents for the Building Permit. It shall be the sole responsibility of the Architect to expedite and secure all required approvals of Plans and Specifications including but not limited to Department of Environmental Management, Department of Health, Department of Fire and Rescue, Water Authority, Virginia Department of Transportation, Virginia Department of Education, etc. The Architect shall provide weekly plan review status reports in writing to the Owner.

D. Bidding or Negotiation Phase

1. The Architect, following the Owner's approval of the Construction Documents and of the latest Statement of Probable Construction Cost, shall assist the Owner in obtaining bids or negotiated proposals, and in awarding and preparing construction contracts.

E. Construction Phase - Administration of the Construction Contract

1. The Construction Phase will commence with the award of the Construction Contract and will terminate when the final Certificate of Payment is issued by the Contractor.

2. The Architect shall provide administration of the Construction contracts as set forth in the

Owner prepared General conditions of the Contract for construction.

3. The Architect shall advise and consult with the Owner. The Architect shall have authority to act on behalf of the Owner to the extent provided in the General Conditions unless otherwise modified in writing.

4. The Architect shall at all times have access to the Work wherever it is in preparation or progress.

5. The Architect and consultants will attend construction progress meetings every week or more often if necessary, take minutes of the meetings, and provide written project status reports. On the basis of on-site observations, the architect shall endeavor to guard the Owner against defects and deficiencies in the work of the Contractor. The Architect may be required to meet at the site in emergency situations. The Architect shall not be responsible for construction means, methods, techniques, sequences, or procedures, or for safety precautions and programs in connection with the work, and shall not be responsible for the Contractor's failure to carry out the work in accordance with the contract documents.

6. The Architect shall review the Contractor's Applications for payment and shall issue Certificates of payment based on project progress.

7. The Architect is the interpreter of the requirements of the Contract Documents and the impartial judge of the performance thereunder by both the Owner and contractor. The architect shall assist the Owner in making decisions on all claims of the Owner or Contractor relating to the execution and progress of the work and on all other matters or questions related thereto.

8. The Architect shall have authority to reject Work that does not conform to the Contract Documents. Whenever, in the Architect's reasonable opinion, it is necessary or advisable to ensure the proper implementation of the intent of the Contract Documents, the Architect will have authority to require special inspection or testing of any Work in accordance with the provisions of the Contract Documents whether or not such Work be then fabricated, installed, or completed.

9. The Architect shall expeditiously review and approve shop drawings, samples, and other submissions of the contractor only for conformance with the design concept of the Project and for compliance with information given in the Contract Documents. The Architect shall coordinate with the Owner prior to approving any items that are in variance with the approved Contract Documents.

10. The Architect shall prepare Proposed Modifications and Change Orders.

11. The Architect shall not be responsible for the acts or omissions of the contractor, or any Subcontractors, or any of the agents of the Contractor or subcontractors or any other person performing any of the Work.

F. Project Close Out

1. The Architect shall conduct inspections to determine the dates of Substantial Completion and final completion, prepare the punch list, shall receive and review written guarantees and related documents assembled by the contractor, and shall issue a final Certificate for Payment.
2. The Architect shall prepare a set of reproducible record drawings showing significant changes in the work made during the construction process based on marked-up prints, drawings, and other data furnished by the Contractor to the Architect. The reproducible record drawings shall also include all addenda items and change orders issued during the construction process. The reproducible record drawings shall be Mylar.
3. The Architect shall provide extensive assistance in the utilization of any equipment or system such as initial start-up or testing, adjusting and balancing, review and approval of operation and maintenance manuals, training personnel for operation and maintenance, and consultation during operation.

II. THE OWNER'S RESPONSIBILITY

A. The Owner shall provide full information, including a general scope of work regarding requirements for the project.
B. The owner shall designate a representative authorized to act in behalf of the school board in respect to the Project.
C. The Owner shall furnish a certified land survey of the site.
D. The Owner shall pay for the services of a soils engineer or other consultant when such services are deemed necessary by the Architect.
E. The Owner shall furnish structural, mechanical, chemical, and other laboratory tests, inspections and reports as required by law or the Contract Documents.
F. If the Owner becomes aware of any fault or defect in the Project or non-conformance with the Contract Documents, prompt written notice will be given to the Architect.
G. The Owner shall furnish information required as expeditiously as necessary for the orderly progress of the Work.

III. CONSTRUCTION COST

A. Construction cost shall be used as the basis for determining the Architect's compensation for Basic Services.
B. Construction Cost does not include the compensation of the Architect and consultants, cost of land, or any other cost.
C. Detailed Cost Estimates prepared by the Architect represents the best judgement as a design professional familiar with the construction industry.
D. A fixed limit on Construction Cost is established as a condition of this contract. The Owner and Architect together will determine what materials, equipment, component systems, and types of construction are to be included in the Contract Documents.

V. PAYMENT TO THE ARCHITECT

A. Payments on account of the Architect's Basic Services shall be made as follows:

1. Payments for Basic Services shall be made monthly in proportion to services performed so that the compensation at the completion of each Phase, shall equal the following percentages of the total Basic Compensation:

Schematic Design Phase..................15%
Design Development Phase................35%
Construction Documents..................75%
Bidding or Negotiation Phase............77%
Construction Phase....................100%

2. No deductions shall be made from the Architect's compensation on account of penalty, liquidated damages, or other sums withheld from payments to contractors.

VI. TERMINATION OF AGREEMENT

A. This agreement may be terminated by either party upon seven day's written notice should the other party fail substantially to perform in accordance with its terms through no fault of the party initiating the termination.

B. In the event of termination due to the fault of parties other than the Architect, the Architect shall be paid compensation for services performed to termination date, including reimbursable expenses then due.

VII. OWNERSHIP OF DOCUMENTS

A. Drawings and Specifications as instruments of service are and shall remain the property of the Architect whether the Project for which they are made is executed or not. The Owner shall be permitted to use the Drawings and Specifications for other projects on its property, for additions to this project and/or for completion of this Project by others.

This Agreement executed the day and year first written above. This Agreement is executed in three counterparts, each of which is deemed as original.

OWNER   **ARCHITECT**

_____   _____
Chairman   Clerk

(seal)   (seal)

Washington County Schools

Agreement made as of the sixth day of March in the year Two Thousand.

BETWEEN THE OWNER: Washington County Schools
Washington City, Virginia

and the CONTRACTOR: Tidewater Contractors, Inc.

The Project: New High School
Maple Road and Hamilton Avenue

The Architect: Jones and Jones, Architects, Inc.

The Owner and the Contractor agree as set forth below.

Article 1—The Contract Documents
The Contract Documents consist of this Agreement, the Conditions of the Contract (General Supplementary and other Conditions), the Architectural Drawings, the Technical Specifications, all Addenda issued prior to and all Modifications issued after execution of this Agreement. These form the Contract, and all are as fully a part of the contract as if attached to this Agreement or repeated herein. An enumeration of the Contract Documents appears in Article 7.

Article 2—The Work
The Contractor shall perform all the Work required by the Contract Documents for *The New High School.*

Article 3—Time of Commencement and Substantial Completion
The work to be performed under this Contract shall be commenced and, subject to authorized adjustments, Substantial Completion shall be achieved not later than *Twenty-four (24) months from the date of this contract.*

Article 4—Contract Sum
The Owner shall pay the Contractor in current funds for the performance of the work, subject to additions and deductions by Change Order as provided in the Contract Documents, the Contract Sum of *$24,497,000.*

The Contract sum is determined as follows:

Article 5—Progress Payments

Based upon Applications for Payment submitted to the Architect by the Contractor and Certificates for Payment issued by the Architect, the Owner shall make progress payments on account of the Contract Sum to the Contractor as provided in the Contract Documents for the period ending the *fifth* day of the month as follows: *beginning with April 5, 2000.*

Not later than ____days following the end of the period covered by the Application for Payment _____ percent (___%) of the portion of the Contract Sum properly allocable to labor, materials, and equipment incorporated in the Work and ____ percent (____%) of the portion of the Contract Sum properly allocable to materials and equipment suitably stored at the site or at some other location agreed upon in writing, for the period covered by the Application for Payment, less the aggregate of previous payments made by the Owner; and upon substantial Completion of the entire work, a sum sufficient to increase the total payments to____ percent (____%) of the Contract Sum, less such amounts as the Architect shall determine for all incomplete work and unsettled claims as provided in the Contract Documents.

Article 6—Final Payment

Final payment, constituting the entire unpaid balance of the contract Sum, shall be paid by the Owner to the Contractor when the work has been completed, the contract fully performed, and a final Certificate for Payments has been issued by the Architect.

Article 7—Miscellaneous Provisions

7.1 Terms used in this Agreement, which are defined in the Conditions of the Contract, shall have the meanings designated in those Conditions.

7.2 The Contract Documents, which constitute the entire agreement between the Owner and the Contractor, as listed in Article 1 and , except for Modifications issued after execution of this Agreement, are enumerated as follows:

This agreement entered into as of the day and year first written above.

_____   _____
OWNER   **CONTRACTOR**

Lexington/Rockbridge Public Schools

Date_____

School_____

Location_____

Grades_____

Number of Teachers: Regular_____SpEd_____Itinerant_____

Special Programs_____

_____

Stated Building Capacity_____

Enrollment_____ as of _____/_____/_____

_____Number of GP Classroom	_____SpecEd Resource Rm
_____Library/Support Areas	_____SpecEd Self-Contain
_____Music Room	_____Art Room
_____Technology Room	_____Home Arts Lab
_____Computer Lab	_____Exploratory Lab
_____Cafeteria	_____Auditorium (seating___)
_____Boy's Gym/Lockers	_____Girl's Gym/Lockers
_____Office	_____Conference Room

SITE (size, general appearance, equipment, parking, traffic, etc.)

BUILDING APPEARANCE (general upkeep, outside maintenance)

GENERAL CONDITION (inside upkeep, maintenance needs)

BUILDING CONFIGURATION AND ORGANIZATION (room configuration, size, adequacy for program)

LIMITED ENROLLMENT CLASSES (adequacy of space, number of spaces, access for handicapped)

POTENTIAL FOR CONTINUED USE (suggested building changes to convert to middle school organization)

APPENDIX E Site Selection Flow Chart

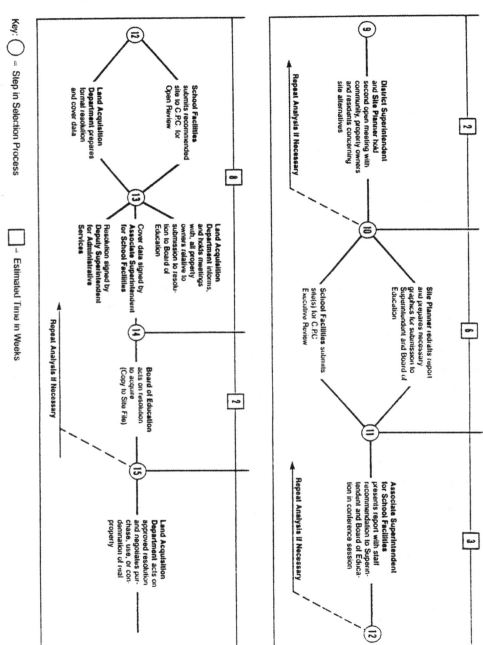

Key: ◯ = Step in Selection Process

☐ = Estimated Time in Weeks

Step 9: District Superintendent and Site Planner hold second open meeting with community, property owners and residents concerning site alternatives

Repeat Analysis if Necessary

Step 10: Site Planner redrafts report and prepares necessary graphics for submission to Superintendent and Board of Education

School Facilities submits site(s) for C.P.C. Executive Review

Step 11: Associate Superintendent for School Facilities presents report with staff recommendation to Superintendent and Board of Education in conference session

Repeat Analysis if Necessary

Step 12: School Facilities submits recommended site to C.P.C. for Open Review

Land Acquisition Department prepares formal resolution and cover data

Step 13: Land Acquisition Department informs, and holds meetings with, all property owners relative to submission to resolution to Board of Education

Cover data signed by Associate Superintendent for School Facilities

Resolution signed by Deputy Superintendent for Administrative Services

Step 14: Board of Education acts on resolution to acquire (Copy to Site File)

Repeat Analysis if Necessary

Step 15: Land Acquisition Department acts on approved resolution and negotiates purchase, use, or condemnation of real property

2   6   3   8   2

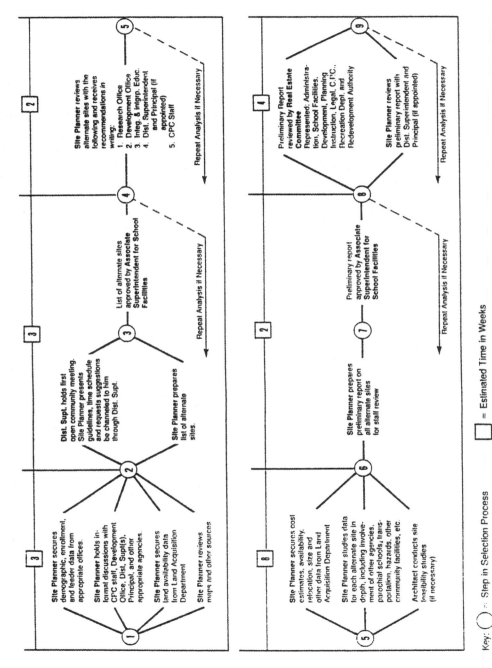

1

Site Planner secures demographic, enrollment, and feeder data from appropriate offices.

Site Planner holds informal discussions with CPC staff, Development Office, Dist. Supt(s), Principal, and other appropriate agencies.

Site Planner secures land availability data from Land Acquisition Department

Site Planner reviews maps and other sources

[3]

2

Dist. Supt. holds first open community meeting. Site Planner presents guidelines, time schedule and requests suggestions be channeled to him through Dist. Supt.

Site Planner prepares list of alternate sites.

[3]

3

List of alternate sites approved by Associate Superintendent for School Facilities

Repeat Analysis if Necessary

4

[2]

5

Site Planner reviews alternate sites with the following and receives recommendations in writing:
1. Research Office
2. Development Office
3. Integ. & Intgrp. Educ.
4. Dist. Superintendent and Principal (if appointed)
5. CPC Staff

Repeat Analysis if Necessary

5

Site Planner secures cost estimates, availability, relocation, size and other data from Land Acquisition Department

Site Planner studies data for each alternate site in depth, including involvement of other agencies, parochial schools, transportation, hazards, other community facilities, etc.

Architect conducts site feasibility studies (if necessary)

[8]

6

Site Planner prepares preliminary report on all alternate sites for staff review

[2]

7

Preliminary report approved by Associate Superintendent for School Facilities

Repeat Analysis if Necessary

8

[4]

9

Preliminary Report reviewed by Real Estate Committee Represented: Administration, School Facilities, Development, Planning Instruction, Legal, CPC., Recreation Dept. and Redevelopment Authority

Site Planner reviews preliminary report with Dist. Superintendent and Principal (if appointed)

Repeat Analysis if Necessary

Key: ◯ = Step in Selection Process   ▢ = Estimated Time in Weeks

APPENDIX F

Flow Chart for Developing Educational Specifications

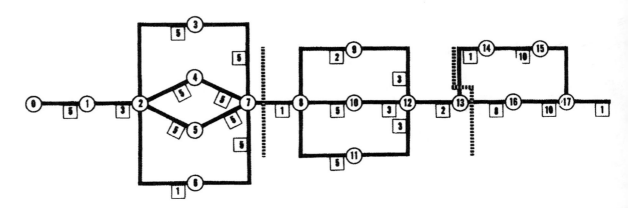

DATA COLLECTION

0 – BUDGET APPROVAL FOR DESIGN
1 – PROJECT ASSIGNED TO PLANNER – 5
2 – CONFER WITH SITE SPECIALIST – 3
3 – CONFER WITH DISTRICT SUPERINTENDENT AND PRINCIPAL – 5
4 – CONFER WITH SCHOOL STAFF – 5
5 – MEET WITH COMMUNITY GROUPS – 5
6 – CONFER WITH CURRICULUM DEPARTMENT – 1
7 – DEVELOPMENT OF ROUGH DRAFT OF EDUCATIONAL SPECIFICATIONS – 5

PROGRAM CONFIRMATION

8 – REVIEW BY SCHOOL PLANNING DIRECTOR – 1
9 – REVIEW BY DISTRICT SUPERINTENDENT AND PRINCIPAL – 2
10 – MEET WITH STAFF – 5
11 – MEET WITH COMMUNITY GROUPS – 5
12 – REVISION OF EDUCATIONAL SPECIFICATIONS – 3
13 – FINAL APPROVAL BY DIRECTOR OF SCHOOL PLANNING – 2

PRODUCTION/DISTRIBUTION

14 – CONFER WITH SCHOOL PLANNING DRAFTSMAN – 1
15 – GRAPHICS COMPLETED – 10
16 – TYPE EDUCATIONAL SPECIFICATIONS FOR PRINTER – 8
17 – SEND DOCUMENT TO PRINTER – 10
18 – DISTRIBUTION OF EDUCATIONAL SPECIFICATIONS – 1

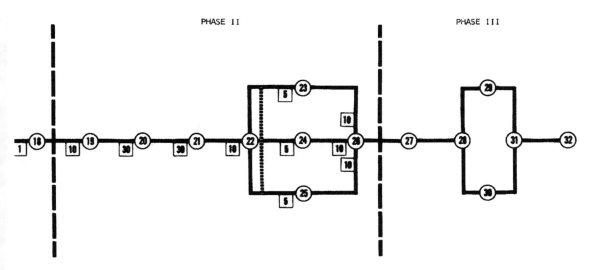

PHASE II

PHASE III

○ = ACTIVITIES

☐ = NUMBER OF WORK DAYS

Job Description for Construction Supervisor

POSITION TITLE: Construction Supervisor

EFFECTIVE DATE: July 1, 1999

REPORTS TO: Director of Construction

QUALIFICATIONS: A degree in engineering/engineering related field preferred, or comparable experience in design and construction and five years experience involving planning, design, and supervision of construction activities.

STATE REQUIREMENTS/QUALIFICATIONS: None

BASIC FUNCTION: Performance of construction management activities in the planning, design, construction of educational facilities.

DIMENSIONS:
Budget responsibilities: None
Employees supervised: None

DUTIES AND RESPONSIBILITIES:

This position encompasses coordination of activities and resolution of problems among contractor-supervisory personnel, architect/ engineers, School Board staff, and governmental officials concerning technical matters related to building foundations, structures, mechanical systems, electrical and communications systems, grading, paving, and drainage. Resolving problems concerning scheduling and coordinating diverse construction activities.

This position requires comprehensive knowledge of standards and procedures for planning, design, scheduling, and quality control of school building programs.

Represents the owner on construction project sites by administering contracts between the School Board and general contractors, separate contractors, and architect/engineers.

Consults with representatives of governmental agencies, School Board staff architects, contractors, and other interested officials to resolve problems concerning interpretation of contract documents.

Establishes coordination and procedural policies for project accomplishment.

Conducts pre-construction conferences and weekly job site meetings.
Resolves on-going construction site problems.

Establishes and maintains a continuous quality control program to assure that facilities are constructed acceptable standards.

Directs improvement in standards of work.

Approves quality of completed work.

Determines adequacy of and recommends approval of payment requests.

Assesses work progress and scheduling and recommends actions for improvement.

Prepares progress reports and maintains project records.

Reviews and approves shop drawings, product data and samples.

Observes testing procedures, reviews test and inspection reports and expenditures corrective action.

Determines the need for contract changes, make recommendations for accomplishment of the change and processes change orders.

Directs installation and inspection of owner furnished equipment and material.

Directs the work of separate contractors.

Conducts final inspections with contractors and architects/ engineers.

Coordinates project acceptance, building occupation and start-up educational activities with staff and governmental agencies.

Coordinates the orientation of maintenance and operational personnel on school plant operation.

Supervises contractor activitity during the guarantee period.

Reviews and verifies project closeout documents, as-built drawings, operation manuals, and project releases.

Assists in the development of contract specifications and contract documents.

Reviews architect/engineer submissions for preliminary, intermediate and final design stages and makes recommendations for design changes.

Assists in the coordination of design review by appropriate governmental agencies.

Coordinates new facilities requirements with the staff.

Prepares cost estimates.

Provides architect/engineer with design parameters including minimum standards and building systems (type, size, model, quality, etc.).

Prepares design and construction schedules.

Makes recommendations on construction procedures and contracting methods.

APPENDIX**H**
Planning Process Evaluation Form

Virginia Polytechnic Institute and State University Office of Educational Services

Prince William County Educational Specifications Planning Project

1. What is your sex?   Male _____   Female _____

2. What is your age?   Age _____

3. Do you have a child/children currently enrolled in the Prince William County School System?

4. How many committee planning sessions were you able to attend?

5. Do you feel these planning efforts were worthwhile?   Yes _____ No _____

6. Do you believe the recommendations of the committee will have significant impact on the final decisions concerning the new secondary facilities? Yes _____ No _____ Don't Know _____

7. Were you basically satisfied with the assistance you received from the VPI&SU consultants? Yes _____ No _____ Don't Know _____

8. Were there additional services the consultants could have provided? Yes _____ No _____

If you answered yes, please state what services could have been provided.

_____

_____

_____

9. Do you feel the community was adequately represented on the planning committee? Yes _____ No _____

If not, what segment should have been included?

_____

_____

10. Was there sufficient time for the committee to prepare an accurate and complete report? Yes _____ No _____

11. If you were involved in a similar planning process, what improvements or changes would you recommend?

_____

_____

12. Do you believe the school will reflect exactly the recommendations of the advisory committee? Yes _____ No _____

13. Do you think the completed secondary facilities will be different from existing secondary schools? Yes _____ No _____

_____

_____

14. Were there any constraints which you believe prevented the advisory committee from having a more significant input into the educational specifications document?
Yes _____ No _____

If yes, what were those constraints?

_____

_____

_____

15. Did your work and involvement on the advisory committee help to clarify or change your opinion about the goals or objectives of the Prince William County School Division?
Yes _____ No _____

APPENDIX I
School Planning Checklist

School Division: _____   Date: _____

Please answer Yes / No to the following questions

I. Capital Improvement Program:

    a.   Contained direct input from citizens/teachers

    b.   Listed all needed projects of School Division

    c.   Reviewed by citizens in open meetings

    d.   Reviewed by School Board

    e.   Reviewed by Planning Authority

    f.   Formally adopted by School Board

    g.   Plan projected for 6-10 years

II. Site Selection:

    a.   Was citizen input obtained in open meetings

    b.   Was the recommended acreage contained in site selection

    c.   Was criteria established in meeting selected site

    d.   Was site reviewed by local governmental units

    e.   Was architect or engineer involved in selection process

    f.   Was selected site free of legal entanglements

    g.   Was site obtained in a timely fashion

III. Architect Selection:

    a.   Were citizens recommendations solicited by School Board

    b.   Were citizens involved in the interview process

    c.   Were architects at both the local and national levels invited to apply

    d.   Were visits made to architect's office and building

IV. Educational Specifications Development

    a.   Was there citizen/teacher involvement in developing an educational program

    b.   Was the final document written by an educator

    c.   Were all essential elements contained in the document

    d.   Was the document reviewed by citizens/teachers

    e.   Was the document formally adopted by the School Board

V. Design

    a. Was a review schedule established by the architect

    b. Was there citizen/teacher involvement in design review meetings

    c. Was the Educational Specification document utilized by the architect

    d. Were the users of the facilities consulted

    e. Was the design reviewed by the proper local and state governmental branch

    f. Was the design reviewed and adopted by the School Board in the preliminary stage

    g. Were the final plans adopted by the School Board

    h. Were citizens, teachers and administrators apprised of compromise and/or changes in design

    i. Were all local, state, and federal laws observed in the design

VI. Bidding and Construction:

    a. Was the bidding process controlled by the School Board

    b. Were citizens present at bid opening

    c. Were bids within the budget

    d. Was construction started within 10 days

    e. Were there minimum change orders during construction

    f. Was the building completed on time

VII. Orientation:

    a. Was a program of orientation held for teachers

    b. Was a program of orientation held for community members

    c. Was the architect involved in the orientation

    d. Was an orientation program designed to include an Open House

VIII. Evaluation:

    a. Was an evaluation of the building completed

    b. Was an evaluation of the planning process completed

    c. Were community members involved in either

List of States Credit Enhancement Programs

California	Eligible city and county bonds
Colorado	Local school bonds
Georgia	Eligible local school bonds
Indiana	Local school bonds, leases
Kentucky	Local school bonds, leases
Michigan	Qualified local school bonds
Minnesota	Eligible local school bonds
Mississippi	Eligible local school bonds
Missouri	Eligible local school bonds
Nevada	Eligible local school bonds
New Jersey	local school bonds
New York	local school bonds
Ohio	Eligible local school bonds
Oklahoma	Eligible local school bonds
Pennsylvania	Local school bonds
South Carolina	Local school bonds
South Dakota	Local school Bonds
Texas	Approved local school bonds
Utah	Qualified local school bonds
Virginia	All local G.O. debt
West Virginia	All local G.O. debt
Wyoming	Eligible local school bonds

Chapter I Organization and Policy Planning

Castaldi, Basil. (1994, 4th edition) *Educational Facilities: Planning, Modernization, and Management.* Needham Heights, MA: Allyn and Bacon, Inc.

Kowalski, Theodore J. (1989). *Planning and Managing School Facilities.* Westport, CT: Greenwood Publishing Group, PP 1-285.

Chapter 2 Planning Considerations

Adams, Don (1991). "Planning Models and Paradigms." In R. V. Carlson and Gary Awkerman (Eds.) *Educational Planning: Concepts, Strategies, and Practices.* PP 5-20, New York: Longman Publishing Group.

Kaufman, Roger and Herman, Jerry. (1991). Strategic Planning in Education, Rethinking, Restructuring, Revitalizing. Lancaster, PA: Technomic Publishing Company, PP. 1-332.

Donsky, Aaron P. (Winter, 1996). "IPEM: An Integrated Planning, Effectiveness Model," *Educational Planning*, Vol. 10, No. 1, PP.19-26.

Lewis, James (1983). *Long Range and Short Range Planning for Educational Administrators.* Boston: Allyn and Bacon, Inc.

Norris, Donald M. and Poulton, Nick L. (1991 edition). *A Guide for New Planners.* Ann Arbor, MI: The Society for College and University Planning, PP 1-102.

Chapter 4 Long-Range Planning: Program Development

Graves, Ben E. (1993). *School Ways: The Planning and Design of America's Schools.* New York: McGraw-Hill, Inc. PP 1-237.

Mackenzie, Donald G. (1989). *Planning Educational Facilities.* Lanham, MD: University Press of America, PP 1-189.

Romney, Valerie A., (1996). *Strategic Planning and Needs Assessment for Schools and Communities.* Fairfax, VA: National Community Education Association, PP 1-90.

Chapter 5 Long-Range Planning: Student Enrollment Projections

Gilmore, W. (1974). *ENSIM: Land Use Analysis Based Enrollment Simulation.* Research Report II, Santa Clara County Schools, San Jose, CA: Office of the Superintendent of Schools.

Hoy, Thomas C. (May 1947). "What Future Needs Are Revealed by School-Population Studies?" *The Education Digest*, Vol 12, No 9, PP 24-26.

MacConnell, James D. (1957). *Planning School Buildings.* Englewood, NJ: Prentice-Hall, Inc.

McKnight, John H. (1990). "The Gradient Cohort Survival Method: A Refinement of the Ratio Forecasting Method for Determining School District Enrollments." Unpublished dissertation, Raleigh, NC: North Carolina Sate University.

Schellenberg, Stephen J. and Stephens, Charles. (April 1987), "Enrollment Projection: Variations on a Theme." Paper presented at the annual meeting of the American Educational Research Association, Washington, DC, cited in Enrollment Projections, Center on Evaluation, Development, Research, Phi Delta Kappa.

Chapter 6 Long-Range Planning: Evaluation of Existing Facilities

Akers, Stephen. (1982). *Appraisal Instrument for School Facilities.* Blacksburg, VA: Unpublished dissertation, Virginia Polytechnic Institute and State University

Earthman, Glen I. (1990). *Administering the Planning Process for Educational Facilities.* Jerico, NY: Wilkerson Press.

Hawkins, Harold and Lilley, Edward (1990). *Appraisal Guide for School Facilities.* Columbus, OH: Council of Educational Facility Planners.

McGuffey, Carroll W. (1974). *MEEB: Model for the Evaluation of Educational Buildings.* Chicago: Board of Education.

Thurston, Rodger (1979). *Model to Assess School Buildings and Facilities for the Physically Handicapped.* Boston: Unpublished dissertation, Boston College.

Chapter 7 Long-Range Planning: Financial Planning

Alexander, Kern and Alexander, M. David. (1992). *American Public School Law*. St. Paul, MN: West Publishing Company.

Appalachian Regional Development Act - 1965 (P.L. 89-4).

Appendix A. (Winter, 1997). "School Facilities," *The Future of Children*, Vol. 7, No. 3.

Camp, William. (1983). "Public School Bonding Corporations financing Public Elementary and Secondary Facilities." Unpublished dissertation, Blacksburg, VA: Virginia Polytechnic Institute and State University.

Council of Infrastructure Financing Authorities. (January 1998). "State Revolving Fund: A Decade of Successful SFR Performance, 1987-1997," Washington, DC: The Council.

Ducker, Richard D. (1994). "Using Impact Fees for Public Schools: The Orange County Experiment," *School Law Bulletin*, Vol.25, No. 2, PP 1-14.

Education for All Handicapped Children Act 1976 (P.L. 94-142).

Educational Writers Association. (1989). *Wolves at the Schoolhouse door: An Investigation of the condition of the Public School Buildings*. Washington, DC: The Association.

Emergency Relief Act - 1974 (P.L. 93-288).

Emergency Relief Act - 1983 (100-707).

Federal Surplus Property Act - 1941 (P.L. 94-519).

Higher Education Facilities Act - 1992 (92-318).

Housing & Community Development Act - 1968 (P.L. 90-448)

Impact Aid Act - 1941 (P.L. 81-874).

Improving America's Schools Act - 1994 (P.L. 103-382).

Partners to Rebuild America's Schools Act - 1997 (S. 456).

Rehabilitation Act - 1973 (P.L. 93-112). Sections 502 and 504

School District of Philadelphia. (1973) *Capital Improvement Program, 1973-1978.* Philadelphia: The School District.

Standard and Poor. (1998). "State Credit Enhancement Programs," Tax-Backed Debt, NYC: Standard and Poor's Municipal Finance Criteria.

United States General Accounting Office. (June 1996). School Facilities: *America's Schools Report Differing Conditions*: Washington, DC: GAO/HEHS-96-103, PP 1-105.

United States General Accounting Office. (April 1995). *School Facilities: America's Schools Not Designed or Equipped for 21st Century.* Washington, DC: GAO/HEHS-95-95, PP 1-67.

United States General Accounting Office. (February 1995). *School Facilities: Condition of America's Schools.* Washington, DC: GAO/HEHS-95-61, PP 1-65.

Taxpayers Relief Act - 1997 (P.L.

Chapter 8 Development of the Capital Improvement Program

Castaldi, Basil. (1994, 4th edition). *Educational Facilities: Planning, Modernization and Management.* New York: McGraw-Hill, Inc.

Kowalski, Theodore J. (1989). *Planning and Managing School Facilities.* Westport, CT: Greenwood Publishing Group.

Montgomery County Public Schools, (1998). *FY Educational Facilities Master Plan:1999-2004.* Rockville, MD: School Facilities Department.

Chapter 9 Employing The Architect

Brubaker, C. William.(1998). *Planning and Designing Schools.* New York: McGraw-Hill Publishers, pp 1-201.

Graves, Ben E. (1993). *School Ways, The Planning and Design of America's Schools.* New York: McGraw-Hill, Inc.

Holcomb, John H. (1995). *A Guide to the Planning of Educational Facilities.* 3rd edition, Lanham, MD: University Press of America.

Vickery, Robert L., (1998). *Finding the Right Architect.* Charlottesville, VA: The Thomas Jefferson Center for Educational Design, University of Virginia.

Chapter 10 School Site Selection and Acquisition

Council of Educational Facility Planners, international. (1991). Guide for Planning Educational Facilities. Scottsdale, AZ: The Council.

Earthman, Glen I. (1990). *Administering the Planning Process for Educational Facilities.* Jerico, NY: Wilkerson Press.

Earthman, Glen I. (1976). "The Politics of Site Selection." *CEFPI Journal,* Vol.14, No. 5.

Grabe, K. (1975). "Economic Advantages in Site Selection." Paper presented at the 52nd Annual conference of Council of Educational Facility Planners, international, Houston, TX.

School District of Philadelphia. (1973). *Capital Improvement Program 1973-1978.* Philadelphia, PA: School Facilities Department.

Chapter 11 Developing Educational Specifications

Earthman, Glen I. (1976). *The Process of Developing Educational Specifications.* Blacksburg, VA: College of Education, Virginia Polytechnic Institute and State University.

Hawkins, Harold. (1991). "Developing Educational Specifications." Unit F, *Guide for Planning Educational Facilities.* Scottsdale, AZ: Council of Educational Facility Planners, international.

Herman, Jerry J. and Herman, Janice L. (1995). *Effective School Facilities, A Development Guidebook.* Lancaster, PA: Technomic Publishing Company.

Holcomb, John H. (1995). *A Guide to the Planning of Educational Facilities.* Lanham, MD: University Press of America.

Alexander, Kern and Alexander, M. David. (1992). *American Public School Law*. St. Paul, MN: West Publishing Company.

Americans with Disabilities Act (ADA). (1990). Public Law No. 101-336, codified at 42 U.S.C. Sec. 12101.

Battaglia, D.H. (1992). *The Impact of the Americans with Disabilities Act on Historic Buildings and Facilities*. Washington, DC: Hunton & Williams. Presentation to the Preservation Alliance of Virginia, November 14, 1992, p. 20.

Civil Rights Act - 1994 (P.L. 88-352)

Earthman, Glen I. (1994). School Renovation Handbook: Investing in America. Lancaster, PA: Technomics Publishing, Inc.

Education for All Handicapped Children Act - 1995 (P.L. 94-142).

Guthrie, James W. and Rodney J. Reed. (1991). *Educational Administration and Policy*. Boston: Allyn and Bacon, Inc. p. 159.

Individuals With Disabilities Education Act - 1975 (P.L. 101-476).

Mayer, C. L. (1982). *Educational Administration and Special Education: A Handbook for School Administrators*. Boston: Allyn and Bacon, Inc. p. 382.

Rehabilitation Act - 1973 (P.L. 93-112).

Sergiovanni, Thomas J., Martin Burlingame, Fred Coombs, and Paul Thurston. (1987). *Educational Governance and Administration, 2nd edition*. Englewood Cliffs, NJ: Prentice-Hall, Inc, p. 226.

Tucker, B.P. and B. A. Goldstein. (1993). *Legal Rights of Persons With Disabilities: An Analysis of Federal Law*. Horsham, PA: LRP Publications.

U.S. Architectural and Transportation Barriers Compliance Board. (1992). *Recommendations for Accessibility Standards for Children's Environment*. Technical Report. Washington, DC: USATBCB, five chapters and appendices.

U.S. Department of Justice. (1992). Title II Highlights. Washington, D.C.: Civil Rights Division, USDOJ.

West, J., ed. (1991). *The Americans With Disabilities Act: From Policy to Practice*. New York: Milbank Memorial Fund, p. 360.

Whisenant, Jay R. (1993). "Access, Public Schools, and The Americans with Disabilities Act." *The Educational Facility Planner,* Vol. 31, No. 1, p 12.

Chapter 13 Monitoring the Design Phase

Brubaker, C. William. (1998). *Planning and Designing Schools*. New York: McGraw-Hill Publishers, PP1-201.

Earthman, Glen I. (1990). *Administering the Planning Process for Educational Facilities*. Jerico, NY: Wilkerson Press.

Earthman, Glen I. (1994). *Renovation Handbook: An Investment in Education*. Lancaster, PA: Technomic Publishers, Inc. pp. 1-180.

Chapter 16 Orientation and Evaluation

Council of Educational Facility Planners (1991). *Guide for Planning Educational Facilities*. Columbus, OH: The Council.

Chapter 17 Planning for Technology

Barron, A. and G. Orwig. (1995). *New Technologies for Education: A Beginners Guide*. Englewood, CO: Libraries Unlimited.

Durost, R. (September, 1994). "Integrating Computer Technology: Planning, Training, and Support." *NASSP Bulletin*, 78, 49-54.

Loveless, T. (December, 1996) "Why aren't computers used more in schools?" *Educational Policy*, 10, 448-67.

U.S. General Accounting Office. (April, 1995). *School Facilities: America's Schools Not Designed or Equipped For 21st Century*. Washington, D.C., GAO/HEHS-95-95.

American Association of School Administrators. (1983). *The Maintenance Gap: Deferred Repair and Renovation in the Nation's Elementary and Secondary Schools*. Arlington, VA: AASA, Council of Great City Schools, National School Boards Association, pp 1-15.

American Association of School Administrators. (1992). *Schoolhouse in the Red*. Arlington, VA: The Association, pp 1-40.

Cash, Carol S. (1993). "Building condition and student achievement and behavior." Unpublished dissertation, Blacksburg, VA: Virginia Polytechnic Institute and State University.

Earthman, Glen I., Carol S. Cash, and Denny Van Berkum. (1996). "Student achievement and behavior and school building condition." *The Journal of School Business Management*. Vol. 8, No. 3, pp 26-37.

Educational Writers Association. (1989). *Wolves at the Schoolhouse Door*. Washington, DC: The Association.

Edwards, Maureen. (1991). "Building conditions, parental involvement and student achievement in the D.C. public school system," Unpublished master's thesis, Washington, DC: Georgetown University.

General Accounting Office. (1995). *School Facilities: Condition of America's Schools*. Washington, DC: GAO/HEHS, B-259307.

General Accounting Office. (1996). *School Facilities: America's Schools Report Differing Conditions*. Washington, DC: GAO/HEHS, B-260872.

Hines, Eric W. (1996). "Building condition and student achievement and behavior." Unpublished dissertation, Blacksburg, VA: Virginia Polytechnic Institute and State University.

"Improving America's Schools Act of 1994." (P. L. 103-382).

McGuffey, C. W. (1982). "Facilities." Chapter 10 in H. Walberg, (Ed), *Improving Educational Standards and Productivity*. (pp. 237-288). Berkeley, CA: McCutchan Publishing Corp.

"Nations Schools Not on Track to Meet Goals 2000 Panel Reports." (December 11, 1998). Associated Press Release. Roanoke, VA: The Roanoke Times, p. A9.

"Partnership to Rebuild America's School Act of 1997." (S. 456).

Pauley v. Bailey. (May 11, 1982). Circuit Court of Kanawah County, West Virginia, No. 75-1268.

Phillips, Runsel M. (1997) "Educational facility age and the academic achievement and attendance of upper elementary school students." Unpublished dissertation, Athens, G.A: University of Georgia.

Roosevelt Elementary School District No. 66 v. Bishop, 179 Arizona 233; 877 P .2d 806 (1994).

Tofler, Alvin. (1980). Third Wave. New York: William Morrow Company, Inc.

index

T

U

V